The Observer's Pocket Series

SOCCER

To Edward

from

Graham

1982

Observer's Books

NATURAL HISTORY
Birds · Birds' Eggs · Wild Animals · Zoo Animals
Farm Animals · Freshwater Fishes · Sea Fishes
Tropical Fishes · Butterflies · Larger Moths
Insects and Spiders · Pond Life · Sea and Seashore
Seashells · Dogs · Horses and Ponies · Cats · Pets
Wild Flowers · Grasses · Mushrooms · Lichens
Cacti · Garden Flowers · Flowering Shrubs · Trees
House Plants · Vegetables · Geology · Fossils
Weather · Astronomy

SPORT
Soccer · Cricket · Golf · Coarse Fishing · Fly Fishing
Show Jumping · Motor Sport

TRANSPORT
Automobiles · Aircraft · Commercial Vehicles
Motorcycles · Steam Locomotives · Small Craft
Ships · Manned Spaceflight · Unmanned Spaceflight

ARCHITECTURE
Architecture · Churches · Cathedrals

COLLECTING
Awards and Medals · Coins · Postage Stamps
Glass · Pottery and Porcelain

ARTS AND CRAFTS
Music · Painting · Modern Art · Furniture
Sewing

HISTORY AND GENERAL INTEREST
Ancient Britain · Flags · Heraldry
European Costume

TRAVEL
London · Tourist Atlas GB · Lake District
Cotswolds and Shakespeare Country

The Observer's Book of

SOCCER

ALBERT SEWELL

Revised by Alan Hughes

WITH 16 COLOUR PLATES AND
12 BLACK AND WHITE ILLUSTRATIONS

FREDERICK WARNE

LONDON

Published by
Frederick Warne (Publishers) Ltd, London, England

Copyright © 1978 Frederick Warne & Co. Ltd

First Edition 1972
Second Edition 1974
Third Edition 1976
Fourth Edition 1978

Library of Congress
Catalog Card No. 72–81144

ISBN 0 7232 1587 1

Printed and bound in Great Britain by
Morrison & Gibb Ltd, London and Edinburgh

Contents

Acknowledgements

The author and publishers wish to thank the following for their kind permission to reproduce photographs: Syndication International for pages 13, 15, 118, 119, 120; Glasgow Rangers Club for page 14; The Press Association for page 133 (left), 150; The Associated Press Ltd for page 133 (right); Sports Press Pictures for page 154; Topix for page 157.

The History of the Game

It is impossible to say exactly when football began, because its origins are lost, literally, in the mists of time. Some say men (and women) first began kicking 'an object' around as far back as the twelfth century. Perhaps they did, but it took a long time for the game to become organized.

The first real stirrings were in the middle of last century, when boys at established English public schools, and at universities such as Cambridge, began to play a form of soccer which at least bore some resemblance to our modern game. It is surprising that a game thought of mainly as a working man's pastime should have originated in the very bastions of the so-called privileged classes.

However, such was the popularity of football that it was not long before it appealed to a wider audience. The oldest Football League club was founded in 1862—26 years before the inauguration of the League itself—Notts County, who came into existence three years before their arch-rivals Nottingham Forest.

The following year, 1863, saw the formation of the Football Association—in a public house in central London. This was the world's first organized attempt at controlling the game at national level, and it was from the new body's title that Association football, or soccer, got its name.

Many people north of the Border believe that Scotland, not England, gave football to the world. With due respect to the Scots, who have contributed so much to the game, this is not so. The first Scottish club, the famous and once powerful Queen's Park, did not appear on the field until 1867, and the Scottish Football Association waited until 1873 for its inception.

Brazil, West Germany, Hungary may come and go. England and Scotland go on for ever in the international soccer sense, despite misguided attempts in the past to belittle the annual clash between these two. The first match was played in November 1872, in Glasgow, and resulted in a goalless draw (it was to be 98 years before the next similar result).

As for Wales, they reached their centenary in 1976 with prospects brighter than at any time in their history. By beating Austria 1–0 at Wrexham, they qualified for the first time for the European Championship quarter-finals, as Britain's lone hopes. Under new manager Mike Smith (an Englishman in charge of Welsh football!), they dominated a qualifying group that also included Hungary, and won five of the six games. This finest achievement by Wales since their participation in the 1958 World Cup quarter-finals came at a time when England were still searching for the right formula.

The violent political climate of the seventies deepened Ireland's soccer problems. These have long included a need to supply players for two international sides—Northern Ireland and the Republic—and the recurring loss of promising players to Football League clubs. But season 1974–75 gave Irish soccer a 'welcome uplift'—the visit of Yugoslavia in April was the first International staged in Belfast since October 1971, and a few weeks later Home Championship football returned to the province after a four-year boycott.

The Home Championship was first played for in season 1883–84 and Scotland had a clean sweep, winning all three matches. In 1885 professionalism was legalized in English soccer, and a year later Arbroath carved their own slice of history by winning a Scottish Cup tie 36–0 against the luckless, and long-since defunct, Bon Accord. This remains the highest score in any official senior football match in Britain. The present-day off-side law and the system of early-round elimination of weak teams both help to ensure that this kind of farce will never be seen again.

In October 1887, Preston North End made a brave effort to challenge Arbroath's feat when they annihilated Hyde 26–0 in an F.A. Cup match. Whether the Preston players had their eye on the record will never be known, but they certainly had no mercy on poor Hyde.

Soccer moved fast in the eighties. The Football League was formed in 1888 and for those who wonder why it should be honoured with the title The Football League, and not the English Football League, the answer is that it was the first such body in the world.

How many of today's soccer followers can reel off the names of those famous twelve clubs which formed the basis of what has become the world's greatest league competition? They were Accrington, Aston Villa, Blackburn Rovers, Bolton Wanderers, Burnley, Derby County, Everton, Notts County, Preston North End, Stoke City, West Bromwich Albion and Wolverhampton Wanderers. Of that number, only Accrington are not still members; they left the League in March 1962, after struggling through the years since the Second World War as Accrington Stanley.

In 1970 two other founder members, Aston Villa and Preston, were relegated to Division Three for the first time in their history. The following year Blackburn Rovers went down for the first time, along with Bolton, another of the famous originals. Such is the swing of fortune in soccer across the decades.

Modern fans think of Tottenham Hotspur in 1961 and Arsenal ten years later as the 'double clubs', i.e. those which have won both the League Championship and the F.A. Cup in the same season. But as long ago as 1888–89, the year in which the League began, Preston won the Cup without conceding a goal, and the Championship without losing a game. This was quite an achievement, even if competition was a lot less fierce in those days, and Aston Villa were the only other side before Tottenham, in 1960–61, to win both trophies in one season. They did it in the season 1896–97.

Floodlights are now part of every club's equipment. But how many people realize that matches were being played under artificial light long before the end of last century? The first reference to a 'floodlit' game is found in records dated 1887, which tells of a game being played at Sheffield by *candlelight*! This is a difficult scene to imagine, but the players must have managed somehow.

As the nineteenth century drew to a close, the game continued to boom. Attendances rose each year, and while there was no sign yet of international competition against foreign opponents, soccer was slowly being introduced abroad.

It is impossible to tell when football was first taught to other countries—to the Brazilians for example—but we do know that British sailors had a lot to do with it. The British Navies, Royal and Merchant, were at the height of their power and influence in the fifty years between 1875 and 1925, and it was during this half century that the game was taken round the world. Sailors on leave abroad often played football among themselves; local inhabitants watched with interest, learned quickly, and soon challenged the soccer 'missionaries' and sometimes beat them.

The first International match between England and a foreign country took place on 6 June 1908. England met Austria in Vienna and won handsomely 6–1. Two days later the teams met again at the same venue and this time the Austrians were beaten 11–1. England then went on to Budapest, and crushed Hungary 7–0, before moving finally to Prague and soundly defeating Bohemia (now Czechoslovakia) 4–0 to end a highly successful first professional tour abroad.

The following year the Austrians invited England back, no doubt hoping for revenge. This time they lost 8–1, so in three games in twelve months against the Austrians, all of them in Vienna, England piled up an aggregate of 25 goals and lost only three. However, and significantly in terms of the improvement in soccer standards abroad, when the teams met next, in May 1930—again in Vienna —there was a goalless draw, and when Austria first played here (at Chelsea in December 1932) England only just scraped home 4–3.

England should have been warned during the year between those two games, when the Scots crashed by a humiliating 5–0 in Vienna !

Despite that 1908 England tour, international football with overseas countries competing did not become established until the early thirties. The 1914–18 War had much to do with that, and throughout the twenties the total of matches played abroad by England was no more than sixteen.

It was not until the summer of 1950 that any British country played a team from the Americas. This was when England participated in the World Cup for the first time. They beat Chile 2–0 in their opening match of the final series in Brazil, but 29 June marked the most embarrassing day in the entire playing history of British soccer. From Belo Horizonte came what must rate as the most fantastic scoreline in the international game: England 0, U.S.A. 1. It was a result which rocked the football world. Perhaps the least excited country was the United States itself, so little interest did they show in the game of Association Football. To the North Americans soccer was a minority sport, and that freak result was as unlikely as, say England beating the U.S.A. at baseball. But it happened!

This match belongs, however, to soccer's comparatively modern history, and there is reason here to go back to the turn of the century. In the season 1898–99 a feat occurred which almost certainly will never be repeated in British soccer. Rangers, over the years Scotland's most successful club until the modern dominance of Celtic, took the Scottish League title in a canter. They won every one of the 18 games they played in the competition, and even allowing for the relatively low standard of Scottish club soccer, it was a tremendous achievement.

The overall standards of play in Scotland are certainly low. A look at past winners of the Scottish League Championship tells the tale. In 1932 Motherwell won the title for the first and only time. Apart from that year, the championship was shared between Rangers and Celtic from 1904, when it was won by Third Lanark, to 1948 when Hibernian took it. During those years the title went to Rangers no fewer than 20 times, and to Celtic 15. Indeed Motherwell's surprise victory in 1932 prevented what would otherwise have been a run of eight consecutive successes for Rangers.

Rangers' Championship success in 1964 gave them a world record total of 34 League titles, but from season 1965–66 Celtic dominated, and when they triumphed yet again in 1974, they brought Scotland a share in another world record—nine consecutive League Championships—previously held jointly by MTK Budapest, who won the Hungarian title from 1917–25 inclusive, and CDNA Sofia, when they were Champions of Bulgaria from 1954–62.

Celtic's long reign ended when Rangers returned to the top in 1975, at which point the Scottish League took one of its most ambitious steps by shaping itself into three sections, headed by a premier division of ten clubs.

If, in the past, Scottish football tended to stagnate because of the great strength of Rangers and Celtic, the game elsewhere grew in power. The development that was to make soccer a world game came in 1904, when F.I.F.A.—the Federation of International Football Associations—was founded in Paris. Seven countries—France, Belgium, Holland, Switzerland, Spain, Denmark and Sweden—were the original members. Today there are more than 150 members of the world body.

Amateur soccer, or rather a twentieth century version of the original amateur game, came along in 1907 when the Amateur F.A.

was formed and the following year Britain put a team in the Olympic Games and won the final at London's White City, beating Denmark 2–0.

The 1974 Amateur Cup Final, won at Wembley by Bishop's Stortford, was the last. Ever-increasing infringement of amateur status by many players led to the Football Association, after years of deliberation, dispensing with the word 'amateur'. Its eradication meant the end of the Amateur Cup and Amateur Internationals. All footballers became 'players', with the professionals contracted, the rest known as non-contract players.

A look at the 1920s tells us that. . . . *In* 1923 Wembley staged its first Cup Final, with an attendance of 126,000, many of whom stormed the gates and broke in. *In* 1926 Huddersfield Town won the League Championship for the third successive year, the first team to do so, and a feat as yet emulated only by Arsenal in 1933–34–35. Huddersfield were also runners-up in 1927, and again in 1928, the greatest period in their history.

In 1927 Cardiff City beat Arsenal 1–0 at Wembley and became the first, and only, side to take the F.A. Cup out of England. This feat is still reckoned to be the most outstanding in Welsh soccer, which has always had to take second place in popularity to rugby. *In* 1929 England lost for the first time on foreign soil, Spain triumphing 4–3 in Madrid, and the following year the World Cup was launched.

Uruguay beat Argentina 4–2 in the Final, and South America was on the world soccer map. And so into the thirties.

The record individual number of goals in any British senior League or Cup match was set in April 1936 when Joe Payne, Luton Town centre-forward, scored ten in his club's 12–0 win against Bristol Rovers in a Division 3 match.

A year later the largest crowd ever to watch a match in Britain squeezed into Hampden Park for the Scotland–England International. The official attendance was 149,547, and unless a new stadium is built it is a British record which will never be broken. Still in Scotland, Celtic's Jimmy McGrory retired in 1938 after scoring an all-time record 550 goals in first-class soccer. This was a record for Britain; overseas players have scored more—Brazil's Pele topped the 1000 mark.

If Scottish club soccer was often overshadowed on the field by its English counterpart, the largest crowds were to be found north of the Border. Manchester United and Arsenal set up the still-existing record for an English League match—82,950. That was on 17 January 1948, at Maine Road (United were still using Manchester City's ground while their own at Old Trafford was being restored after bomb damage during the War). In March of the same year Rangers and Hibernian met in the Scottish Cup semi-final at Hampden Park in front of 143,570. Then, in the Final, nearly a quarter of a million fans saw the two matches Rangers needed to beat Greenock Morton. Those were the days of the great crowds, after years when people had been starved of top-class competition.

Coming more up to date—although that depends to a large extent on the age of the reader—in 1953 Stanley Mortensen scored a hat-trick in the Coronation Year F.A. Cup Final against Bolton Wanderers. He was the first man to achieve such a feat, but even his success was overshadowed by that of his partner, Stanley (now Sir Stanley) Matthews.

Bolton, led by Nat Lofthouse, were 3–1 ahead well into the second half. It seemed all over for Blackpool, and for the genius Matthews who had never won a Cup-winners' medal, and was playing in what was to be his last Final. Then the two Stanleys broke loose. Matthews mesmerized a Bolton side playing one short after injury—there were no substitutes then—and Blackpool triumphed 4–3 in one of the all-time classic Finals.

The 'Matthews Final' could be regarded as almost the end of an era in British football. Six months later, at Wembley in November 1953, came the 6–3 slaughter of England by Hungary—those magnificent Magyars—which led to a vast re-thinking on the game's tactics and economics.

A new competitive dimension was brought to the game in 1955 with the launching of the European Cup, and both in that and the two other big European tournaments—the Cup-Winners' Cup and Fairs Cup (now the U.E.F.A. Cup)—British clubs have figured prominently among the honours, as will be seen from reference to the European section of this book.

One of the most important factors in the revolution within British football was the removal of the maximum wage in 1961. This ensured that our stars did not need to go to Italy to earn salaries commensurate with their skills, as world-class players like John Charles, Denis Law, Jimmy Greaves and others had done.

The long-overdue acceptance of substitutes in League football was at last approved in 1965. A year later came the greatest achievement of all for British soccer, with England's triumph at Wembley as host nation in the World Cup. In Mexico in 1970 the world crown was taken by Brazil for the third time.

In 1974 West Germany, emulating England eight years before, became the second successive European host nation to take the World Cup. Whatever the quality of Scotland's performance in Argentina in 1978 is of secondary importance to the state of the modern game in these Islands, where the most urgent requirement is an injection of tactical enterprise by coaches and managers if football is to provide the level of entertainment necessary to hold its appeal.

Liverpool's great night of triumph. Their long-serving players Tommy Smith (left) and Ian Callaghan celebrate in traditional style.

Glasgow Rangers are invariably one of Scotland's successful clubs, and the present players carry on the tradition set by their predecessors. Left to right—*Back row:* Alan Boyd, Alex Miller, Derek Parlane, Colin Jackson, Ronnie Lowrie, Peter McCloy, Stewart Kennedy, Martin Henderson, Tom Forsyth, Ken Watson, Ally Dawson. *Middle row:* Physiotherapist Tom Craig, Gordon Boyd, Eric Morris, Ralph Brand, Chris Robertson, Derek Johnstone, Colin Stein, Davie Armour, Alex O'Hara, Jim Denny, coach Joe Mason. *Front row:* Manager Jock Wallace, Billy Mackay, Tommy McLean, Iain Munro, Bobby Russell, Sandy Jardine, John Greig, Davie Cooper, Alex Mac-Donald, Bobby McKean, Johnny Hamilton, Derek Strickland.

The goal that clinched Scotland's place in the 1978 World Cup finals. The dark-shirted Kenny Dalglish watches his header beat Wales goalkeeper Dai Davies.

Guide to the 92 Football League Clubs in England and Wales

as at the end of the 1976–77 season

ALDERSHOT

Recreation Ground, Aldershot, Aldershot 20211

Shirts: red, blue and white trim. *Shorts:* white. *Stockings:* red, blue and white tops. *Second colours:* white shirts, blue shorts.

The years of the Second World War provided Aldershot with the most colourful teams in their history. Many of the game's best names were on military service in the garrison town and appeared as guests for the club. Among them were Frank Swift, Tommy Lawton, Matt Busby, Denis Compton, and the full England half-back line of that era, Cliff Britton, Stan Cullis and Joe Mercer.

In more settled times Aldershot rarely achieved much of distinction until, by attaining fourth place in Division Four in season 1972–73, they won promotion for the first time. Before that, their most successful season was in 1969–70 when they were sixth in Division Four. That was the season, too, when they attracted their record attendance to the Recreation Ground, 19,138 watching their fourth round F.A. Cup replay against Carlisle.

Another notable Cup triumph occurred in 1963–64 when they defeated Aston Villa, then a Division One team, 2–1 after a goalless draw at Villa Park. Aldershot can claim a share of at least one record—that of the quickest goal. Albert Mundy scored six seconds after the kick-off at Hartlepool on 25 October 1958.

Record attendance: 19,138 v. Carlisle (F.A. Cup), January 1970.
Modern Capacity: 20,000. **Nickname:** 'Shots.'
Entered Football League: 1932—Div. 3 (South).
Biggest win: 8–1 v. Gateshead (Div. 4), September 1958.
Heaviest defeat: 0–9 v. Bristol City (Div. 3 South), December 1946.
Highest final League position: 4th in Div. 4, 1972–73.
Best in F.A. Cup: 5th Round, 1932–33.
Best in League Cup: 2nd Round, 1960–61, 1962–63, 1963–64, 1965–66, 1966–67, 1970–71, 1971–72.
Pitch measurements: $117\frac{1}{2}$ x 76 yd.
Highest League Scorer in Single Season: Ron Fogg—24 in 1963–64 (Div. 4).
Transfers—
  Highest fee paid: £13,500—Joe Jopling (from Leicester), March 1974.
  Highest fee received: £50,000—Joe Jopling (to Leicester), September 1970.

ARSENAL

Arsenal Stadium, Highbury, London, N5 1BU, 01–226 0304

Shirts: red, white sleeves. *Shorts:* white. *Stockings:* red, with thin white band. *Second colours:* gold shirts, blue shorts.

By performing the League Championship–F.A. Cup double in 1971, Arsenal not only caught up with their illustrious past—they exceeded it. They became the first club to win the Championship eight times, and the 'double' was signalled by Bertie Mee being voted 'Manager of the Year' and captain Frank McLintock winning the 'Footballer of the Year' award.

Arsenal have been constant members of Division One since 1919, and their greatest era until the seventies occurred during the 1930s when they 'came to power' under the managership of Herbert Chapman. They were League Champions in 1931, 1933, 1934, 1935, and 1938, and won the F.A. Cup in 1930 and 1936.

After the war, under Tom Whittaker, they won the First Division title in 1948 and 1953, and the F.A. Cup again in 1950. But then came a long period of non-success from which the way back to former glory followed two losing appearances in the Football League Cup Final.

In the 1970 Fairs Cup they won their first European prize and a year later they completed the double—a feat which not even the club's great honours-winning teams of the thirties could achieve, and against which subsequent Arsenal performances paled.

The Double (League Champions, F.A. Cup Winners): 1970–71.
League Champions: 1930–31, 1932–33, 1933–34, 1934–35, 1937–38, 1947–48, 1952–53, 1970–71.
F.A. Cup Winners: 1929–30, 1935–36, 1949–50, 1970–71.
European Fairs Cup Winners: 1969–70.
Record attendance: 73,295 v. Sunderland (League), March 1935.
Modern Capacity: 63,000. **Nickname:** 'Gunners.'
Entered Football League: 1893—Div. 2.
Biggest win: 12–0 v. Loughborough T. (Div. 2), March 1900, and 12–0 v. Ashford United (F.A. Cup), 1893–94.
Heaviest defeat: 0–8 v. Loughborough T. (Div. 2), December 1896.
Best in League Cup: Runners-up 1967–68, 1968–69.
Pitch measurements: 110 x 71 yd.
Highest League Scorer in Single Season: Ted Drake—43 in 1934–35 (Div. 1).
Transfers—
  Highest fee paid: £333,333—Malcolm Macdonald (from Newcastle), August 1976.
  Highest fee received: £200,000—Ray Kennedy (to Liverpool), July 1974.

ASTON VILLA

Villa Park, Birmingham B6 6HE, 021–327 6604

Shirts: claret, light blue sleeves, claret & light blue collars and cuffs. *Shorts:* white, claret & blue stripes. *Stockings:* light blue, claret & white tops. *Second colours:* white shirts & shorts, claret & blue trim.

Aston Villa were among the 12 founder members of the Football League in 1888; they were Champions 6 times between 1894 and 1910, and in 1897 they achieved the 'double' of League title and F.A. Cup, a feat previously performed by Preston N.E. in 1888–89 and which Tottenham Hotspur (1960–61) and Arsenal (1970–71) have since equalled. When they finished runners-up to Arsenal in 1930–31, they scored 128 League goals, still a record for a First Division club. Villa also hold the record of 7 F.A. Cup wins, but in 1970 they fell into the Third Division for the first time. Two years later they were Champions of that division, and in 1975 new manager Ron Saunders took them to a notable 'double'—the League Cup and promotion to the First Division.

Certainly, those lads of the Aston Villa Wesleyan Church could never have realized in 1874 what glories the club they formed would achieve. It would need many pages to record Villa's great players: Charlie Wallace, Harold Halse, Harry Hampton, Clem Stephenson and Joe Bache (the 1913 Cup Final attack); Sam Hardy, Frank Barson, Andy Ducat, Frank Moss, 'Pongo' Waring, Billy Walker, Jimmy Hagan, Alex Massie, Trevor Ford, Peter McParland. These are but a few.

The Double (League Champions, F.A. Cup Winners): 1896–97.
League Champions: 1893–94, 1895–96, 1896–97, 1898–99, 1899–1900, 1909–10.
Division 2 Champions: 1937–38, 1959–60.
Division 3 Champions: 1971–72.
F.A. Cup Winners: 1886–87, 1894–95, 1896–97, 1904–05, 1912–13, 1919–20, 1956–57.
League Cup Winners: 1960–61, 1974–75, 1976–77.
Record attendance: 76,588 v. Derby County (F.A. Cup), March 1946.
Modern Capacity: 64,000. **Nickname:** 'Villans.'
Entered Football League: 1888—Div. 1.
Biggest win: 13–0 v. Wednesday Old Ath. (F.A. Cup), 1886–87.
Heaviest defeat: 1–8 v. Blackburn R. (F.A. Cup), 1888–89.
Pitch measurements: 115 x 75 yd.
Highest League Scorer in Single Season: T. ('Pongo') Waring —49 in 1930–31 (Div. 1).
Transfers—
    Highest fee paid: £250,000—Tommy Craig (from Newcastle), January 1978.
    Highest fee received: £200,000—Bruce Rioch (to Derby), February 1974.

BARNSLEY

Oakwell Ground, Grove Street, Barnsley, Barnsley 84113

Shirts: red. *Shorts:* white. *Stockings:* white. *Second colours:* white shirts & black shorts.

Ever since their formation, Barnsley have known the extremes of fortune. Often, it must be said, the emphasis has been on the struggle to make ends meet. Yet there have been great occasions such as winning the F.A. Cup as a Second Division side in 1912 after herculean efforts against West Bromwich Albion. The teams met first at the old Crystal Palace in a goalless draw, and Barnsley snatched victory by the only goal during extra time in the replay at Bramall Lane, Sheffield. This was deserved compensation for their 2–0 defeat by Newcastle, in the Final two years earlier, when a second match was also required to decide the outcome.

One of their biggest disappointments was missing promotion to Division One in 1922 on goal average. Three times Barnsley were Third Division North Champions: in 1933–34, when they scored 118 goals; in 1938–39, when they won 30 and drew 7 of their 42 League games; and in 1954–55.

Like other clubs living in the shadows of better-known neighbours, Barnsley have discovered many stars, among them Eric Brook and Fred Tilson, who together played in Manchester City's 1934 F.A. Cup-winning team; George Hunt, Wilf Copping, Dick Spence, Danny Blanchflower and Tommy Taylor, who lost his life in the Munich air disaster involving Manchester United in February 1958.

F.A. Cup Winners: 1911–12.
Division 3 (North) Champions: 1933–34, 1938–39, 1954–55.
Record attendance: 42,056 v. Stoke (F.A. Cup), February 1935.
Modern Capacity: 38,500. **Nickname:** 'Tykes.'
Entered Football League: 1898—Div. 2.
Biggest win: 9–0 v. Loughborough T. (Div. 2), January 1899 and 9–0 v. Accrington Stanley (Div. 3 North), February 1934.
Heaviest defeat: 0–9 v. Notts County (Div. 2), November 1927.
Best in League Cup: 3rd Round, 1962–63.
Pitch measurements: 110 x 74 yd.
Highest League Scorer in Single Season: Cecil McCormack —33 in 1950–51 (Div. 2).
Transfers—
  Highest fee paid: £20,000 (joint fee)—Frank Sharp and Leslie Lea (from Cardiff), August 1970.
  Highest fee received: £60,000—Anton Otulakowski (to West Ham), October 1976.

BIRMINGHAM CITY

St Andrew's, Birmingham B9 4NH, 021–772 0101/2689

Shirts: royal blue, white stripes on sleeves. *Shorts:* white with blue trim. *Stockings:* white with blue hoops. *Second colours:* yellow shirts & shorts with blue trim.

Although the League Championship, F.A. Cup and European prizes still elude them, Birmingham City have seldom been short of class players in one or more key positions. Their speciality has been goalkeepers of international calibre, among them Dan Tremelling, Harry Hibbs, Gil Merrick and Jim Herriot.

As Small Heath, the club were founder members of Division Two in 1892. They stepped into Division One in 1894, but slipped back two years later. Promotion came once more in 1901, but this time they lasted only one season. They climbed again in 1903; the name Small Heath was dropped in favour of Birmingham in 1905, and a year later they moved to their present St Andrew's home from Muntz Street.

Since the last war, as Birmingham City, they have been F.A. Cup Finalists (1956), Fairs Cup Finalists twice (1960, 1961), League Cup Winners (1963) and promoted three times to the First Division —in 1948, 1955 and 1972. In February 1974, facing the threat of relegation again, City transferred 22-year-old striker Bob Latchford to Everton to set a new British record equivalent of £350,000 (for details see foot of page).

Division 2 Champions: 1892–93, 1920–21, 1947–48, 1954–55.
League Cup Winners: 1962–63.
Record attendance: 66,844 v. Everton (F.A. Cup), February 1939.
Modern capacity: 52,500. **Nickname:** 'Blues.'
Entered Football League: 1892—Div. 2.
Biggest win: 12–0 v. Walsall Town Swifts (Div. 2), December 1892 and 12–0 v. Doncaster Rovers (Div. 2), April 1903.
Heaviest defeat: 1–9 v. Sheffield Wednesday (Div. 1), December 1930.
Best in F.A. Cup: Final, 1930–31, 1955–56.
Pitch measurements: 115 x 74 yd.
Highest League Scorer in Single Season: Joe Bradford—29 in 1927–28 (Div. 1).
Transfers—
  Highest fee paid: £180,000—Howard Kendall (from Everton), February 1974.
  Highest fee received: £350,000 equivalent (British record)— Bob Latchford (to Everton—£80,000 cash plus Howard Kendall, valued £180,000, and Archie Styles, valued £90,000), February 1974.

BLACKBURN ROVERS

Ewood Park, Blackburn BB2 4JF, Blackburn 55432/3

Shirts: blue & white halves. *Shorts:* white. *Stockings:* blue with red and white tops. *Second colours:* red shirts, blue shorts.

The F.A. Cup was almost the exclusive property of Blackburn Rovers during the latter part of the last century. They won the trophy in three successive years, 1884–86, and again in 1890 and 1891, then had to wait 37 years to win it for the sixth time by beating Huddersfield 3–1 at Wembley in 1928.

Rovers were original members of the Football League in 1888 and carried off the First Division Championship in 1912 and 1914. They remained continuously in the top flight of League clubs until 1936. Since then, however, they have had varying spells in the Second Division and their fortunes slumped to a new low in 1970–71 when, together with Bolton Wanderers, another Lancashire club steeped in tradition, they dropped into Division Three. As Champions of that section, they returned to the Second Division in 1975.

Many chroniclers of the game—and certainly those old enough to remember—maintain that Bob Crompton was the finest full-back of any era. In the early part of the century he was capped 41 times for England and played for Rovers for 23 years.

Since the 1939–45 war Rovers most-capped players, both for England, have been winger Bryan Douglas (36 Internationals) and half-back Ronnie Clayton (35), who holds the Blackburn record of 580 League appearances.

League Champions: 1911–12, 1913–14.
Division 2 Champions: 1938–39.
Division 3 Champions: 1974–75.
F.A. Cup Winners: 1883–84, 1884–85, 1885–86, 1889–90, 1890–91, 1927–28.
Record attendance: 61,783 v. Bolton (F.A. Cup), March 1929.
Modern Capacity: 52,000.
Entered Football League: 1888—Div. 1.
Biggest win: 11–0 v. Rossendale United (F.A. Cup), 1884–85.
Heaviest defeat: 0–8 v. Arsenal (Div. 1), February 1933.
Best in League Cup: Semi-final 1961–62.
Pitch measurements: 116 x 72 yd.
Highest League Scorer in Single Season: Ted Harper—43 in 1925–26 (Div. 1).
Transfers—
  Highest fee paid: £60,000—Jimmy Kerr (from Bury), May 1970.
  Highest fee received: £150,000—Paul Bradshaw (to Wolves), September 1977.

BLACKPOOL

Bloomfield Road, Blackpool FY1 6JJ, Blackpool 46118

Shirts: tangerine with white stripe on sleeves. *Shorts:* white with tangerine stripe. *Stockings:* white with tangerine hoop. *Second colours:* white shirts, tangerine shorts.

Their appearances at Wembley in the years immediately after the Second World War will remain treasured memories for all associated with the Blackpool club. They went down 4–2 to Manchester United in the 1948 F.A. Cup Final, which has a place among Wembley's finest games; then they lost 2–0 to Newcastle in 1951 and finally came their memorable 4–3 triumph over Bolton in 1953. That was the match in which Stanley Matthews inspired his team-mates to snatch victory.

Stanley Mortensen, who achieved a hat-trick in the Bolton final, scored nearly 200 League goals for the club he later managed. Another notable personality of that era was the captain, Harry Johnston, who received the 'Footballer of the Year' award in 1951 —of which Matthews was the first holder in 1948.

Blackpool came closest to taking the First Division title in 1956 when they finished runners-up. They continued as a power through the fifties when much of the credit was due to their astute manager Joe Smith, the former England and Bolton inside forward who served from 1935 to 1958.

After being relegated in 1967, they bounced back again in 1970, but their comeback lasted only one season as they finished bottom of Division One—a sad ending to the Blackpool career of one of their finest ever players, Jimmy Armfield, who made more than 550 League appearances for the club and was capped 43 times at full-back for England.

F.A. Cup Winners: 1952–53.
Division 2 Champions: 1929–30.
Record attendance: 39,118 v. Man. Utd. (League), April 1952.
Modern Capacity: 38,000. **Nickname:** 'Tangerines.'
Entered Football League: 1896—Div. 2.
Biggest win: 8–4 v. Charlton Ath. (Div. 1), September 1952.
Heaviest defeat: 1–10 v. Small Heath (Div. 2), March 1901, and 1–10 v. Huddersfield Town (Div. 1), December 1930.
Best in League Cup: Semi-final 1961–62.
Pitch measurements: 111 x 73 yd.
Highest League Scorer in Single Season: Jimmy Hampson— 45 in 1929–30 (Div. 2).
Transfers—
  Highest fee paid: £60,000—Alan Suddick (from Newcastle), December 1966.
  Highest fee received: £300,000—Paul Hart (to Leeds), March 1978.

BOLTON WANDERERS

Burnden Park, Bolton BL3 2QR, Bolton 21101

Shirts: white. *Shorts:* navy blue. *Stockings:* white. *Second colours:* red shirts, white shorts.

Three times between 1923—the first Wembley F.A. Cup Final—and 1929, Bolton Wanderers won the game's most coveted domestic trophy. They did so without conceding a goal at Wembley. Five Wanderers players took part in each of those successful Finals—against West Ham in 1923 (2–0), Manchester City 1926 (1–0) and Portsmouth 1929 (2–0). They were Pym in goal, Haworth, Nuttall, Seddon and Butler.

Curiously, for all their Cup-fighting prowess and as founder-members of the Football League, Bolton have never won the Championship. Relegated in 1964, they sank into Division Three in 1971, but two years later began the climb back as Third Division Champions and in 1976 and 1977 they just missed promotion back to the First Division.

Bolton's individual League scoring record for a season (38 goals by Joe Smith) has stood longer than that of any other club—since 1920–21.

No one ever typified the fighting spirit of Wanderers better than centre-forward Nat Lofthouse, who played 33 times for England and, between 1946–61, scored 255 League goals—the club record.

Tragedy struck Burnden Park on 9 March 1946, when crush barriers broke at an F.A. Cup-tie between Bolton and Stoke City. Thirty-three people were killed and more than four hundred injured in the worst football disaster ever known in England.

F.A. Cup Winners: 1922–23, 1925–26, 1928–29, 1957–58.
Division 2 Champions: 1908–09.
Division 3 Champions: 1972–73.
Record attendance: 69,912 v. Manchester City (F.A. Cup), February 1933.
Modern Capacity: 60,000. **Nickname:** 'Trotters.'
Entered Football League: 1888—Div. 1.
Biggest win: 13–0 v. Sheffield United (F.A. Cup), February 1890.
Heaviest defeat: 0–7 v. Manchester City (Div. 1), March 1936.
Best in League Cup: Semi-final, 1976–77.
Pitch measurements: 112½ x 76 yd.
Highest League Scorer in Single Season: Joe Smith—38 in 1920–21 (Div. 1).
Transfers—
  Highest fee paid: £120,000—Alan Gowling (from Newcastle), March 1978.
  Highest fee received: £90,000—Barry Siddall (to Sunderland), September 1976.

A.F.C. BOURNEMOUTH

Dean Court, Bournemouth, Dorset BH7 7AF, Bournemouth 35381

Shirts: red with white trimmings. *Shorts:* white. *Stockings:* black with red tops & white band. *Second colours:* navy blue & white striped shirts, navy blue shorts.

No era has been more exciting or rewarding for Bournemouth than the early seventies. Their promotion from the Fourth Division in 1971 was followed by three more good seasons, in each of which they challenged for a Second Division place, but in 1974–75 they slumped and were relegated to the Fourth Division on goal average.

Centre-forward Ted MacDougall broke several Bournemouth goal-scoring records, among them most goals in a season, previously held by Ron Eyre with 32 in season 1928–29. During the successful 1970–71 season MacDougall was the Football League's highest scorer with 42, and the following season scored nine goals in a match—a new F.A. Cup record—when Bournemouth beat Margate 11–0 in the first round, their record victory.

But eventually the club was unable to hold him any more than opposing defences could, and in September 1972 sold their shooting star to Manchester United for £220,000. MacDougall soon moved on from Old Trafford to West Ham and then to Norwich where, inspired by manager John Bond as in his Bournemouth days, he scored prolifically in the mid-seventies.

The club was originally known simply as Boscombe, but when elected to the Third Division (South) in 1923, Bournemouth was incorporated in the title. In 1972 they 'went Continental' by changing their name to A.F.C. Bournemouth.

Record attendance: 28,799 v. Manchester United (F.A. Cup), March 1957.
Modern Capacity: 24,000. **Nickname:** 'Cherries.'
Entered Football League: 1923—Div. 3 (South).
Biggest win: 11–0 v. Margate (F.A. Cup), November 1971.
Heaviest defeat: 1–8 v. Bradford City (Div. 3), January 1970.
Highest final League position: 2nd in Div. 3 South, 1947–48.
Best in F.A. Cup: 6th Round 1956–57.
Best in League Cup: 4th Round 1961–62, 1963–64.
Pitch measurements: 115 x 75 yd.
Highest League Scorer in Single Season: Ted MacDougall— 42 in 1970–71 (Div. 4).
Transfers—
    Highest fee paid: £70,000 Brian Clark (from Cardiff), October 1972.
    Highest fee received: £220,000—Ted MacDougall (to Manchester United), September 1972.

BRADFORD CITY

Valley Parade, Bradford BD8 7DY, Bradford 306062

Shirts: amber with maroon panel, collar & cuffs. *Shorts:* maroon with amber piping. *Stockings:* white. *Second colours:* maroon shirts & white shorts.

Bradford City have been striving hard to keep first-class Association football alive in the area since neighbours Bradford Park Avenue lost their membership of the Football League in 1970.

Yet most of City's glories belong to the past. They were in Division One between 1908 and 1922, and became the first holders of the present F.A. Cup in 1911 when they defeated Newcastle United 1–0 at Old Trafford, after a goalless draw at the old Crystal Palace. During seasons 1910–11 and 1911–12, Bradford City played 12 consecutive F.A. Cup ties without conceding a goal, and there were echoes of long ago when, in 1976, while struggling in the Fourth Division, they beat First Division Norwich 2–1 away to reach the sixth round.

When they won the Third Division North title in season 1928–29, City scored 128 goals and obtained 63 points, by far their best statistics in League football.

Not surprisingly in an area noted for the handling game, Bradford City F.C. developed in 1903 from a Rugby club—Manningham. Since then a number of fine players have worn City's colours, among them Sam Barkas, Tommy Cairns, Arthur Whitehurst (who scored seven goals v. Tranmere in 1929), Willie Watson and Trevor Hockey.

City paid their record fee of £12,500 in July 1974, when Welsh International Hockey returned to Valley Parade (where his career began) after serving six other clubs.

F.A. Cup Winners: 1910–11.
Division 2 Champions: 1907–08.
Division 3 (North) Champions: 1928–29.
Record attendance: 39,146 v. Burnley (F.A. Cup), March 1911.
Modern Capacity: 24,000. **Nickname:** 'Paraders.'
Entered Football League: 1903—Div. 2.
Biggest win: 11–1 v. Rotherham (Div. 3 North), August 1928.
Heaviest defeat: 1–9 v. Colchester Utd. (Div. 4) December 1961.
Best in League Cup: 5th Round 1964–65.
Pitch measurements: 112 x 71 yd.
Highest League Scorer in Single Season: David Layne—34 in 1961–62 (Div. 4).
Transfers—
  Highest fee paid: £30,000—David McNiven (from Leeds), February 1978.
  Highest fee received: £23,000—Bruce Bannister (to Bristol Rovers), November 1971.

BRENTFORD

Griffin Park, Braemar Road, Brentford, Middlesex TW8 0NT
01–560 2021

Shirts: red & white stripes. *Shorts:* black. *Stockings:* black with red & white tops. *Second colours:* royal blue shirts & white shorts.

Formed in 1888, when by one vote they decided against setting up as a Rugby club, Brentford turned professional in 1900, and after successes in the Southern League became founder members of the Third Division in 1920. Under the progressive management of Harry Curtis they began a long period of success which took them into Division One in 1935.

Among their achievements was to win all 21 home League matches in the Third Division (South) in season 1929–30—no club has since won every home game in a season—but, curiously, they failed to win promotion that year, finishing runners-up. In 1932–33 they took the title and added the Second Division crown two seasons later.

After the Second World War, Brentford slipped from First to Fourth Division. In January 1967 they were near to going out of existence, but they resisted a take-over bid by Queen's Park Rangers, and by November 1971 they had cleared a debt of £104,000. The struggle has continued on the field, for promotion to Division Three in 1972 lasted only one season.

Division 2 Champions: 1934–35.
Division 3 (South) Champions: 1932–33.
Division 4 Champions: 1962–63.
Record attendance: 39,626 v. Preston N.E. (F.A. Cup), March 1938.
Modern Capacity: 38,000. **Nickname:** 'Bees.'
Entered Football League: 1920—Div. 3.
Biggest win: 9–0 v. Wrexham (Div. 3), October 1963.
Heaviest defeat: 0–7 v. Swansea (Div. 3 South), November 1924, and 0–7 v. Walsall (Div. 3 South), January 1957.
Best in F.A. Cup: 6th Round 1937–38, 1945–46, 1948–49.
Best in League Cup: 3rd Round 1960–61, 1968–69.
Pitch measurements: 114 x 75 yd.
Highest League Scorer in Single Season: Jack Holliday—36 in 1932–33 (Div. 3 South).
Transfers—
  Highest fee paid: £25,000—Andy McCulloch (from Oxford United), March 1976.
  Highest fee received: £50,000—Stewart Houston (to Manchester United), December 1973.

BRIGHTON AND HOVE ALBION

Goldstone Ground, Hove, Sussex BN3 7DE, Brighton 739535

Shirts: blue & white stripes. *Shorts:* blue with white seams. *Stockings:* white, blue trimmed top. *Second colours:* red or blue shirts with white trim, white shorts.

Relegated in 1973 after only a one-season stay in the Second Division and situated near the foot of the Third six months later, Brighton sought a big-name manager to improve their image. They appointed Brian Clough on November 1, less than three weeks after his resignation at Derby, where he had won Second and First Division Championships. Clough's arrival sent interest booming at Brighton, but they went out of the F.A. Cup in the first round, beaten 4–0 in a home replay by amateurs Walton and Hersham, and three days later suffered further humiliation before their own supporters, crashing 8–2 to Third Division leaders Bristol Rovers —the heaviest home defeat in Brighton's history.

Within seven months Clough had gone, for in June 1974 he returned to the First Division scene in charge of Leeds United, an appointment that lasted 44 days. He was succeeded by his assistant Peter Taylor who built the side that narrowly missed promotion in 1975–76. When he rejoined Clough at Nottingham Forest, former England star Alan Mullery was given his first managerial appointment and he took Brighton back into the Second Division at the end of 1976–77.

Division 3 (South) Champions: 1957–58.
Division 4 Champions: 1964–65.
Record attendance: 36,747 v. Fulham (League), December 1958.
Modern Capacity: 38,000.
Entered Football League: 1920—Div. 3.
Biggest win: 10–1 v. Wisbech (F.A. Cup), November 1965.
Heaviest defeat: 0–9 v. Middlesbrough (League), August 1958.
Best in F.A. Cup: 5th Round 1929–30, 1932–33, 1945–46, 1959–60.
Best in League Cup: 4th Round 1966–67, 1976–77.
Pitch measurements: 112 x 75 yd.
Highest League Scorer in Single Season: Peter Ward—32 in 1976–77 (Div. 3).
Transfers—
  Highest fee paid: £200,000—Teddy Maybank (from Fulham), November 1977.
  Highest fee received: £26,000—Ken Beamish (to Blackburn), May 1974.

BRISTOL CITY

Ashton Gate, Bristol BS3 2EJ, Bristol 632812

Shirts: red, white trim. *Shorts:* white. *Stockings:* red & white. *Second colours:* white shirts, black shorts.

In their first season in Division One, in 1906–07, Bristol City finished runners-up to Newcastle, and two years later reached the F.A. Cup Final for the only time in their history.

First Division status was surrendered in 1911 and they alternated between Divisions Two and Three during the next 60 years with seasons of occasional brilliance, such as 1954–55 when they strode away with the old Third Division (South) title. They obtained 70 points—nine more than the second club.

City's most celebrated international was centre-half Billy Wedlock, who played 26 times for England from 1907–12. Another England cap, John Atyeo, holds the club's records for most League appearances (597) and most League goals (315) between 1951 and 1966. He also scored 35 Cup goals.

But the City team of 1974 gave Bristol reasons to dwell more on the present than the past, knocking out F.A. Cup favourites and runaway First Division leaders Leeds 1–0 in a fifth round replay at Elland Road to reach the last eight for the first time in 53 years.

Under manager Alan Dicks, the steadily-improving City side finished fifth in the Second Division in 1973 and 1975. Then, in season 1975–76, they made a magnificent attempt to bring First Division football back to Ashton Gate after 65 years—and succeeded. At the height of the promotion effort they resisted Arsenal's £250,000 offer for captain Geoff Merrick and top scorer Tom Ritchie, a decision that was to influence City's destiny, as much as their impressive football did.

Division 2 Champions: 1905–06.
Division 3 (South) Champions: 1922–23, 1926–27, 1954–55.
Record attendance: 43,335 v. Preston N.E. (F.A. Cup), Feb. 1935.
Modern Capacity: 40,500. **Nickname:** 'Robins.'
Entered Football League: 1901—Div. 2.
Biggest win: 11–0 v. Chichester (F.A. Cup), November 1960.
Heaviest defeat: 0–9 v. Coventry City (League), April 1934.
Best in F.A. Cup: Final 1908–09.
Best in League Cup: Semi-final 1970–71.
Pitch measurements: 115 x 78 yd.
Highest League Scorer in Single Season: Don Clark—36 in 1946–47 (Div. 3 South).
Transfers—
  Highest fee paid: £110,000—Chris Garland (from Leicester), November 1976.
  Highest fee received: £100,000—Chris Garland (to Chelsea), September 1971.

BRISTOL ROVERS

Eastville, Bristol BS5 6NN, Bristol 558620

Shirts: blue & white quarters. *Shorts:* white. *Stockings:* blue & white. *Second colours:* yellow shirts, black shorts.

Although twice in the 1950s Bristol Rovers finished sixth in Division Two, most of their existence has been spent in Third Division company, but season 1973–74 raised hopes of a shining new era at Eastville. From kick-off day in August, Rovers were unbeaten in 27 League games until February 1, a sequence stretched to 32 by five matches without defeat at the end of the previous season.

On the strength of such a run, which was highlighted by the free scoring of Alan Warboys and Bruce Bannister, Rovers set up a long lead in the Third Division. The 8–2 win at Brighton on December 1 was the biggest victory in their history, and with City doing great deeds in the F.A. Cup, Bristol became a region of intense football interest in 1973–74. It ended with Rovers promoted on goal average as runners-up to Oldham.

Rovers have always had a reputation for developing their own players, and Ronnie Dix, Phil Taylor, Roy Bentley and Larry Lloyd are just a few who have achieved distinction elsewhere.

Unlike their neighbours, Bristol City, the Rovers have never reached the Final of the F.A. Cup. The furthest they have gone is the sixth round, in 1951 and 1958—the year in which they knocked out Burnley, then a First Division side.

Division 3 (South) Champions: 1952–53.
Record attendance: 38,472 v. Preston N.E. (F.A. Cup), January 1960.
Modern Capacity: 40,000. **Nickname:** 'Pirates.'
Entered Football League: 1920—Div. 3.
Biggest win: 8–2 v. Brighton (Div. 3), December 1973.
Heaviest defeat: 0–12 v. Luton Town (Div. 3 South), April 1936.
Best in F.A. Cup: 6th Round 1950–51, 1957–58.
Best in League Cup: 5th Round 1970–71, 1971–72.
Pitch measurements: 112 x 76 yd.
Highest League Scorer in Single Season: Geoff Bradford—33 in 1952–53 (Div. 3 South).
Transfers—
    Highest fee paid: £35,000—Alan Warboys (from Sheffield United), March 1973.
    Highest fee received: £55,000—Phil Roberts (to Portsmouth), May 1973.

BURNLEY

Turf Moor, Burnley, Lancs. BB10 4BX, Burnley 27777 & 38021

Shirts: claret with sky blue V. *Shorts:* white. *Stockings:* white with claret top. *Second colours:* blue shirts with claret trim, blue shorts.

Burnley returned to the First Division in 1973 after two seasons' absence. They did so as Second Division Champions, but suffered another playing slump in 1975–76. In January that season, a few weeks after transferring Welsh international left-winger Leighton James to Derby for £310,000, Burnley also parted company with Jimmy Adamson, whose resignation ended 30 years with the club as player, coach and manager. The season ended with relegation at Turf Moor for the second time in six seasons.

Burnley, one of the League's founder clubs in 1888, shattered all records in season 1920–21, by playing 30 consecutive matches without defeat. This memorable League record from 6 September to 25 March read: played 30, won 21, drawn 9, goals 68–17, points 51. Thus Burnley won the First Division title for the first time in their history, and their record unbeaten sequence was not surpassed until 1969–70 when Leeds played 34 matches before losing.

Burnley have consistently operated the transfer market to survive in the shadow of the two glamour clubs of Manchester, and James's departure meant that in eight seasons they had earned £1½ million from major deals including: Willie Morgan to Manchester United (£100,000), Ralph Coates to Tottenham (£190,000), Steve Kindon to Wolverhampton (£100,000), Dave Thomas to Queen's Park Rangers (£165,000), Martin Dobson to Everton (£300,000) and Geoff Nulty to Newcastle (£120,000).

League Champions: 1920–21, 1959–60.

Division 2 Champions: 1897–98, 1972–73.

F.A. Cup Winners: 1913–14.

Record attendance: 54,775 v. Huddersfield Town (F.A. Cup), February 1924.

Modern Capacity: 39,000. **Nickname:** 'Clarets.'

Entered Football League: 1888—Div. 1.

Biggest League win: 9–0 v. Darwen (Div. 1), January 1892; 9–0 v. Crystal Palace (F.A. Cup), 1908–09; 9–0 v. New Brighton (F.A. Cup), January 1957.

Heaviest League defeat: 0–10 v. Aston Villa (Div. 1), August 1925 and 0–10 v. Sheffield United (Div. 1), January 1929.

Best in League Cup: Semi-final 1960–61, 1968–69.

Pitch measurements: 115½ x 73 yd.

Highest League Scorer in Single Season: George Beel—35 in 1927–28 (Div. 1).

Transfers—

  Highest fee paid: £100,000—Tony Morley (from Preston), February 1976.

  Highest fee received: £310,000—Leighton James (to Derby) November 1975.

BURY

Gigg Lane, Bury BL9 9HR, 061-764 4881/2

Shirts: white with royal blue collar. *Shorts:* royal blue. *Stockings:* royal blue. *Second colours:* yellow shirts & shorts.

Bury, nicknamed 'The Shakers', have certainly stirred the football world in their time, starting from season 1894–95, when they won the Second Division championship in their first year as League members. Five years later they defeated Southampton 4–0 in the F.A. Cup Final at the old Crystal Palace, and in 1903 they caused an even bigger stir by winning the trophy again without conceding a goal in any of their ties. They trounced Derby County on the same ground by six goals to nil—which remains the biggest winning margin in the Final.

Bury stayed in the First Division for seventeen seasons; they dropped to the Second Division in 1912 and regained higher status in 1924, but this time they survived for only five seasons. Since then they have achieved occasional periods of glory such as winning the Division Three title in 1960–61 by a margin of six points. They reached the semi-final of the Football League Cup in season 1962–63 before losing 4–3 on aggregate to Birmingham City, the eventual winners of the trophy. Bury showed their tenacity as Cup fighters in 1955 when they played Stoke City for a record 9 hours 22 minutes, in five meetings in the F.A. Cup third round before Stoke won 3–2 at Old Trafford.

'The Shakers' were themselves shaken as they slipped to the Third Division in 1967 and in 1971 to the Fourth, but within three years they were back in the Third.

F.A. Cup Winners: 1899–1900, 1902–03.
Division 2 Champions: 1894–95.
Division 3 Champions: 1960–61.
Record attendance: 35,000 v. Bolton Wanderers (F.A. Cup), January 1960.
Modern Capacity: 35,000. **Nickname:** 'Shakers.'
Entered Football League: 1894—Div. 2.
Biggest win: 12–1 v. Stockton (F.A. Cup), 1896–97.
Heaviest defeat: 0–10 v. Blackburn Rovers (F.A. Cup), 1887–88.
Best in League Cup: Semi-final 1962–63.
Pitch measurements: 116 x 80 yd.
Highest League Scorer in Single Season: Norman Bullock—31 in 1925–26 (Div. 1).
Transfers—
  Highest fee paid: £25,000—Jimmy McIlwraith (from Motherwell), December 1975; £25,000—Ian Robins (from Oldham), July 1977.
  Highest fee received: £60,000—Alec Lindsay (to Liverpool), March 1969.

CAMBRIDGE UNITED

The Abbey Stadium, Newmarket Road, Cambridge CB5 8LL
Teversham 2170

Shirts: black & amber stripes. *Shorts:* black. *Stockings:* black with amber & white turnovers. *Second colours:* white shirts & shorts.

From the moment they turned professional in 1946, Cambridge United rapidly established a reputation as a progressive-thinking club while playing in the Cambridgeshire, Eastern Counties and Southern Leagues. They won the Southern League Championship in successive years, 1968–69 and 1969–70, and by then their credentials had so impressed Football League clubs that at the annual meeting, in June 1970, they were elected to the Fourth Division in place of Bradford Park Avenue.

Understandably the switch to higher class football produced many fresh challenges for Cambridge and the first season in the League was very much one of trial and error. United finished 20th, only one place clear of the re-election zone, but in 1972 they improved to tenth and a year later third place in the final table took them up to Division Three. They dropped again to the Fourth, however, in 1974. That set-back was only temporary. In 1976–77 they came back as Fourth Division champions.

One of the highlights of their inaugural year as a Football League club was a fixture with Chelsea, in May 1970, which attracted a crowd of 14,000. The match was Chelsea's 'thank you' for signing Ian Hutchinson, who had joined them from Cambridge in July 1968, and this is the only instance of an existing official attendance record for a League club being set at a friendly game.

Division 4 Champions: 1976–77.
Record attendance: 14,000 v. Chelsea (Friendly), May 1970.
Modern Capacity: 14,000
Entered Football League: 1970—Div. 4.
Biggest League win: 6–0 v. Darlington (Div. 4), September 1971.
Heaviest defeat: 0–6 v. Aldershot (Div. 4), April 1974, and 0–6 v. Darlington (Div. 4), September 1974.
Best in F.A. Cup: 3rd Round 1973–74.
Best in League Cup: 2nd Round 1973–74, 1976–77.
Pitch measurements: 112 × 75 yd.
Highest League Scorer in Single Season: Brian Greenhalgh —19 in 1971–72 (Div. 4), and Alan Biley—19 in 1976–77.
Transfers—
    Highest fee paid: £30,000—Bobby Shinton (from Walsall), March 1974; £30,000 Gordon Swetzer (from Brentford), March 1978.
    Highest fee received: £40,000—Brian Greenhalgh (to Bournemouth), February 1974.

CARDIFF CITY

Ninian Park, Cardiff CF1 8SX, Cardiff 28501 & 33230

Shirts: blue with yellow & white stripe on chest. *Shorts:* blue.
Stockings: blue with yellow & white band. *Second colours:* yellow
shirts & shorts.

The most memorable event in Cardiff City's history occurred in
1927, when they became the first non-English club to win the
F.A. Cup. That year they beat Arsenal 1–0 at Wembley and the
drama of the occasion was heightened by the fact that the Arsenal
goalkeeper, Dan Lewis, whose error allowed Cardiff to triumph, was
himself a Welshman.

Three years earlier another mistake—this time by a City player—
cost Cardiff the First Division Championship. They needed two
points from their final match against Birmingham, but missed a
penalty late in the game and could only draw.

In the Cardiff goal, during their First Division days of the 1920s,
was Tom Farquharson their longest-serving player. He made nearly
450 League appearances between 1922 and 1935.

Cardiff's star waned, however, and the club slipped into the
Second Division in 1929 and the Third (South) two seasons later,
but re-emerged as Southern Section Champions in 1947. Since the
last war they have had two spells totalling seven years in the First
Division, from 1952–57 and 1960–62, but at the end of 1974–75,
after narrowly escaping relegation for three seasons, they dropped
into Division 3 again. Under manager Jimmy Andrews they were
promoted back to the Second Division in 1976.

As Welsh Cup winners, Cardiff have made frequent appearances
in the European Cup-Winners' Cup and become one of Britain's
most travelled clubs. In 1967–68 they reached the semi-finals.

F.A. Cup Winners: 1926–27.
Division 3 (South) Champions: 1946–47.
Record attendance: 61,566 Wales v. England (International),
October 1961.
Modern Capacity: 60,000. **Nickname:** 'Bluebirds.'
Entered Football League: 1920—Div. 2.
Biggest win: 9–2 v. Thames (Div. 3 South), February 1932.
Heaviest defeat: 2–11 v. Sheffield United (Div. 1), January 1926.
Best in League Cup: Semi-final 1965–66.
Pitch measurements: 112 x 76 yd.
Highest League Scorer in Single Season: Stan Richards—31
in 1946–47 (Div. 3 South).
Transfers—
  Highest fee paid: £60,000—Willie Anderson (from Aston
  Villa), February 1973.
  Highest fee received: £110,000—John Toshack (to Liverpool),
  November 1970.

CARLISLE UNITED

Brunton Park, Carlisle CA1 1LL, Carlisle 26237

Shirts: blue with broad white stripe, red piping. *Shorts:* white.
Stockings: red. *Second colours:* yellow shirts, blue shorts.

Carlisle United's progress was unspectacular following their
formation in 1903. In 1928 they were elected to Division Three
(North) in place of Durham City and finished eighth in their first
campaign. But they had to seek re-election in 1934–35.

They were third in 1951, but when Division Four was formed
from the bottom 12 clubs of each section of the Third in 1958,
Carlisle were among them.

They gained promotion in 1962, dropped straight back the
following season, but immediately went up again, with Hugh
McIlmoyle scoring 39 out of a grand total of 113 League goals.

Carlisle, situated so close to the Border that at one time there was
speculation about their joining the Scottish League, swept on into
Division Two in 1965, just twelve months after leaving the Fourth
Division. In 1967 they finished only one place from the First Division,
and in 1974 they at last brought top-division football to their North-
west outpost by finishing third in Div. 2—a wonderful achievement
for a club of their size.

Life in the First Division began astonishingly, with 1–0 wins in
the first three games, at Chelsea, at Middlesbrough and at home to
Tottenham. But they could not play above themselves indefinitely,
and for Carlisle it proved a one-season stay in the top company.
The bubble burst and they finished bottom.

Division 3 Champions: 1964–65.
Record attendance: 27,500 v. Birmingham City (F.A. Cup),
January 1957, and 27,500 v. Middlesbrough (F.A. Cup), February
1970.
Modern Capacity: 30,000. **Nickname:** 'Cumbrians.'
Entered Football League: 1928—Div. 3 (North).
Biggest win: 8–0 v. Hartlepool (Div. 3 North), September 1928,
and 8–0 v. Scunthorpe United (Div. 3 North), December 1952.
Heaviest League defeat: 1–11 v. Hull City (Div. 3 North),
January 1939.
Best in F.A. Cup: 6th Round 1974–75.
Best in League Cup: Semi-final 1969–70.
Pitch measurements: 117 x 78 yd.
Highest League Scorer in Single Season: Jimmy McConnell
—42 in 1928–29 (Div. 3 North).
Transfers—
  Highest fee paid: £75,000—David Kemp (from Portsmouth),
March 1978.
  Highest fee received: £125,000—Billy Rafferty (to Wolves),
March 1978.

CHARLTON ATHLETIC

The Valley, Floyd Road, Charlton, London SE7 8AW, 01-858 3711/2

Shirts: red, white trim. *Shorts:* white. *Stockings:* red. *Second colours* yellow shirts & shorts.

Charlton Athletic was a name to conjure with between 1935 and 1947 when the London club distinguished themselves in League and Cup. They came within touching distance of a memorable League hat-trick after winning the Division Three (South) Championship in 1935. The following season they gained promotion to Division One, and twelve months later they were runners-up for the Championship itself.

Beaten in extra time in the F.A. Cup Final of 1946 by Derby, Charlton returned to Wembley the following season and beat Burnley 1–0 after extra time. But after the glories of the forties came the slump with Charlton falling into Division Two in 1957 and then, in 1972, to Division Three, which they had left in 1935. They returned to the Second Division in 1975.

Among Charlton's best-known players were Sam Bartram, who kept goal for them in 583 League games from 1934–56, and South Africans John Hewie (capped 19 times by Scotland at full-back) and Stuart Leary, who holds the club scoring record with 153 goals between 1953–62.

In December 1957 Charlton staged one of the most amazing recoveries in football history. With 20 minutes left in a Second Division match at home to Huddersfield, they were losing 5–1 and reduced to ten men—yet finished winners by 7–6, with Johnny Summers scoring five of the goals.

F.A. Cup Winners: 1946–47.
Division 3 (South) Champions: 1928–29, 1934–35.
Record attendance: 75,031 v. Aston Villa (F.A. Cup), February 1938.
Modern Capacity: 67,000. **Nickname:** 'Robins.'
Entered Football League: 1921—Div. 3 (South).
Biggest win: 8–1 v. Middlesbrough (Div. 1), September 1953.
Heaviest defeat: 1–11 v. Aston Villa (Div. 2), November 1959.
Best in League Cup: 4th Round 1962–63, 1964–65.
Pitch measurements: 114 x 73 yd.
Highest League Scorer in Single Season: Ralph Allen—32 in 1934–35 (Div. 3 South).
Transfers—
   Highest fee paid: £65,000—Dick Tydeman (from Gillingham), December 1976.
   Highest fee received: £280,000—Derek Hales (to Derby), December 1976.

CHELSEA

Stamford Bridge Grounds, Fulham Road, London SW6 1HS.
01–385 5545/6

Shirts: royal blue. *Shorts:* royal blue. *Stockings:* white. *Second colours:* yellow shirts & shorts.

For the first fifty years of their existence Chelsea did not win a single prize. Then they celebrated their golden jubilee by taking the League Championship of 1954–55 under the managership of Ted Drake. Under his successor, Tommy Docherty, they won the League Cup in 1964–65 and, guided by Dave Sexton, they collected two more trophies in successive seasons.

In 1970 Chelsea at last lifted the F.A. Cup, dramatically beating Leeds 2–1 in extra time at Old Trafford in the first replayed Final since 1912. That victory qualified them for the Cup-Winners' Cup, and led them a year later to their first European prize, Real Madrid being beaten in the replayed Final in Athens. In 1972 they reached their third successive Final—this time in the League Cup—but Stoke beat them 2–1, so Chelsea have still to win a peacetime trophy at Wembley.

They have forfeited top-class status twice since the last war. In 1962–63 they won back a First Division place first time but in the middle seventies, after committing themselves to a multi-million pound ground redevelopment scheme, Chelsea swiftly disintegrated on the field and were relegated in 1975. But after two years they were back in the First Division, a fine achievement since their financial difficulties prevented them buying players.

League Champions: 1954–55.
F.A. Cup Winners: 1969–70.
League Cup Winners: 1964–65.
Winners of European Cup-Winners' Cup: 1970–71.
Record attendance: 82,905 v. Arsenal (League), October 1935.
Modern Capacity: 55,000. **Nickname:** 'Blues.'
Entered Football League: 1905—Div. 2.
Biggest win: 13–0 v. Jeunesse Hautcharage, Luxembourg (European Cup-Winners' Cup), September 1971.
Heaviest defeat: 1–8 v. Wolves (Div. 1), September 1953.
Pitch measurements: 114 x 71½ yd.
Highest League Scorer in Single Season: Jimmy Greaves—41 in 1960–61 (Div. 1).
Transfers—
   Highest fee paid: £225,000—David Hay (from Celtic), July 1974.
   Highest fee received: £275,000—Peter Osgood (to Southampton), March 1974.

CHESTER

Sealand Road, Chester CH1 4LW, Chester 21048

Shirts: royal blue & white stripes. *Shorts:* royal blue with red & white stripes. *Second colours:* yellow shirts & shorts.

For Chester F.C., proximity to those two great Merseyside clubs, Everton and Liverpool, has always meant severe competition for players and supporters. The club was formed in 1884—four years before the Football League began—but did not gain election to the old Third Division North until 1931. The early seasons were full of promise. The team finished third in their debut year, fourth the following season, third in 1934–35, were runners-up in 1935–36, and third in 1936–37.

A number of international players, among them Tommy Lawton and Don Welsh, assisted the club while on military service during the Second World War. On the resumption of peace-time League football in 1946–47, Chester filled third place once more, but a succession of managers, including Frank Brown, Louis Page and John Harris, were unable to bring the Cheshire club much success.

It came, however, in season 1974–75. In their finest-ever effort in knock-out football, Chester dismissed First Division giants Leeds 3–0 and Newcastle 1–0 (after drawing 0–0 away) to reach the League Cup semi-final. Aston Villa then stopped them 5–4 on aggregate, but major compensation for manager Ken Roberts and his players was only weeks away—a place in Division 3 and the first time promotion had been won in Chester's history, albeit by four-hundredths of a goal.

Record attendance: 20,500 v. Chelsea (F.A. Cup), January 1952.
Modern Capacity: 20,000. **Nickname:** 'Seals.'
Entered Football League: 1931—Div. 3 (North).
Biggest win: 12–0 v. York City (Div. 3 North), February 1936.
Heaviest defeat: 2–11 v. Oldham Athletic (Div. 3 North), January 1952.
Highest final League position: 2nd in Div. 3 (North), 1935–36.
Best in F.A. Cup: 5th Round 1976–77.
Best in League Cup: Semi-final 1974–75.
Pitch measurements: 114 x 75 yd.
Highest League Scorer in Single Season: Dick Yates—36 in 1946–47 (Div. 3 North).
Transfers—
 Highest fee paid: £30,000—Ian Mellor (from Brighton), February 1978.
 Highest fee received: £110,000—Paul Futcher (to Luton), May 1974.

CHESTERFIELD

Saltergate, Chesterfield S40 4SX, Chesterfield 32318

Shirts: royal blue. *Shorts:* white. *Stockings:* white with two blue rings. *Second colours:* amber shirts & shorts.

Membership of Chesterfield F.C. in their formation year of 1866 cost a couple of shillings or ten new pence. Exactly 100 years later the club's most distinguished product, Gordon Banks, kept goal for England in their World Cup Final victory over West Germany at Wembley. Banks, later of Leicester City and Stoke City, always acknowledged the value of those early days with Chesterfield. He was one of two outstanding goalkeepers developed post-war by the club. The other was Ray Middleton, who became a Justice of the Peace following his work for local youth organizations. Other well-known players in the town of the Crooked Spire have included members of the Milburn family, 'Legs' Linacre, Tommy Capel and Gordon Dale.

Chesterfield played in Division Two between 1899 and 1909 but then dropped out of the League until 1921, when they re-entered as members of Division Three (North), a section which they won in 1931 and 1936.

They have spent two separate periods in Division Two since those early days, and in 1947 finished fourth—the highest final placing they have attained in the Football League. Fourth Division Champions in 1970, they have finished fifth twice since in a bid to win back the Second Division place they last held in 1951.

Division 3 (North) Champions: 1930–31, 1935–36.
Division 4 Champions: 1969–70.
Record attendance: 30,968 v. Newcastle (League), April 1939.
Modern Capacity: 28,500. **Nickname:** 'Blues.'
Entered Football League: 1899—Div. 2.
Biggest win: 10–0 v. Glossop N.E. (Div. 2), January 1903.
Heaviest defeat: 1–9 v. Port Vale (Div. 2), September 1932.
Best in F.A. Cup: 5th Round 1932–33, 1937–38, 1949–50.
Best in League Cup: 4th Round 1964–65.
Pitch measurements: 114 x 73 yd.
Highest League Scorer in Single Season: Jimmy Cookson—44 in 1925–26 (Div. 3 North).
Transfers—
    Highest fee paid: £20,000—Stuart Parker (from Southend), February 1977; £20,000—Richard Green (from Scunthorpe), February 1977.
    Highest fee received: £80,000—Steve Hardwick (to Newcastle), December 1976.

COLCHESTER UNITED

Layer Road, Colchester CO2 7JJ, Colchester 74042

Shirts: blue & white stripes. *Shorts:* blue. *Stockings:* white. *Second colours:* red shirts, black shorts.

Colchester United first made an impact on soccer in England in 1948, when they achieved a series of astonishing F.A. Cup giant-killing acts. While still members of the Southern League, they knocked out Huddersfield Town and Bradford (who had previously defeated Arsenal) before finally falling at Blackpool in the fifth round. Their manager then was Ted Fenton, who later guided West Ham back to the First Division.

Not surprisingly after such impressive evidence of their talents, Colchester were elected to the Football League in 1950. And 21 years later, in the fifth round of season 1970–71, they celebrated their 'coming of age' with another incredible Cup triumph. This time they defeated Leeds United 3–2 at Layer Road, and by now even Wembley seemed a possibility for manager Dick Graham's team of Fourth Division enthusiasts, but in the quarter-finals Colchester were drawn away to Everton and beaten 5–0.

Three times in the sixties Colchester lost their place in Division Three, but they returned again at the end of season 1973–74 on the strength of magnificent home form and the individual scoring power of 24-goal Bobby Svarc. He repeated that total in 1974–75 and Svarc's transfer to Blackburn in October 1975 set a record for Colchester at £25,000.

Record attendance: 19,072 v. Reading (F.A. Cup), November 1948.

Modern Capacity: 16,000. **Nickname:** 'U's.'

Entered Football League: 1950—Div. 3 (South).

Biggest win: 9–1 v. Bradford City (Div. 4), December 1961.

Heaviest defeat: 0–7 v. Leyton Orient (Div. 3 South), January 1952; 0–7 v. Reading (Div. 3 South), September 1957.

Highest final League position: 2nd in Div. 4, 1961–62.

Best in F.A. Cup: 6th Round 1970–71.

Best in League Cup: 5th Round 1974–75.

Pitch measurements: 110 x 74 yd.

Highest League Scorer in Single Season: Bobby Hunt—37 in 1961–62 (Div. 4).

Transfers—
  Highest fee paid: £15,000—Dave Simmons (from Aston Villa), December 1970; £15,000—Eddie Rowles (from Darlington), December 1977.

  Highest fee received: £25,000—Bobby Svarc (to Blackburn), October 1975.

COVENTRY CITY

Highfield Road, Coventry CV2 4GU, Coventry 57171

Shirts: sky blue with navy & white trim. *Shorts:* sky blue with navy & white trim. *Stockings:* sky blue. *Second colours:* red shirts with navy blue collar & cuffs, navy blue shorts.

The rise of Coventry City from the obscurity of the Fourth Division in 1959, to the glamour of the First Division eight years later, is one of the success stories of post-war soccer.

From the old Southern League, they gained admission to the Football League in 1919 and just avoided relegation from the Second Division in their first season. They dropped down to the Third Division in 1925 and took eleven seasons to get back into the Second, finishing 1935–36 as Third Division South Champions.

Coventry slipped again in 1952 and became founder members of the Fourth Division in 1958. After only one season in the Fourth, however, the new-look City gained promotion and began the thrilling climb that took them into the First Division in 1967. Thus they became the only club to have played in six divisions of the Football League (3N, 3S, 4, 3, 2, 1).

That ebullient manager, Jimmy Hill, led the Sky Blue revolution of the sixties, and having reached the First Division for the first time, City had to survive a two-season threat of relegation before they could breathe more comfortably in the top section. Then, caught up in the car industry's depression in the mid-seventies, Coventry found the need to sell players at big fees and buy moderately—a delicate balancing act between solvency, First Division survival and diminishing gates.

Division 2 Champions: 1966–67.
Division 3 (South) Champions: 1935–36.
Division 3 Champions: 1963–64.
Record attendance: 51,455 v. Wolves (League), April 1967.
Modern Capacity: 52,000. **Nickname:** 'Sky Blues.'
Entered Football League: 1919—Div. 2.
Biggest win: 9–0 v. Bristol City (Div. 3 South), April 1934.
Heaviest defeat: 2–10 v. Norwich City (Div. 3 South), Mar. 1930.
Best in F.A. Cup: 6th Round 1962–63, 1972–73 (also reached the last eight in old 4th Round 1909–10).
Best in League Cup: 5th Round 1964–65, 1970–71, 1973–74.
Pitch measurements: 110 x 72 yd.
Highest League Scorer in Single Season: Clarrie Bourton—49 in 1931–32 (Div. 3 South). .
Transfers—
  Highest fee paid: £240,000—Larry Lloyd (from Liverpool), August 1974.
  Highest fee received: £200,000—Jeff Blockley (to Arsenal), October 1972.

40

CREWE ALEXANDRA

Gresty Road, Crewe CW2 6EB, Crewe 3014

Shirts: red with white trim. *Shorts:* white with red stripe. *Stockings:* red & white. *Second colours:* sky blue shirts with white trim, black shorts.

The club owes its origins to the game of cricket. In 1876 a local cricket team decided to form a football section, and only 12 years later, while still amateurs, Crewe Alexandra—derived from the name of the town and the hotel they used—had reached the semi-final of the F.A. Cup.

They turned professional in 1893, the year after becoming a founder member of Division Two of the Football League. Unhappily, they were not re-elected in 1896 and remained in comparative obscurity until after the First World War when they re-entered the League in Division Three (North) in 1921.

Since then the story of Crewe has almost always been one of hard struggle. Promotion from Division Four in 1962–63, when they were third, and again in 1967–68 (fourth) provided brief periods of reward, and another was the club's remarkable 2–1 F.A. Cup third round win at Chelsea in January 1961.

The most melancholy period in Crewe's long history occurred during 1956–57 when they played a record 30 consecutive League matches without a win. One of the finest players produced by Crewe was Frank Blunstone, who moved to Chelsea as a boy winger in February 1953 and went on to gain five full caps for England.

Record attendance: 20,000 v. Tottenham (F.A. Cup), January 1960.
Modern Capacity: 16,000. **Nickname:** 'Railwaymen.
Entered Football League: 1892—Div. 2.
Biggest win: 8–0 v. Rotherham United (Div. 3 North), October 1932.
Heaviest defeat: 2–13 v. Tottenham (F.A. Cup), February 1960.
Highest final League position: 3rd in Div. 4, 1962–63.
Best in F.A. Cup: Semi-final 1887–88.
Best in League Cup: 3rd Round 1960–61, 1974–75.
Pitch measurements: 112 x 75 yd.
Highest League Scorer in Single Season: Terry Harkin—35 in 1964–65 (Div. 4).
Transfers—
  Highest fee paid: £5000—Gordon Wallace (from Liverpool), October 1967.
  Highest fee received: £30,000—Brian Parker (to Arsenal), August 1975.

CRYSTAL PALACE

Selhurst Park, London SE25 6PU, 01–653 2223

Shirts: white with red diagonal band from left shoulder. *Shorts:* white. *Stockings:* white. *Second colours:* red & blue vertical striped shirts, royal blue shorts.

The progress of Crystal Palace to First Division status became more than a dream from April 1966, when they appointed Bert Head as manager. He joined them from Bury, but first made his mark in football management at Swindon, where he built a star-studded team from nothing, and by 1969 Palace completed the astonishing climb from Fourth Division to First in only eight years.

Selhurst Park was redeveloped to match the club's proudly-won status, but despite enormous spending in the transfer market Palace were always struggling to stay in top company. In March 1973 the flamboyant Malcolm Allison was appointed manager, but he could not save the club from relegation that season or the next.

In 1975–76 Palace approached Christmas seven points clear in the Third Division and, with remarkable wins away to Leeds, Chelsea and Sunderland, they reached the F.A. Cup semi-final for the first time. But their decline was even more spectacular, and after losing the semi-final to Southampton they faded to fifth in the final table. Manager Allison left at the end of the season.

At the end of the following season, under the managership of Terry Venables, Palace regained their place in the Second Division.

Division 3 Champions: 1920–21.
Record attendance: 49,498 v. Chelsea (League), December 1969.
Modern Capacity: 52,000. **Nickname:** 'Eagles'.
Entered Football League: 1920—Div. 3.
Biggest win: 9–0 v. Barrow (Div. 4), October 1959.
Heaviest defeat: 4–11 v. Manchester City (F.A. Cup), February 1926.
Best in F.A. Cup: Semi-final 1975–76.
Best in League Cup: 5th Round 1968–69, 1970–71.
Pitch measurements: 110 x 75 yd.
Highest League Scorer in Single Season: Peter Simpson— 46 in 1930–31 (Div. 3 South).
Transfers—
   Highest fee paid: £140,000—Don Rogers (from Swindon), October 1972.
   Highest fee received: £200,000—Peter Taylor (to Tottenham), September 1976.

DARLINGTON

Feethams Ground, Darlington, Co. Durham DL1 5JB
Darlington 65097/67712

Shirts: white with red collar & cuffs. *Shorts:* black with red & white
seam. *Stockings:* black with red & white tops. *Second colours:* royal
blue shirts & shorts.

Eighty pounds would not buy a complete set of team kit today.
Yet in season 1924–25 Darlington won the Third Division North
title with a team assembled for just that modest sum. They finished
five points ahead of the next two clubs, Nelson and New Brighton,
neither of whom are now members of the Football League. Unfortunately they survived only two seasons before being relegated.

Darlington are one of the comparatively few League clubs to have
used only one ground—Feethams—since their formation in 1883.
In their early years they played in the Northern League and became
professional in 1908, when they joined the North-Eastern League.
The club was reformed after the First World War, and in 1921
became one of the original members of the old Division Three North.

They remained there until Division Four was created in 1958, and
in season 1965–66 they delighted their supporters by finishing
runners-up with the same number of points (59) as the champions,
Doncaster Rovers. A year later, however, they were relegated.
Darlington's best-known players have included centre-forward
David Brown (74 League goals in 97 matches from 1923–26) and
Ken Furphy, who went on to manage Workington, Watford,
Blackburn and Sheffield United.

Division 3 (North) Champions: 1924–25.
Record attendance: 21,023 v. Bolton Wanderers (League Cup)
November 1960.
Modern Capacity: 21,000. **Nickname:** 'Quakers.'
Entered Football League: 1921—Div. 3 (North).
Biggest win: 13–1 v. Scarborough (F.A. Cup), 1886.
Heaviest defeat: 0–10 v. Doncaster (Div. 4), January 1964.
Best in F.A. Cup: 5th Round 1957–58.
Best in League Cup: 5th Round 1967–68.
Pitch measurements: 110 x 74 yd.
Highest League Scorer in Single Season: David Brown—39 in
1924–25 (Div. 3 North).
Transfers—
    Highest fee paid: £7,500—Jimmy Seal (from York), November
    1976.
    Highest fee received: £25,000—Martin Burleigh (to Carlisle),
    May 1975.

DERBY COUNTY

The Baseball Ground, Derby DE3 8NB, Derby 40105

Shirts: white, dark blue collars. *Shorts:* dark blue. *Stockings:* white.
Second colours: light blue and dark blue shirts, light blue shorts.

The revival of Derby County began with the appointment of Brian Clough, former Middlesbrough and England centre-forward, in May 1967. Under his inspiring managership (and, on the field, rallied by the captaincy and playing skill of Dave Mackay) Derby roared back to the First Division two years later.

In season 1971–72 they became League Champions for the first time, but in October 1973 Clough sensationally quit the club, and the task of restoring calm after a major upheaval fell upon Mackay, who left Nottingham Forest to return to Derby. He did it with maximum effect, for by the end of the following season (1974–75) County were Champions again.

Why do Derby County—one of the original 12 Football League clubs in 1888—have a home with the unlikely name of the Baseball Ground? In 1895 a wealthy businessman, Sir Francis Ley, formed a baseball club in the town and built a fine ground, but the American game did not catch on. After a few months, the baseball club was disbanded, and County moved in. Previously they had played at the Derby racecourse ground.

In 1946 Derby with, world-class inside-forwards in Raich Carter and Peter Doherty, won their first major trophy, beating Charlton 4–1 in extra time in the F.A. Cup Final.

League Champions: 1971–72, 1974–75.
Division 2 Champions: 1911–12, 1914–15, 1968–69.
Division 3 (North) Champions: 1956–57.
F.A. Cup Winners: 1945–46.
Record attendance: 41,826 v. Tottenham (League), September 1969.
Modern Capacity: 42,000. **Nickname:** 'Rams.'
Entered Football League: 1888—Div. 1.
Biggest win: 12–0 v. Finn Harps (UEFA Cup), September 1976.
Heaviest defeat: 2–11 v. Everton (F.A. Cup), 1889–90.
Best in League Cup: Semi-final 1967–68.
Pitch measurements: 110 x 71 yd.
Highest League Scorer in Single Season: Jack Bowers—37 in 1930–31 (Div. 1) ; Ray Straw—37 in 1956–57 (Div. 3 North).
Transfers—
  Highest fee paid: £310,000—Leighton James (from Burnley), November 1975.
  Highest fee received: £200,000—Bruce Rioch (to Everton), December 1976.

DONCASTER ROVERS

Belle Vue Ground, Doncaster DN4 5HT, Doncaster 55281

Shirts: red with white trimmings. *Shorts:* white. *Stockings:* red & white. *Second colours:* yellow shirts, brown shorts.

Doncaster Rovers' past is crowded with players of distinction: the Keetley brothers, Frank, Harold, Joe and Tom (who still holds the club record for the most League goals—178); Fred Emery, later manager; Sam Cowan who won England caps with Manchester City; Jack Lambert, Arsenal's centre-forward in the 1930 and 1932 F.A. Cup Finals; Peter Doherty, rated by many as the most skilful inside-forward of his era; Clarrie Jordan (42 League goals in 1946–47); Manchester United and Northern Ireland goalkeeper Harry Gregg; England Under-23 forward Alick Jeffrey, with 36 goals, was the League's top scorer in 1964–65.

The Belle Vue ground, opposite Doncaster racecourse, is at 118½ by 79 yards the largest pitch in the League and no more notable performances have been achieved on it than in 1946–47. That season Rovers took the old Third Division North title with 33 wins—a Football League record—and the astonishing total of 72 points from 42 League matches, including 37 from away games. That points tally remained a League record for 29 years—until beaten by Lincoln City in 1975–76.

Twice in the past decade (in 1966 and 1969) Doncaster won the Fourth Division Championship, but each time Division 3 proved above their station and in 1974 they had to apply for re-election for the second time in their history.

Division 3 (North) Champions: 1934–35, 1946–47, 1949–50.
Division 4 Champions: 1965–66, 1968–69.
Record attendance: 37,149 v. Hull (League), October 1948.
Modern Capacity: 40,000.
Entered Football League: 1901—Div. 2.
Biggest win: 10–0 v. Darlington (Div. 4), January 1964.
Heaviest defeat: 0–12 v. Small Heath (Div. 2), April 1903.
Best in F.A. Cup: 5th Round 1951–52, 1953–54, 1954–55, 1955–56.
Best in League Cup: 5th Round 1975–76.
Pitch measurements: 118½ x 79 yd.
Highest League Scorer in Single Season: Clarrie Jordan—42 in 1946–47 (Div. 3 North).
Transfers—
   Highest fee paid: £10,000—John Flowers (from Stoke), July 1966; £10,000—Dick Habbin (from Rotherham), September 1977.
   Highest fee received: £70,000—Mike Elwiss (to Preston), February 1974.

45

EVERTON

Goodison Park, Liverpool L4 4EL, 051–521 2020

Shirts: royal blue, white trim. *Shorts:* white with blue trim. *Stockings:* white. *Second colours:* amber shirts with blue trim, amber shorts.

In 1888 Everton became one of the original members of the Football League and were Division One champions in 1890–91. Fifteen years later they won the F.A. Cup for the first time. Everton stayed in the First Division for 42 years until 1930, then spent only one season in the Second before returning to win the First Division twice more (1932 and 1939) before the Second World War.

Twice during Harry Catterick's managership, in 1963 and 1970, Everton won the Championship, making seven League titles in all for the Goodison Park club, and in 1966 they took the F.A. Cup for the third time. But in May 1973, after three moderate seasons, Everton appointed a new manager—Billy Bingham, their former Irish International right-winger.

Everton broke all British transfer records in February 1974 when, in a part-exchange deal with Birmingham City, they paid the equivalent of £350,000 for striker Bob Latchford. Six months later they set a new British cash record of £300,000 when signing Martin Dobson from Burnley.

Despite such big signings, Everton failed to shift the power of Merseyside football from Anfield, although in April 1976 they became the first club in Football League history to reach the milestone of 3000 First Division points.

League Champions: 1890–91, 1914–15, 1927–28, 1931–32, 1938–39, 1962–63, 1969–70.
Division 2 Champions: 1930–31.
F.A. Cup Winners: 1905–06, 1932–33, 1965–66.
Record attendance: 78,299 v. Liverpool (League), September 1948.
Modern Capacity: 56,000. **Nickname:** 'Toffees.'
Entered Football League: 1888—Div. 1.
Biggest win: 11–2 v. Derby County (F.A. Cup), 1889–90.
Heaviest defeat: 4–10 v. Tottenham (Div. 1), October 1958.
Best in League Cup: Finalists 1976–77.
Pitch measurements: 112 x 75 yd.
Highest League Scorer in Single Season: Bill ('Dixie') Dean 60 in 1927–28 (Div. 1).
Transfers—
    Highest fee paid: £350,000 equivalent (British record)—Bob Latchford (from Birmingham City—£80,000 cash plus Howard Kendall, valued £180,000 and Archie Styles, valued £90,000), February 1974.
    Highest fee received: £220,000—Alan Ball (to Arsenal), December 1971.

EXETER CITY

St James's Park, Exeter EX4 6PX, 0392–54073

Shirts: white with red stripes on sleeve. *Shorts:* white with red seams. *Stockings:* white with red stripes. *Second colours:* blue shirts & shorts.

No one would suggest that life has been easy for the City club which has never journeyed above the Third Division. Nevertheless, a number of distinguished players began their careers at St James's Park. They include left-winger Cliff Bastin, who became an England international and collected F.A. Cup-winning and First Division Championship medals with Arsenal before he was 20; Dick Pym, Bolton's goalkeeper in three successful Cup Finals at Wembley in the 1920s; and the modern Fourth Division hero of Exeter's schoolboys was Fred Binney, City's leading scorer in seasons 1971–72, 1972–73 and 1973–74, but then transferred to Brighton.

Who among Exeter's older supporters will forget the wonderful Cup run in 1931? After fighting through to the competition proper, they beat First Division Derby 3–2 at Exeter; next they won 2–1 at Bury and then, in front of their own followers again, defeated Leeds United 3–1. That victory put Exeter in the last eight for the only time, and when the 'Grecians' held Sunderland 1–1 at Roker Park, it seemed they were heading for the semi-finals. But before a record crowd of nearly 21,000 the replay was lost by four goals to two.

Record attendance: 20,984 v. Sunderland (F.A. Cup), March 1931.
Modern Capacity: 18,500. **Nickname:** 'Grecians.'
Entered Football League: 1920—Div. 3.
Biggest win: 8–1 v. Coventry City (Div. 3 South), December 1926; 8–1 v. Aldershot (Div. 3 South), May 1935.
Heaviest defeat: 0–9 v. Notts County (Div. 3 South), October 1948; 0–9 v. Northampton (Div. 3 South), April 1958.
Highest final League position: Runners-up Division 3 (South) 1932–33. Runners-up Division 4 1976–77.
Best in F.A. Cup: 6th Round 1930–31.
Best in League Cup: 4th Round 1973–74.
Pitch measurements: 115 x 75 yd.
Highest League Scorer in Single Season: Fred Whitlow—34 in 1932–33 (Div. 3 South).
Transfers—
  Highest fee paid: £15,000—John Delve (from Plymouth), March 1978.
  Highest fee received: £40,000 equivalent (£25,000 plus two players in exchange)—Fred Binney (to Brighton), May 1974.

FULHAM

Craven Cottage, Stevenage Road, London SW6, 01-736 6561

Shirts: white with black trim. *Shorts:* black with white seams. *Stockings:* white with black hoops. *Second colours:* red shirts & shorts.

For years Fulham have been known as 'London's friendliest club', but few took them seriously as contenders for prizes until 1975, when they reached Wembley for the first time after four F.A. Cup semi-final disappointments. After Sunderland in 1973, they became the second Second Division finalists in three seasons, and although beaten 2–0 by London rivals West Ham, Fulham's appearance at Wembley reflected enormous credit on the club, on manager Alec Stock and on captain Alan Mullery, who was also voted 'Footballer of the Year'.

Fulham have experienced two brief spells of First Division football, but after losing top status in 1968 they dropped straight through to the Third Division for two seasons.

In 1961 Fulham made their England captain, Johnny Haynes, Britain's first £100-a-week footballer; in 1966 they supplied right-back George Cohen to England's triumphant World Cup team; in March 1974 they paid West Ham £25,000 for that World Cup-winning captain, Bobby Moore, at the end of his record 108-cap international career. A year later Moore was back in familiar surroundings at Wembley, playing against his old club in the Cup Final. And they said there was no romance left in football!

Division 2 Champions: 1948–49.
Division 3 (South) Champions: 1931–32.
Record attendance: 49,335 v. Millwall (League), October 1938.
Modern Capacity: 45,000. **Nickname:** 'Cottagers.'
Entered Football League: 1907—Div. 2.
Biggest win: 10–1 v. Ipswich (Div. 1), December 1963.
Heaviest defeat: 0–9 v. Wolves (Div. 1), September 1959.
Best in F.A. Cup: Runners-up 1974–75.
Best in League Cup: 5th Round 1967–68, 1970–71.
Pitch measurements: 110 x 75 yd.
Highest League Scorer in Single Season: Frank Newton—41 in 1931–32 (Div. 3 South).
Transfers—
    Highest fee paid: £80,000—Paul Went (from Charlton), July 1972.
    Highest fee received: £200,000—Teddy Maybank (to Brighton), November 1977.

GILLINGHAM

Priestfield Stadium, Gillingham, Kent ME7 4DD, Medway 51854

Shirts: blue with white collar & cuffs. *Shorts:* white with blue stripe. *Stockings:* blue with white tops. *Second colours:* white shirts & blue shorts.

When Gillingham were voted out of the Football League in 1938 and replaced by Ipswich Town, their existence as a senior club seemed to be over. But after the war, under an energetic and far-seeing management, they became a force in the Southern League. When, in 1950, the Football League decided to increase membership from 88 to 92 clubs, by extending each Third Division section (North and South) from 22 to 24 teams, 'The Gills' were readmitted.

The club started life as New Brompton Excelsior, changing their name to Gillingham in 1913. The subsequent playing years until they left the League provided little of distinction. In fact, the club had to wait until season 1963–64 for their first major success—the Championship of the Fourth Division. They lost only nine of their 46 matches and beat Carlisle United to the title on goal average, each club obtaining 60 points.

Gillingham were relegated in 1971, but returned to the Third Division in 1974 as the season's highest-scoring team with 90 goals. Their sharpshooter was Brian Yeo, whose 31 League goals equalled the club record set 19 years earlier by Ernie Morgan.

Division 4 Champions: 1963–64.
Record attendance: 23,002 v. Queen's Park Rangers (F.A. Cup), January 1948.
Modern Capacity: 22,000. **Nickname:** 'Gills.'
Entered Football League: 1920—Div. 3.
Biggest win: 10–1 v. Gorleston (F.A. Cup), November 1957.
Heaviest defeat: 2–9 v. Nottingham Forest (Div. 3 South), November 1950.
Best in F.A. Cup: 5th Round 1969–70.
Best in League Cup: 4th Round 1963–64.
Pitch measurements: 114 x 75 yd.
Highest League Scorer in Single Season: Ernie Morgan—31 in 1954–55 (Div. 3 South); Brian Yeo—31 in 1973–74 (Div. 4).
Transfers—
   Highest fee paid: £18,000—Danny Westwood (from Queen's Park Rangers), December 1975.
   Highest fee received: £65,000—Dick Tydeman (to Charlton), December 1976.

49

GRIMSBY TOWN

Blundell Park, Cleethorpes, S. Humberside DN35 7PY
Cleethorpes 61420/61803

Shirts: black & white stripes. *Shorts:* black. *Stockings:* red. *Second colours:* red shirts & white shorts.

In the period between the two wars Grimsby Town, whose ground is situated in the town of Cleethorpes, played in four sections of the Football League—the Third Division and Third North, as well as the First and Second Divisions.

They were still in Division One immediately after the Second World War, but finished bottom in 1948, and after ups and downs between Divisions Two and Four, they found themselves having to seek re-election through finishing 91st on the League ladder in season 1968–69. Three years later they were Fourth Division champions.

The club was founded as Grimsby Pelham in 1878, but after a year dropped the name of Pelham. They won the Division Two Championship in 1901 and again in 1934. Two years later they lost to Arsenal by the only goal in the semi-final of the F.A. Cup. They again reached the last four in 1939, this time crashing 5–0 to Wolverhampton Wanderers.

Grimsby have produced many first-class forwards, none better than Ernest (Pat) Glover, who scored 42 League goals in 1933–34, and Jackie Bestall, the finest creator of attacks in the club's history.

Division 2 Champions: 1900–01, 1933–34.
Division 3 (North) Champions: 1925–26, 1955–56.
Division 4 Champions: 1971–72.
Record attendance: 31,650 v. Wolves (F.A. Cup), February 1937.
Modern Capacity: 28,000. **Nickname:** 'Mariners.'
Entered Football League: 1892—Div. 2.
Biggest win: 9–2 v. Darwen (Div. 2), April 1899.
Heaviest defeat: 1–9 v. Arsenal (Div. 1), January 1931.
Best in F.A. Cup: Semi-final 1935–36, 1938–39.
Best in League Cup: 5th Round 1965–66.
Pitch measurements: 111 x 74 yd.
Highest League Scorer in Single Season: Pat Glover—42 in 1975–76 (Div. 2).
Transfers—
    Highest fee paid: £20,000—Phil Hubbard (from Norwich), October 1972; £20,000—Ron Wigg (from Rotherham), January 1975; £20,000—Malcolm Partridge (from Leicester), March 1975.
    Highest fee received: £20,000—Doug Collins (to Burnley), September 1968.

HALIFAX TOWN

Shay Ground, Halifax, W. Yorkshire, HX1 2YS, Halifax 53423

Shirts: blue with white motifs. *Shorts:* white with blue motif. *Stockings:* royal blue with white hoops. *Second colours:* green & yellow striped shirts, green shorts.

The seasons of reward have been strictly limited for Halifax Town since their early days in the Yorkshire Combination and Midland League. So there was understandable excitement in 1971 when the club made a sustained bid to bring Second Division football to The Shay for the first time. In the end, they had to be content with third place behind Preston and Fulham.

Two seasons earlier the Town side had won their way into the Third Division as runners-up to Doncaster Rovers after an unbroken sequence as members of the Third Division (North) and then the Fourth Division. In those bleak days Halifax had to seek re-election seven times, and it says much for their perseverance that they were repeatedly voted back.

The Shay bulged at its sides one February day in 1953, when nearly 37,000 turned up to watch Tottenham Hotspur in the F.A. Cup fifth round. Halifax had made the most of their luck in being drawn at home in every tie, and after dealing with Ashton and Southport, they put out First Division 'giants' Cardiff and Stoke. But for all the urgings of their record crowd they went down 3–0 to Spurs.

Record attendance: 36,885 v. Tottenham (F.A. Cup), February 1953.
Modern Capacity: 38,000.
Entered Football League: 1921—Div. 3 (North).
Biggest win: 7–0 v. Bishop Auckland (F.A. Cup), January 1967.
Heaviest defeat: 0–13 v. Stockport County (Div. 3 North), January 1934.
Highest final League position: Runners-up Div. 3 (North) 1934–35; runners-up Div. 4 1968–69.
Best in F.A. Cup: 5th Round 1932–33, 1952–53.
Best in League Cup: 4th Round 1963–64.
Pitch measurements: 110 x 70 yd.
Highest League Scorer in Single Season: Albert Valentine— 34 in 1934–35 (Div. 3 North).
Transfers—
  Highest fee paid: £14,000—Fred Kemp (from Blackpool), January 1972.
  Highest fee received: £45,000—Alan Waddle (to Liverpool), June 1973.

HARTLEPOOL UNITED

18 Scarborough Street, Hartlepool TS24 7DA
Hartlepool 72584/3492

Shirts: blue with white trim on sleeves. *Shorts:* white. *Stockings:* blue.
Second colours: red with white trim & red shorts.

Overshadowed throughout their existence by their powerful north-eastern neighbours, Newcastle and Sunderland, the Hartlepool club have known more of life's struggles than success. Indeed, they have had to apply ten times for re-election.

They joined the old Division Three North on its formation in 1921, and stayed in this section until they moved into the newly created Fourth Division in 1958. They did finish runners-up in 1956–57, but in those days only one club gained promotion from each Third Division section. They scored 90 goals in their 46 matches that season, and on that form they were unlucky to miss a higher grade.

They had to wait another 11 years, until 1968, before they experienced promotion. Then they took third place in Division Four behind Luton and Barnsley. Unfortunately, at the end of the following season they were relegated. In April 1959, they briefly commanded attention by thrashing Barrow 10–1; three years later they lost by the same margin to Wrexham.

One of Hartlepool's longest-serving managers was Fred Westgarth in the after-war years, and the club also launched Brian Clough on his managerial career.

Record attendance: 17,420 v. Manchester United (F.A. Cup), January 1957.
Modern Capacity: 18,000. **Nickname:** 'Pool.'
Entered Football League: 1921—Div. 3 (North).
Biggest win: 10–1 v. Barrow (Div. 4), April 1959.
Heaviest defeat: 1–10 v. Wrexham (Div. 4), May 1962.
Highest final League position: Runners-up Div. 3 (North) 1956–57.
Best in F.A. Cup: 4th Round 1954–55.
Best in League Cup: 4th Round 1974–75.
Pitch measurements: 113 x 76 yd.
Highest League Scorer in Single Season: Bill Robinson—28 in 1927–28 (Div. 3 North).
Transfers—
 Highest fee paid: £10,000—Ambrose Fogarty (from Sunderland), November 1963.
 Highest fee received: £60,000—Malcolm Poskett (to Brighton), February 1978.

HEREFORD UNITED

Edgar Street, Hereford HR4 9JU, Hereford 4037

Shirts: white with black & red trim. *Shorts:* black with red & white stripes. *Stockings:* white, black & red trim. *Second colours:* red shirts with white & black trim, white shorts with black & red stripes.

After striving for years for Football League membership, Southern League Hereford United so captured the public imagination with spectacular deeds in the 1971–72 F.A. Cup that, four months later, they were voted into the Fourth Division, displacing Barrow.

By knocking out Newcastle United (six times winners of the F.A. Cup) 2–1 in the third round after drawing 2–2 at St James's Park, Hereford became the first non-League club to dismiss First Division opponents since Yeovil in 1949. The success story continued on their entry to the Football League, for their first season ended with promotion as Fourth Division runners-up.

Of Hereford's 64 Third Division goals in their run in 1974–75, Dixie McNeil scored 31, a record for the club in his first season with them, and there was another milestone in 1975–76 as United aimed for the Second Division. On October 25, 36-year-old Terry Paine (ex-Southampton & England) played his 765th League game, so beating the all-time appearance record set up by Jimmy Dickinson (Portsmouth, 1946–65). The season ended triumphantly with Hereford runaway champions—and promoted to the Second Division only four years after leaving the Southern League.

This was the complete answer to anyone who doubted whether rurally-situated Hereford could make their mark in League football on a population of 300,000 in and around the cathedral city on the banks of the River Wye.

Division 3 Champions: 1975–76.
Record attendance: 18,114 v. Sheffield Wednesday (F.A. Cup) January 1958.
Modern Capacity: 20,000.
Entered Football League: 1972—Div. 4.
Biggest win: 11–0 v. Thynnes (F.A. Cup), September 1947.
Heaviest defeat: 2–9 v. Yeovil Town (S. League), September 1955.
Best in F.A. Cup: 4th Round 1971–72, 1973–74.
Best in League Cup: 3rd Round 1974–75.
Pitch measurements: 111 x 80 yd.
Highest League Scorer in Single Season: Dixie McNeil—35 in 1975–76 (Div. 3).
Transfers—
  Highest fee paid: £20,000—Dixie McNeil (from Lincoln), August 1974; £20,000—Dave Rylands (from Liverpool), September 1974.
  Highest fee received: £60,000—Dixie McNeil (to Wrexham), September 1977.

HUDDERSFIELD TOWN

Leeds Road, Huddersfield HD1 6PE, Huddersfield 20335/6

Shirts: blue & white stripes. *Shorts:* white. *Stockings:* white.
Second colours: yellow shirts & shorts.

In the mid-twenties Huddersfield reigned supreme as First Division
Champions for three successive years (1924–25–26), the finest era
in their history. Yet not many years earlier the club had struggled
through periods of financial crisis.

The appointment of Herbert Chapman as manager (1922–25)
heralded the club's dominant period. In that great team of the
twenties which Chapman created were the captain Clem Stephenson,
who had played for Aston Villa, winger Billy Smith, who made nearly
500 appearances in 15 years, full-backs Roy Goodall and Sam
Wadsworth.

Having won the F.A. Cup for the first time in 1922, Town went on
to their Championship treble, the first in League history.

They stayed in Division One until 1952, then won back their place
first time. In 1956 they dropped again and spent 14 years in the
Second Division. Their return as Div. 2 champions was but a
fleeting revival, for by 1973 Huddersfield had tumbled for the first
time into the Third Division.

Even worse was to follow, for Town finished season 1974–75
bottom of the table by five points . . . and a club steeped in tradition,
and one of the greatest names in football half a century earlier, went
into Fourth Division obscurity.

League Champions: 1923–24, 1924–25, 1925–26.
Division 2 Champions: 1969–70.
F.A. Cup Winners: 1921–22.
Record attendance: 67,037 v. Arsenal (F.A. Cup), February 1932.
Modern Capacity: 52,000.
Entered Football League: 1910—Div. 2.
Biggest win: 10–1 v. Blackpool (Div. 1), December 1930.
Heaviest defeat: 0–8 v. Middlesbrough (Div. 1), September 1950.
Best in League Cup: Semi-final 1967–68.
Pitch measurements: 116 x 76 yd.
Highest League Scorer in Single Season: Sam Taylor—35 in
   1919–20 (Div. 2) ; George Brown—35 in 1925–26 (Div. 1).
Transfers—
   Highest fee paid: £70,000—Alan Gowling (from Manchester
   United), June 1972.
   Highest fee received: £100,000—Trevor Cherry (to Leeds),
   June 1972.

HULL CITY

Boothferry Park, Hull HU4 6EU, 0482–52195/7

Shirts: black & amber stripes with white collar. *Shorts:* white.
Stockings: white. *Second colours:* white shirts, black shorts.

Hull City were formed as an amateur club in 1904 and gained admission to the Second Division in 1905. Four times up to 1960 they dropped into the Third Division, then regained their status in the higher grade in 1966, scoring 31 victories and 109 goals in winning the Third Division title that year.

They came closest to promotion to Division One in 1910 when Oldham Athletic pipped them for second place by ·286 of a goal. During the Second World War Hull's ground in Anlaby Road was hit by enemy bombs, and in 1946 the club was reformed and acquired their present impressive home, Boothferry Park, which has its own railway station.

The list of City's post-war managers includes Frank Buckley, Raich Carter, Cliff Britton and Terry Neill, and since 1966 they have been members of the Second Division.

Hull have often been impressive F.A. Cup fighters. They were semi-finalists in 1930 (despite being on their way down to the Third Division North), and as a Second Division side in 1921 sprang a sensation in the third round by beating Burnley 3–0.

That season Burnley won the First Division title and, their defeat by Hull apart, played 30 matches between September and March without being beaten.

Division 3 (North) Champions: 1932–33, 1948–49.
Division 3 Champions: 1965–66.
Record attendance: 55,019 v. Manchester United (F.A. Cup), February 1949.
Modern Capacity: 42,000. **Nickname:** 'Tigers.'
Entered Football League: 1905—Div. 2.
Biggest win: 11–1 v. Carlisle (Div. 3 North), January 1939.
Heaviest defeat: 0–8 v. Wolves (Div. 2), November 1911.
Best in F.A. Cup: Semi-final 1929–30.
Best in League Cup: 4th Round 1973–74, 1975–76.
Pitch measurements: 113 x 73 yd.
Highest League Scorer in Single Season: Bill McNaughton—39 in 1932–33 (Div. 3 North).
Transfers—
    Highest fee paid: £75,000—Alf Wood (from Millwall), November 1974; £75,000—Dave Roberts (from Oxford), February 1975.
    Highest fee received: £200,000 equivalent (£170,000 plus a player)—Stuart Pearson (to Manchester United), May 1974.

IPSWICH TOWN

Portman Road, Ipswich IP1 2DA, Ipswich 51306 & 57107

Shirts: royal blue with white motif. *Shorts:* white with blue stripes.
Stockings: royal blue with white hoops. *Second colours:* white shirts
with black motif, black shorts.

Football fame came to Ipswich in 1962 when they won the League
Championship in their first season in Division One. Under Alf
Ramsey the club had a remarkable rise.

Ramsey took over as manager in August 1955, after Town had
gone down to the Third Division. Two years later they were back in
the Second Division. They won promotion to the First as Champions
after four more seasons, and a year later surprised the whole soccer
world by winning the League Championship.

After their shock Championship triumph in 1962, with Ray
Crawford (33) and Ted Phillips (28) scoring 61 of their 93 goals,
Ipswich slipped down to the Second Division in 1964 and it took
them four seasons to fight their way back.

Crawford holds the aggregate goal record (203) for Ipswich and
Phillips, who also played a great part in their meteoric rise to fame,
set a new club record for the most goals in a season—41 in the
Third Division South, 1956–57.

U.E.F.A. Cup victories over Real Madrid and Lazio in season
1973–74 confirmed the extent of the Suffolk club's revival under the
managership of Bobby Robson, and in 1975 they achieved their
best-ever F.A. Cup run, losing lucklessly to West Ham in a semi-final
replay.

League Champions: 1961–62.
Division 2 Champions: 1960–61, 1967–68.
Division 3 (South) Champions: 1953–54, 1956–57.
Record attendance: 38,010 v. Leeds (F.A. Cup), March 1975.
Modern Capacity: 38,000. **Nickname:** 'Blues.'
Entered Football League: 1938—Div. 3 (South).
Biggest win: 10–0 v. Floriana, Malta (European Cup), September
1962.
Heaviest defeat: 1–10 v. Fulham (Div. 1), December 1963.
Best in F.A. Cup: Semi-final 1974–75.
Best in League Cup: 5th Round 1965–66, 1974–75.
Pitch measurements: 112 x 75 yd.
Highest League Scorer in Single Season: Ted Phillips—41 in
1956–57 (Div. 3 South).
Transfers—
  Highest fee paid: £220,000—Paul Mariner (from Plymouth),
  October 1976.
  Highest fee received: £200,000—David Johnson (to Liver-
  pool), August 1976.

LEEDS UNITED

Elland Road, Leeds LS11 0ES, Leeds 716037

Shirts: white with blue & yellow trim. *Shorts:* white with blue & yellow trim. *Stockings:* white with blue & yellow trim. *Second colours:* yellow shirts, with blue & white striped sleeves, yellow shorts.

Since the late sixties, Leeds have established a reputation as one of the most consistent and powerful clubs in Europe. Between 1964 and 1975 they won seven major prizes: Second Division, League Cup, two League Championships, the Fairs Cup twice and the F.A. Cup. Over the same period they were runners-up eleven times in domestic and European competitions.

In 1969 they set a new First Division points record (67) and under Don Revie they became a major all-international force.

In July 1974 Revie left Elland Road to manage England. His successor, Brian Clough, was sacked after 44 days and replaced by Jimmy Armfield, from Bolton. His arrival brought stability and the season ended with Leeds only the third British club to reach the European Cup Final, but they lost 2–0 to Bayern Munich and suffered further by being banned from European football because of misconduct by supporters at the Final in Paris.

Three times Leeds have been close to completing the League Championship–F.A. Cup double (1965, 1970, 1972). Though the Cup was at last won in 1972, this competition has provided United's biggest upsets, with odd-goal defeats from Fourth Division Colchester (1971), Second Division Sunderland (in the 1973 Final), another Second Division side, Bristol City, in 1974 and Third Division Crystal Palace in 1976.

League Champions: 1968–69, 1973–74.
Division 2 Champions: 1923–24, 1963–64.
F.A. Cup Winners: 1971–72.
League Cup Winners: 1967–68.
European Fairs Cup Winners: 1967–68, 1970–71.
Record attendance: 57,892 v. Sunderland (F.A. Cup), March 1967.
Modern Capacity: 48,000.
Entered Football League: 1905—Div. 2 (as Leeds City).
Biggest win: 10–0 v. Lyn Oslo (European Cup), September 1969.
Heaviest defeat: 1–8 v. Stoke City (Div. 1), August 1934.
Pitch measurements: 115 x 76 yd.
Highest League Scorer in Single Season: John Charles—42 in 1953–54 (Div. 2).
Transfers—
  Highest fee paid: £300,000—Paul Hart (from Blackpool), March 1978.
  Highest fee received: £500,000—Gordon McQueen (to Manchester United), February 1978.

LEICESTER CITY

Filbert Street, Leicester, Leicester 57111/2

Shirts: blue. *Shorts:* white. *Stockings:* white. *Second colours:* white shirts with blue trim, blue shorts.

A dozen old boys of Wyggeston School paid ninepence each to buy a football and start a soccer team in 1884. They called themselves Leicester Fosse. At first they used the Leicester rugby ground, but in 1889 moved to Filbert Street and five years later they were elected to the Second Division.

The name was changed from Fosse to City in 1919. By then they were a well-established Second Division club. They have won the Division Two championship five times and got their first taste of First Division football in 1925. They have played in the F.A. Cup Final four times—thrice in the sixties—and never won it. In 1964 they won the League Cup and were runners-up in the following season.

Two Arthurs have been principal goalscoring heroes of Leicester. Arthur Chandler achieved a total of 262 between 1923 and 1935 —his feat of scoring in 16 consecutive matches in season 1924–25 (Div. Two) remains a British record—and Arthur Rowley scored 44 League goals in the 1956–57 season to help them to the Second Division title.

Goalkeepers, too, have thrilled the fans at Filbert Street. In 1967 City transferred England's World Cup-winning 'keeper Gordon Banks to Stoke and replaced him with Peter Shilton. He followed Banks into the England team . . . and to Stoke in November 1974 at a fee of £340,000.

Division 2 Champions: 1924–25, 1936–37, 1953–54, 1956–57, 1970–71.
League Cup Winners: 1963–64.
Record attendance: 47,298 v. Tottenham (F.A. Cup), February 1928.
Modern Capacity: 42,000. **Nickname:** 'Filberts.'
Entered Football League: 1894—Div. 2 (as Leicester Fosse).
Biggest win: 10–0 v. Portsmouth (Div. 1), October 1928.
Heaviest defeat: 0–12 v. Nottingham Forest (Div. 1), April 1909.
Best in F.A. Cup: Runners-up 1948–49, 1960–61, 1962–63, 1968–69.
Pitch measurements: 112 x 75 yd.
Highest League Scorer in Single Season: Arthur Rowley—44 in 1956–57 (Div. 2).
Transfers—
    Highest fee paid: £160,000—Roger Davies (from Bruges), December 1977.
    Highest fee received: £340,000—Peter Shilton (to Stoke), November 1974.

LINCOLN CITY

Sincil Bank, Lincoln LN5 8LD, Lincoln 22224

Shirts: red & white stripes. *Shorts:* black. *Stockings:* red, white top.
Second colours: yellow shirts with blue trimmings, blue shorts with yellow stripe.

Founder members of Division Two in 1892, Lincoln were voted out after finishing at the foot of the table in 1908 and 1911. Three times they won the Championship of the old Division Three North, and five times they have had to apply for re-election to Division Four.

Andy Graver, who had two spells with the club, scored 144 League goals for Lincoln through the 1950s and for rapid scoring, no one in League history has bettered Frank Keetley's six goals in 21 minutes against Halifax (Div. Three North) at Lincoln in January 1932.

Until 1975–76 Lincoln's most impressive season was in 1951–52. As Third North champions they were the highest-scoring Football League side with 121 goals. Graver, later transferred to Leicester and then bought back again—each time at a record fee for Lincoln—scored 37 of them, including six in the club's biggest ever win of 11–1 against Crewe Alexandra.

In 1975, under impressive young manager Graham Taylor, City missed promotion to Division 3 on goal average. They stepped up their scoring rate in 1975–76, equalled their best-ever F.A. Cup progress by reaching the Fourth Round . . . and took the Fourth Division Championship with 74 points, a new record for any division of the Football League, beating Doncaster's 72 in 1946–47. With 111 goals, Lincoln also became the first club to score a century of League goals since Queen's Park Rangers (Division 3) in 1966–67.

Division 3 (North) Champions: 1931–32, 1947–48, 1951–52.
Division 4 Champions: 1975–76.
Record attendance: 23,196 v. Derby County (League Cup), November 1967.
Modern Capacity: 25,000. **Nickname:** 'Imps.'
Entered Football League: 1892—Div. 2.
Biggest win: 11–1 v. Crewe Alexandra (Div. 3 North), Sept. 1951.
Heaviest defeat: 3–11 v. Manchester City (Div. 2), March 1895.
Best in F.A. Cup: 4th Round 1953–54, 1960–61, 1975–76.
Best in League Cup: 4th Round 1967–68.
Pitch measurements: 110 x 75 yd.
Highest League Scorer in Single Season: Alan Hall—42 in 1931–32 (Div. 3 North).
Transfers—
  Highest fee paid: £20,000—Peter Grotier (from West Ham), October 1974.
  Highest fee received: £29,500—Andy Graver (to Leicester) December 1954.

LIVERPOOL

Anfield Road, Liverpool L4 OTH, 051–263 2361

Shirts: red with white trim. *Shorts:* red. *Stockings:* red. *Second colours:* . white shirts, black shorts.

For football fanaticism there is no place quite like Merseyside, where the game is almost a religion, with Anfield the worshipping shrine for half the city's soccer devotees.

Twice in three seasons (1963–66) Liverpool were crowned League Champions, and in the year between they won their first F.A. Cup.

For sheer consistency they have exceeded Leeds United in modern times, and by winning the Championship in season 1972–73— when also taking the U.E.F.A. Cup—Liverpool equalled Arsenal's record of eight First Division titles.

They took the F.A. Cup again in 1974 and then the architect of it all, manager Bill Shankly, abdicated. In choosing his successor Liverpool went for continuity in the person of 54-year-old assistant manager Bob Paisley. In his second season in charge (1975–76) Liverpool repeated their 1973 double of League Championship (a record ninth title) and U.E.F.A. Cup, and there were individual honours for Paisley (Manager of the Year) and Kevin Keegan (Footballer of the Year).

Yet they surpassed even that in 1976–77 when they won the League title a tenth time, won the European Cup and almost won the F.A. Cup as well, losing the treble only by a 2–1 defeat by Manchester United at Wembley.

League Champions: 1900–01, 1905–06, 1921–22, 1922–23, 1946–47, 1963–64, 1965–66, 1972–73, 1975–76, 1976–77.
Division 2 Champions: 1893–94, 1895–96, 1904–05, 1961–62.
F.A. Cup Winners: 1964–65, 1973–74.
European Cup Winners: 1976–77.
U.E.F.A. Cup Winners: 1972–73, 1975–76.
Record attendance: 61,905 v. Wolves (F.A. Cup), February 1952.
Modern Capacity: 56,000. **Nickname:** 'Reds.'
Entered Football League: 1893—Div. 2.
Biggest win: 11–0 v. Stromsgodset (Cup Winners Cup), September 1974.
Heaviest defeat: 1–9 v. Birmingham (Div. 2), December 1954.
Best in League Cup: 5th Round 1972–73, 1973–74.
Pitch measurements: 110 x 75 yd.
Highest League Scorer in Single Season: Roger Hunt—41 in 1961–62 (Div. 2).
Transfers—
  Highest fee paid: £440,000—Kenny Dalglish (from Celtic), July 1977.
  Highest fee received: £500,000—Kevin Keegan (to S.V. Hamburg), June 1977.

LUTON TOWN

Kenilworth Road, Luton, Beds. LU1 1DH, 0582—411622

Shirts: orange with navy & white stripe. *Shorts:* navy blue. *Stockings:* orange. *Second colours:* white shirts with navy & orange stripe, white shorts.

Luton Town established more than a club record with the sale of centre-forward Malcolm Macdonald to Newcastle United for £185,000 in May 1971. That fee made him the highest-priced player at that time to leave the Second Division.

Thirty-four years before the Macdonald era, Luton had another headline-making centre-forward in Joe Payne, their top scorer, with 55 goals, when they gained promotion to Division Two in 1937. The previous season Payne, who later joined Chelsea, scored *ten* goals as emergency centre-forward in Luton's 12–0 win over Bristol Rovers. It is an individual scoring record that has never been equalled in League or F.A. Cup football.

In 1955 Luton moved up to Division One after a triple tie on points, their superior goal average allowing them, and not Rotherham, to be promoted with Birmingham. Four years later they reached the F.A. Cup Final for the first time, losing 2–1 to Nottingham Forest. But in 1960 Luton were relegated (with Leeds) and continued to drop—to Division Three in 1963 and to the Fourth in 1965.

By 1974 they were back in the First Division, but only for one season. In December 1975, with debts of £724,000, Luton faced the threat of liquidation, and were saved by the dramatic £80,000 transfer of forward Peter Anderson to Belgian club Royal Antwerp.

Division 3 (South) Champions: 1936–37.
Division 4 Champions: 1967–68.
Record attendance: 30,069 v. Blackpool (F.A. Cup), March 1959.
Modern Capacity: 31,000. **Nickname:** 'Hatters.'
Entered Football League: 1897—Div. 2.
Biggest win: 12–0 v. Bristol Rovers (Div. 3 South), April 1936.
Heaviest defeat: 1–9 v. Swindon Town (Div. 3 South), August 1921.
Best in F.A. Cup: Runners-up 1958–59.
Best in League Cup: 4th Round 1962–63, 1973–74.
Pitch measurements: 112 x 72 yd.
Highest League Scorer in Single Season: Joe Payne—55 in 1936–37 (Div. 3 South).
Transfers—
  Highest fee paid: £110,000—Paul Futcher (from Chester), May 1974.
  Highest fee received: £185,000—Malcolm Macdonald (to Newcastle), May 1971.

MANCHESTER CITY

Maine Road, Moss Side, Manchester M14 7WM, 061–226 1191/2

Shirts: sky blue, white trim. *Shorts:* sky blue with white trim. *Stockings:* sky blue with white rings at top. *Second colours:* white shirts with red & black sash, white or blue shorts.

Following their return from the Second Division in 1966, Manchester City became one of Britain's most formidable sides under the dual influence of Joe Mercer as manager and Malcolm Allison, coach. In three seasons they won four of the game's top prizes—the League Championship in 1968, the F.A. Cup in 1969 and, in 1970, the League Cup and Cup-Winners' Cup.

In 1971 Allison took over, but the success formula had gone. In 1973 he moved to Crystal Palace, and after brief spells under Johnny Hart and Ron Saunders, City gave the managership to their former full-back Tony Book in April 1974. His first triumph as manager was the League Cup in 1976.

In the early 1930s City overshadowed United in Manchester's battle for soccer prestige and in 1937 they won their first League Championship. The following season they were relegated in unique circumstances—as the First Division top scorers with 80 goals.

Space permits mention of only a few of the club's great-name players of the past such as Billy Meredith, Jimmy McMullan, Eric Brook, Sam Cowan, Jackie Bray, Peter Doherty, Matt Busby, and two of the finest goalkeepers the game has seen, Frank Swift and German-born Bert Trautmann.

League Champions: 1936–37, 1967–68.
Division 2 Champions: 1898–99, 1902–03, 1909–10, 1927–28, 1946–47, 1965–66.
F.A. Cup Winners: 1903–04, 1933–34, 1955–56, 1968–69.
League Cup Winners: 1969–70, 1975–76.
Winners of European Cup-Winners' Cup: 1969–70.
Record attendance: 84,569 v. Stoke (F.A. Cup), March 1934.
Modern Capacity: 52,000.
Entered Football League: 1892 Div. 2 (as Ardwick).
Biggest win: 11–3 v. Lincoln City (Div. 2), March 1895.
Heaviest defeat: 1–9 v. Everton (Div. 1), September 1906.
Pitch measurements: 117 x 79 yd.
Highest League Scorer in Single Season: Tom Johnson—38 in 1928–29 (Div. 1).
Transfers—
    Highest fee paid: £300,000—Mick Channon (from Southampton), July 1977.
    Highest fee received: £250,000—Dennis Tueart (to New York Cosmos), February 1978.

MANCHESTER UNITED

Old Trafford, Manchester M16 ORA, 061–872 1661/2

Shirts: red, white trim. *Shorts:* white. *Stockings:* black, red & white band. *Second colours:* white shirts with three narrow red stripes on left, black shorts.

Manchester United's is a history of two clubs, not one. The first died on 6 February 1958, when the aircraft bringing them home from a European Cup-tie crashed in snow on take-off from Munich. Eight players were among the 23 killed.

The life of manager Matt Busby was also in the balance, and by the time he was able to return to Old Trafford, a new Manchester United team had been born. Less than three months later they played Bolton in the most emotion-charged F.A. Cup Final of all. In 1963 they returned to Wembley and won the Cup for the third time; they became League Champions again in 1965 and 1967 and, at Wembley a year later, on 29 May 1968, they defeated Benfica 4–1 to become England's first holders of the European Cup.

In 1974, despite massive spending by Tommy Docherty (United's third manager after Sir Matt Busby became a director), they lost the First Division place they had held since 1938, but he took them up again a year later. Though their exciting bid for the double in 1976 ended with third place in the Championship and shock defeat against Southampton in the F.A. Cup Final, Old Trafford was booming again. United topped the attendance charts with an average home League gate of 54,750.

League Champions: 1907–08, 1910–11, 1951–52, 1955–56, 1956–57, 1964–65, 1966–67.

Division 2 Champions: 1935–36, 1974–75.

F.A. Cup Winners: 1908–09, 1947–48, 1962–63, 1976–77.

European Cup Winners: 1967–68.

Record attendance: 76,962—Wolves v. Grimsby (F.A. Cup Semi-final), March 1939. (Record crowd for a League match in England is 82,950 for Manchester United v. Arsenal, January 1948—played on Manchester City's ground.)

Modern Capacity: 61,000. **Nickname:** 'Red Devils.'

Entered Football League: 1892—Div. 1 (as Newton Heath).

Biggest win: 10–0 v. Anderlecht, Belgium (European Cup), September 1956.

Heaviest defeat: 0–7 v. Aston Villa (Div. 1), December 1930.

Best in League Cup: Semi-final 1969–70, 1970–71, 1974–75.

Pitch measurements: 116 x 76 yd.

Highest League Scorer in Single Season: Dennis Viollet—32 in 1959–60 (Div. 1).

Transfers—

 Highest fee paid: £500,000—Gordon McQueen (from Leeds), February 1978.

 Highest fee received: £175,000—Gerry Daly (to Derby), March 1977.

MANSFIELD TOWN

Field Mill Ground, Mansfield, Notts. Mansfield 23567

Shirts: amber with blue trim. *Shorts:* blue with amber stripe. *Stockings:* amber. *Second colours:* white shirts with blue & amber trim, white shorts.

The name of Mansfield Town was on many people's lips one February night in 1969—and no wonder. The Third Division club had astounded the football world by beating West Ham United—who included three World Cup players, Bobby Moore, Geoff Hurst and Martin Peters—3–0 in the F.A. Cup fifth round.

Forty years earlier in 1929 Mansfield, then a non-League club, produced an equally remarkable Cup result by winning 1–0 away to Second Division Wolves in the third round.

Such days of spectacular deeds helped to compensate followers of Mansfield for seasons of comparatively unexciting activity until the club gained promotion to the Second Division for the first time in 1976–77. Since winning the Midland League in 1924, 1925 and 1929, Mansfield had rarely attracted national acclaim.

Entering the League (Division Three South) in 1931, they missed the Second Division by one place in 1951 and 1965. In 1975 Town won the Fourth Division Championship by six points.

Roy Goodall, Freddie Steele, Charlie Mitten, Sam Weaver, Raich Carter and Tommy Cummings are among illustrious names who as managers of Mansfield tried to bring a higher standard of football to Field Mill.

Division 3 Champions: 1976–77.
Division 4 Champions: 1974–75.
Record attendance: 24,467 v. Nottingham Forest (F.A. Cup), January 1953.
Modern Capacity: 22,000. **Nickname:** 'Stags.'
Entered Football League: 1931—Div. 3 (South).
Biggest win: 9–2 v. Rotherham (Div. 3 North), December 1932; 9–2 v. Hounslow Town (F.A. Cup), November 1962.
Heaviest defeat: 1–8 v. Walsall (Div. 3 North), January 1933.
Best in F.A. Cup: 6th Round 1968–69.
Best in League Cup: 5th Round 1975–76.
Pitch measurements: 115 x 72 yd.
Highest League Scorer in Single Season: Ted Harston—55 in 1936–37 (Div. 3 North).
Transfers—
  Highest fee paid: £30,000—Dennis Martin (from Newcastle), March 1978.
  Highest fee received: £80,000—Ray Clarke (to Sparta, Rotterdam), July 1976.

MIDDLESBROUGH

Ayresome Park, Middlesbrough, Teesside TS1 4PB,
Middlesbrough 89659/85996

Shirts: red, with white chestband, white trim. *Shorts:* red, white
stripes on seam. *Stockings:* red. *Second colours:* white shirts with
red motif, white shorts.

Former Leeds and England centre-half Jack Charlton's first season
as a manager ended triumphantly in 1974 with Middlesbrough
returning to the First Division after an interval of 20 years. Charlton
instilled Leeds-type efficiency into 'Boro's play, and they led the
field from the start to give the North-east a second successive year
of triumph following Sunderland's F.A. Cup victory in 1973.

Middlesbrough, the only League club to have won the Amateur
Cup (1895, 1898), joined the Second Division in 1899 and were
promoted three years later. Ayresome Park has been their home
since 1903.

They caused a sensation in 1905, when they paid Sunderland
the game's first transfer fee of £1000 for Alf Common, and not long
afterwards Steve Bloomer, another famous name in soccer history,
joined 'Boro' from Derby.

During their earlier years, Middlesbrough set several records. Two
came in 1926–27 when, after the change in the offside law, they
scored what is still the Division Two record of 122 goals. Local-born
centre-forward George Camsell contributed 59, another unbeaten
record for the same division. In 1927–28, Middlesbrough and
Tottenham shared a less enviable record—the highest points totals
(37 and 38) for teams relegated from the First Division.

Division 2 Champions: 1926–27, 1928–29, 1973–74.
F.A. Amateur Cup Winners: 1894–95, 1897–98.
Record attendance: 53,596 v. Newcastle United (League),
December 1949.
Modern Capacity: 42,500. **Nickname:** 'Boro.'
Entered Football League: 1899—Div. 2.
Biggest win: 10–3 v. Sheffield United (Div. 1), November 1933.
Heaviest defeat: 0–9 v. Blackburn (Div. 2), November 1954.
Best in F.A. Cup: 6th Round 1935–36, 1946–47, 1969–70,
1974–75, 1976–77, 1977–78.
Best in League Cup: Semi-final 1975–76.
Pitch measurements: 115 x 75 yd.
Highest League Scorer in Single Season: George Camsell—
59 in 1926–27 (Div. 2).
Transfers—
  Highest fee paid: £120,000—Billy Ashcroft (from Wrexham),
  August 1977.
  Highest fee received: £352,000—Graeme Souness (to Liver-
  pool), January 1978.

65

MILLWALL

The Den, Coldblow Lane, London SE14 5RH, 01-639 3143/4

Shirts: royal blue with white trim. *Shorts:* white with blue trim. *Stockings:* blue with white rings. *Second colours:* red shirts with black & white trim, black shorts.

Between 1964 and 1967 Millwall established a League record that will not easily be beaten. They played 59 consecutive home matches without defeat, a sequence that started in the Fourth Division on 24 August 1964 and ended in a Second Division match against Plymouth Argyle on 14 January 1967. A much earlier Millwall record was their aggregate of 127 goals in winning the Third Division (South) Championship of 1927–28.

The club was among the original members of the Third Division in 1920. In 1937 they became the first Third Division club to reach the F.A. Cup semi-finals, beating First Division opponents Chelsea, Derby County and Manchester City at The Den, before falling 2–1 to Sunderland at the last hurdle before Wembley.

A year later Millwall were back in Division Two, but after the war their fortunes slumped and they dropped from Second Division to Third and then through the trapdoor to the Fourth. They climbed back to the Second in successive seasons (1964–65–66), but were once more relegated in 1975. A tremendous late run took them up again twelve months later under Gordon Jago's managership.

In May 1970 Millwall transferred forward Keith Weller to Chelsea for £100,000, and that figure was exceeded in January 1973, when they collected £115,000 from the transfer of Derek Possee to Crystal Palace.

Division 3 (South) Champions: 1927–28, 1937–38.
Division 4 Champions: 1961–62.
Record attendance: 48,672 v. Derby County (F.A. Cup), February 1937.
Modern Capacity: 40,000. **Nickname:** 'Lions.'
Entered Football League: 1920—Div. 3.
Biggest win: 9–1 v. Torquay United (Div. 3 South), August 1927; 9–1 v. Coventry City (Div. 3 South), November 1927.
Heaviest defeat: 1–9 v. Aston Villa (F.A. Cup), January 1946.
Best in F.A. Cup: Semi-final 1899–1900, 1902–03, 1936–37.
Best in League Cup: 5th Round 1973–74.
Pitch measurements: 110 x 72½ yd.
Highest League Scorer in Single Season: Dick Parker—37 in 1926–27 (Div. 3 South).
Transfers—
    Highest fee paid: £45,000—Alf Wood (from Shrewsbury), May 1972.
    Highest fee received: £115,000—Derek Possee (to Crystal Palace), January 1973.

NEWCASTLE UNITED

St James's Park, Newcastle-upon-Tyne NE1 4ST, 0632–28361/2

Shirts: black & white stripes, white sleeves. *Shorts:* black, white seam. *Stockings:* white with black rings at top. *Second colours:* yellow shirts with green collar & cuffs, green shorts.

Blaydon Races, the Geordie folk-song, rang out in the unlikely surroundings of Budapest in June 1969. The occasion: Newcastle's 3–2 second-leg victory over the Hungarian side Ujpest Dozsa giving them the Fairs' Cup 6–2 on aggregate at their first attempt in Europe.

Tyneside fans also sang with great gusto at Wembley, in 1951 and 1952, when their club became the first this century to take the F.A. Cup in successive seasons. In 1955 they won it again, for the sixth time, but their 100 per cent Wembley record ended in 1974, when United lost 3–0 to Liverpool in their record eleventh F.A. Cup Final.

In June 1975 Gordon Lee, from Blackburn, replaced Joe Harvey as manager, and in his first season took Newcastle to Wembley for their first League Cup Final.

After the Second World War Tyneside roared to the sharp-shooting of 'Wor Jackie' Milburn, who scored 178 League goals (the club aggregate record) from 1946–57. Together with full-back Bob Cowell and left-winger Bobby Mitchell, he played in the Cup-winning teams of 1951, 1952 and 1955, but Newcastle fans did not see the goalscoring like of Milburn again until the start of season 1971–72, with the £185,000 signing of Malcolm Macdonald from Luton.

League Champions: 1904–05, 1906–07, 1908–09, 1926–27.
Division 2 Champions: 1964–65.
F.A. Cup Winners: 1909–10, 1923–24, 1931–32, 1950–51 1951–52, 1954–55.
European Fairs Cup Winners: 1968–69.
Record attendance: 68,386 v. Chelsea (League), September 1930.
Modern Capacity: 56,000. **Nickname:** 'Magpies.'
Entered Football League: 1893—Div. 2.
Biggest win: 13–0 v. Newport County (Div. 2), October 1946.
Heaviest defeat: 0–9 v. Burton Wanderers (Div. 2), April 1895.
Best in League Cup: Final 1975–76.
Pitch measurements: 110 x 75 yd.
Highest League Scorer in Single Season: Hughie Gallacher—36 in 1926–27 (Div. 1).
Transfers—
  Highest fee paid: £185,000—Malcolm Macdonald (from Luton), May 1971.
  Highest fee received: £333,333—Malcolm Macdonald (to Arsenal), August 1976.

NEWPORT COUNTY

Somerton Park, Newport, Gwent NPT 0HZ, Newport 71543/71271

Shirts: amber with black trim. *Shorts:* black with amber stripe. *Stockings:* amber. *Second colours:* white shirts & shorts.

Older supporters of Newport County still wonder what the club might have achieved but for the outbreak of the Second World War. Their speculation is understandable for in 1938–39, the last full League season before hostilities, Newport won the Division Three South Championship in confident style.

But when, after a seven-year wait, League football resumed in 1946–47, they faced the Second Division with a reshaped team and were promptly relegated. They finished bottom with only 23 points from the 42 fixtures, and conceded 133 goals. At Newcastle, on 5 October 1946, County crashed 13–0, which equalled what is still the heaviest Football League defeat (Stockport County 13, Halifax Town 0 in Division Three North on 6 January 1934).

These statistics gave Newport all the wrong reasons by which to remember their only season in the Second Division, and since then life for them has been an almost continuous struggle for survival in a Rugby Union stronghold.

For clubs such as Newport who are constantly beset by financial problems, a run in the F.A. Cup can be a boon. Unfortunately, such occasions have been rare, though in 1949 Newport reached the fifth round before losing, a little unluckily, 3–2 at Portsmouth. On the way they overcame Leeds United and Huddersfield Town, and that remains their furthest progress in the F.A. Cup.

Division 3 (South) Champions: 1938–39.
Record attendance: 24,268 v. Cardiff City (League), October 1937.
Modern Capacity: 20,000.
Entered Football League: 1920—Div. 3.
Biggest win: 10–0 v. Merthyr Town (Div. 3 South), April 1930.
Heaviest defeat: 0–13 v. Newcastle United (Div. 2), October 1946.
Best in F.A. Cup: 5th Round 1948–49.
Best in League Cup: 3rd Round 1962–63.
Pitch measurements: 110 x 75 yd.
Highest League Scorer in Single Season: Tudor Martin—34 in 1929–30 (Div. 3 South).
Transfers—
  Highest fee paid: £10,000—Brian Godfrey (from Bristol Rovers), June 1973.
  Highest fee received: £15,000—Steve Aizlewood (to Swindon), March 1976.

NORTHAMPTON TOWN

County Ground, Abington Avenue, Northampton NN1 4PS
Northampton 31553

Shirts: white with claret trim. *Shorts:* white. *Stockings:* white.
Second colours: yellow shirts with claret trim, yellow shorts.

Northampton Town are always assured of one significant entry in the history of the Football League. In 1965 they became the first club to rise from the Fourth to the First Division, a feat they achieved in five remarkable seasons. The tragedy was that their return to the lowest reaches of the League should be even swifter. They lasted only one season in Division One and, almost unbelievably, by 1969 were back in Division Four, from which they climbed again in 1976.

The club first tasted success as Southern League champions in 1909 and the man who guided them to that triumph was Herbert Chapman, later to win much wider managerial fame with Huddersfield Town and Arsenal. Strangely, that was Northampton's only notable football prize until they took the Division Three title in 1962–63.

Dave Bowen, the former Wales and Arsenal wing-half, who managed the club through most of the vicissitudes to the 1970s, Cliff Holton, another previously with Arsenal, Ron Flowers and Jack English are just a few of the experienced players who have starred for the 'Cobblers', whose ground is also the home of Northamptonshire County Cricket Club.

Division 3 Champions: 1962–63.
Record attendance: 24,523 v. Fulham (League), April 1966.
Modern Capacity: 25,000. **Nickname:** 'Cobblers.'
Entered Football League: 1920—Div. 3.
Biggest win: 10–0 v. Walsall (Div. 3 South), November 1927.
Heaviest defeat: 0–10 v. Bournemouth (Div. 3 South), September 1939.
Best in F.A. Cup: 5th Round 1933–34, 1949–50, 1969–70.
Best in League Cup: 5th Round 1964–65, 1966–67.
Pitch measurements: 110 x 76 yd.
Highest League Scorer in Single Season: Cliff Holton—36 in 1961–62 (Div. 3).
Transfers—
  Highest fee paid: £27,000—Joe Broadfoot (from Ipswich), November 1965.
  Highest fee received: £60,000—Phil Neal (to Liverpool), October 1974.

NORWICH CITY

Carrow Road, Norwich NR1 1JE, Norwich 612131

Shirts: yellow with green trim. *Shorts:* green with yellow trim. *Stockings:* yellow with green tops. *Second colours:* white shirts & shorts.

The seventies have been the most significant years in Norwich City's history. In 1972 they reached Division One for the first time; in 1973 manager Ron Saunders took them to a first Wembley appearance (they lost the League Cup Final to Tottenham, 1–0); season 1973–74, during which Saunders moved to Manchester City, ended with the 'Canaries' dropping back into Division Two, and a year later, under John Bond, they were back in the top section.

Norwich won the League Cup in only its second season (1961–62), and it is as cup fighters that the East Anglian club are best known. Founded in 1905, they waited only four years before establishing their reputation by knocking out Liverpool at Anfield. Other notable cup 'scalps' included Sunderland in 1910–11, Tottenham in 1914–15, Leeds in 1934–35, Liverpool again in 1950–51, and Arsenal at Highbury in 1953–54.

Their greatest F.A. Cup run came in 1959 when, as a Third Division side, they knocked out Manchester United, Cardiff, Tottenham and Sheffield United before losing 1–0 to Luton after a 1–1 draw in the semi-final.

Norwich, who gained the nickname 'Canaries' when they adopted their green and yellow colours, and moved to a ground called 'The Nest' in 1908, were founder-members of Division Three (South) in 1920. They won promotion to Division Two in 1934, but were relegated in 1939 and stayed down until 1960.

Division 2 Champions: 1971–72.
Division 3 (South) Champions: 1933–34.
League Cup Winners: 1961–62.
Record attendance: 43,984 v. Leicester City (F.A. Cup), March 1963.
Modern Capacity: 42,000. **Nickname:** 'Canaries.'
Entered Football League: 1920—Div. 3.
Biggest win: 10–2 v. Coventry (Div. 3 South), March 1930.
Heaviest defeat: 2–10 v. Swindon Town (Southern League), September 1908.
Best in F.A. Cup: Semi-final 1958–59.
Pitch measurements: 114 x 74 yd.
Highest League Scorer in Single Season: Ralph Hunt—31 in 1955–56 (Div. 3 South).
Transfers—
    Highest fee paid: £145,000—Phil Boyer (from Bournemouth), February 1974.
    Highest fee received: £170,000—Graham Paddon (to West Ham), December 1973.

NOTTINGHAM FOREST

City Ground, Nottingham NG2 5FJ, 0602–868236/7/8

Shirts: red, white trim. *Shorts:* white. *Stockings:* red. *Second colours:* yellow shirts & shorts.

In the strictest sense of the word, Nottingham Forest are the only *true* club in the Football League, run as they are by an elected committee. The other 91 are all limited companies, each with a board of directors.

Forest were founded in 1865, and are the third oldest League club after Notts County and Stoke City. In various ways, Forest helped shape the game's early history. For instance, their England International Sam Widdowson was the first player to wear shin-guards, in 1874. It was in a Forest game four years later that a referee used a whistle for the first time—previously signals were given by handkerchief—and in 1891 the crossbar and nets made their first appearance in soccer, at the Forest ground.

The club's first F.A. Cup success came in 1898, but although they won the trophy again in 1959, the Championship has always eluded them.

Yet they have seldom lacked players of International standing, their more recent caps including Terry Hennessey, Joe Baker, Alan Hinton, Jim Baxter and Ian Moore. Bob McKinlay, former centre-half and captain, set the remarkable club record of 614 League appearances between 1951 and 1969.

In August 1974 Forest sold striker Duncan McKenzie to Leeds for £250,000, during Brian Clough's brief reign at Elland Road; five months later Clough became manager of Forest and took them back into the First Division in 1976–77.

Division 2 Champions: 1906–07, 1921–22.
Division 3 (South) Champions: 1950–51.
F.A. Cup Winners: 1897–98, 1958–59.
Record attendance: 49,945 v. Manchester United (League), October 1967.
Modern Capacity: 49,500.
Entered Football League: 1892—Div. 1.
Biggest win: 14–0 v. Clapton (F.A. Cup), 1890–91.
Heaviest defeat: 1–9 v. Blackburn Rovers (Div. 2), April 1937.
Best in League Cup: 4th Round 1960–61, 1969–70.
Pitch measurements: 115 x 78 yd.
Highest League Scorer in Single Season: Wally Ardron—36 in 1950–51 (Div. 3 South).
Transfers—
  Highest fee paid: £270,000—Peter Shilton (from Stoke), September 1977.
  Highest fee received: £250,000—Duncan McKenzie (to Leeds), August 1974.

NOTTS COUNTY

Meadow Lane, Nottingham NG2 6AG, Nottingham 868494

Shirts: black & white stripes. *Shorts:* black. *Stockings:* white.
Second colours: gold shirts, green shorts.

Notts County are the oldest club in the Football League, formed in
1862 and founder members of the League in 1888. Twice in the
next six years they reached the final of the F.A. Cup. They lost 3–1
to Blackburn Rovers at Kennington Oval in 1891, but in 1894 they
won the trophy by beating Bolton Wanderers 4–1 at Everton. They
spent three separate periods in Division One between 1897 and
1926, but their highest final position was third in 1901.

Few events in County's chequered history have caused greater
comment than the sensational signing of centre forward Tommy
Lawton from Chelsea in November 1947 for £20,000, a figure
which few clubs, let alone a Third Division side, could afford in
those days. Yet the deal paid off for club and player. County soon
won promotion and Lawton gained further caps for England.

Jackie Sewell went from Meadow Lane to Sheffield Wednesday
in March 1951, for the then record fee of £34,500, after scoring
nearly 100 League goals.

Another remarkable County character was the 6 ft 5 in Albert
Iremonger, rated by some as the finest goalkeeper ever to play for
England. He made 564 League appearances for the club from
1904–26.

Division 2 Champions: 1896–97, 1913–14, 1922–23.
Division 3 (South) Champions: 1930–31, 1949–50.
Division 4 Champions: 1970–71.
F.A. Cup Winners: 1893–94.
Record attendance: 47,301 v. York (F.A. Cup), March 1955.
Modern Capacity: 45,000. **Nickname:** 'Magpies.'
Entered Football League: 1888—Div. 1.
Biggest win: 11–1 v. Newport County (Div. 3 South), January
1949.
Heaviest defeat: 1–9 v. Aston Villa (Div. 1), September 1888;
1–9 v. Blackburn Rovers (Div. 1), November 1889; 1–9 v.
Portsmouth (Div. 2), April 1927.
Best in League Cup: 5th Round 1963–64, 1972–73, 1975–76.
Pitch measurements: 117$\frac{1}{3}$ x 76 yd.
Highest League Scorer in Single Season: Tom Keetley—39 in
1930–31 (Div. 3 South).
Transfers—
  Highest fee paid: £45,000—David Hunt (from Derby), March
  1978.
  Highest fee received: £100,000—Don Masson (to Queen's
  Park Rangers), December 1974.

OLDHAM ATHLETIC

Boundary Park, Oldham OL1 2PA, 061–624 4972

Shirts: royal blue. *Shorts:* white. *Stockings:* white. *Second colours:* tangerine shirts, blue shorts.

Although most of Oldham's modern existence has been spent in the Third and Fourth Divisions, they were in the Championship section half a century ago. Indeed, they narrowly failed to carry off the League title in 1914–15, finishing a point behind Everton.

Eric Gemmell performed a notable goalscoring feat for Oldham in season 1951–52. Playing in a Third Division North match against Chester, he scored seven times in an 11–2 win.

In addition to developing goalscorers, Oldham have found a number of International goalkeepers, notably Jack Hacking, Ted Taylor, Albert Gray and Frank Moss, who was one of seven Arsenal players capped against Italy in 1934.

Season 1970–71 was notable in two ways for Oldham. They earned promotion to Division Three and their players also won the one-season Ford Sporting League, bringing the club total prize money of £80,000 for the improvement of spectator facilities.

With a late-season flourish, Oldham snatched the Third Division Championship of 1973–74, returning to the Second Division after an interval of twenty years. Two seasons later, excellent home results at one stage suggested possible further promotion, but the away form was not good enough to take them back to the First Division they left in 1923.

Division 3 (North) Champions: 1952–53.
Division 3 Champions: 1973–74.
Record attendance: 47,671 v. Sheffield Wednesday (F.A. Cup), January 1930.
Modern Capacity: 36,500. **Nickname:** 'Latics.'
Entered Football League: 1907—Div. 2.
Biggest win: 11–0 v. Southport (Div. 4), December 1962.
Heaviest defeat: 4–13 v. Tranmere (Div. 3 North), December 1935.
Best in F.A. Cup: Semi-final 1912–13.
Best in League Cup: 2nd Round 1960–61, 1962–63, 1964–65, 1965–66, 1970–71, 1971–72, 1975–76.
Pitch measurements: 110 x 74 yd.
Highest League Scorer in Single Season: Tom Davis—33 in 1936–37 (Div. 3 North).
Transfers—
  Highest fee paid: £40,000—David Holt (from Bury), December 1974 ; £40,000—Steve Taylor (from Bolton), October 1977.
  Highest fee received: £80,000—David Shaw (to West Bromwich), March 1973.

ORIENT

Leyton Stadium, Brisbane Road, London E10 5NE, 01–539 2223

Shirts: white with broad red stripes. *Shorts:* white with red stripe. *Stockings:* white with red top. *Second colours:* red shirt with white stripes, red shorts with white stripes.

When Orient sold brilliant young half-back Tommy Taylor to West Ham for £80,000 in October 1970, it was a move of considerable financial significance to a club which three years earlier almost foundered. Orient called a Sunday morning public meeting after disclosing accumulated debts of £100,000. The response was generous and Taylor's transfer completed economic recovery.

The club owe their name to the Orient Shipping Company. They were formed in 1881 as Clapton Orient; they became Leyton Orient in 1946 and dropped the prefix 'Leyton' in 1967. Orient made their home at Brisbane Road in 1937, having previously shared Clapton greyhound stadium, the Essex cricket ground at Leyton and the old Lea Bridge speedway stadium.

Alec Stock, who had three spells in charge, took them to second place in Division Three South in 1955 and up into Division Two as Champions 12 months later. In 1962 they gained promotion with Liverpool to Division One, but survived only one season. Under George Petchey—their eleventh post-war manager—Orient just failed to go back to top company in 1974, drawing the final game at home to Aston Villa when they needed victory for promotion.

Division 3 (South) Champions: 1955–56.
Division 3 Champions: 1969–70.
Record attendance: 34,345 v. West Ham United (F.A. Cup), January 1964.
Modern Capacity: 35,000. **Nickname:** 'O's.'
Entered Football League: 1905—Div. 2 (as Clapton Orient).
Biggest win: 9–2 v. Aldershot (Div. 3 South), February 1934; 9–2 v. Chester (League Cup), October 1962.
Heaviest defeat: 0–8 v. Aston Villa (F.A. Cup), January 1929.
Best in F.A. Cup: 6th Round 1925–26, 1953–54, 1971–72.
Best in League Cup: 5th Round 1962–63.
Pitch measurements: 110 x 80 yd.
Highest League Scorer in Single Season: Tom Johnston—35 in 1957–58 (Div. 2).
Transfers—
  Highest fee paid: £60,000—Gerry Queen (from Crystal Palace), September 1972; £60,000—Ricky Heppolette (from Preston), December 1972.
  Highest fee received: £112,000—Dennis Rofe (to Leicester), August 1972.

OXFORD UNITED

Manor Ground, Headington, Oxford OX3 7RS, 0865–61503

Shirts: yellow with blue trim. *Shorts:* blue with yellow stripe.
Stockings: yellow with blue trim. *Second colours:* white shirts
& shorts.

Until 1962 one of the oldest established clubs outside the Football
League, Oxford United were formed in 1896 as Headington United
but did not turn professional until 1949. They took their present
name in 1961 and, after Accrington Stanley withdrew from Division
Four a year later, Oxford got the chance of League status, quickly
proving themselves worthy of it. In 1964 they became the first
Fourth Division side to reach the sixth round of the F.A. Cup, and
in only six seasons of League membership they climbed two
divisions into the Second.

In their first year in Division Two (1968–69) Oxford survived by
only one place. In the next three seasons they finished just below
half-way, and in 1972–73 they attained their highest final Second
Division placing—eighth. Improvement was not maintained, however, and with relegation increased to three clubs, Oxford spent an
uncomfortable season 1973–74 near the foot of the table. There was
another season-long fight against relegation in 1975–76, this time
ending in failure.

When United gained promotion from the Fourth Division in
1964–65 with 61 points, they scored 87 goals. Their results that
season included a record 7–0 success against Barrow.

Division 3 Champions: 1967–68.
Record attendance: 22,730 v. Preston N.E. (F.A. Cup), February
1964.
Modern Capacity: 19,000.
Entered Football League: 1962—Div. 4.
Biggest win: 7–0 v. Barrow (Div. 4), December 1964.
Heaviest defeat: 0–5 v. Cardiff (Div. 2), February 1969 ; 0–5 v.
Cardiff (Div. 2), September 1973.
Best in F.A. Cup: 6th Round 1963–64.
Best in League Cup: 5th Round 1969–70.
Pitch measurements: 112 x 78 yd.
Highest League Scorer in Single Season: Colin Booth—23 in
1964–65 (Div. 4).
Transfers—
  Highest fee paid: £70,000—Andy McCulloch (from Cardiff),
  June 1974.
  Highest fee received: £75,000—Dave Roberts (to Hull),
  February 1975.

PETERBOROUGH UNITED

London Road, Peterborough PE2 8AL, Peterborough 63947

Shirts: blue and white stripes. *Shorts:* blue. *Stockings:* navy blue.
Second colours: yellow shirts, black shorts.

When Peterborough United, an ambitious Southern League club
with a splendidly appointed ground, won admission to the Football
League in 1960–61, the cynics wondered whether they were really
equipped to bridge the gap between the two grades of football.
The 'Posh', as they are familiarly known, gave the best possible
answer: they won the Fourth Division Championship at the first
attempt, and in record-breaking style.

Terry Bly was the chief destroyer of defences in Peterborough's
first season in League football. His tally of 52 goals in 46 games
remains the highest for the division—no other player has topped
50 League goals for any club in post-war football—and the 134
goals obtained by Peterborough is a record for any division of the
Football League. Will it ever be beaten?

The following season they threatened to go straight into the
Second Division. Finally, however, they took fifth place, though
they scored more goals, 107, than either of the promoted teams.

In 1965, Peterborough reached the sixth round of the F.A. Cup,
beating Salisbury, Queen's Park Rangers, Chesterfield, Arsenal and
Swansea before losing to Chelsea.

In 1968 the club was demoted to the Fourth Division because of
alleged irregularities in their books, but at the end of his second
season in 1974, manager Noel Cantwell had inspired another
Peterborough promotion success as Fourth Division winners.

Division 4 Champions: 1960–61, 1973–74.
Record attendance: 30,096 v. Swansea (F.A. Cup), February
1965.
Modern Capacity: 30,000. **Nickname:** 'Posh.'
Entered Football League: 1960—Div. 4.
Biggest win: 8–1 v. Oldham Athletic (Div. 4), November 1969.
Heaviest defeat: 1–8 v. Northampton (F.A. Cup), December
1946.
Best in F.A. Cup: 6th Round 1964–65.
Best in League Cup: Semi-final 1965–66.
Pitch measurements: 113 x 76 yd.
Highest League Scorer in Single Season: Terry Bly—52 in
1960–61 (Div. 4).
Transfers—
  Highest fee paid: £25,000—Ernie Moss (from Chesterfield),
  January 1976.
  Highest fee received: £55,000—David Gregory (to Stoke),
  June 1977.

PLYMOUTH ARGYLE

Home Park, Plymouth PL2 1BQ, Plymouth 52561/2/3

Shirts: white with green & black trimmings. *Shorts:* white with green & black trimmings. *Stockings:* white with green & black turnover. *Second colours:* yellow shirts & shorts.

Plymouth Argyle achieved some extraordinary feats in their early years in the old Southern Section of the Third Division. For six consecutive years between 1921 and 1927 they finished runners-up, twice missing promotion by a point and once on goal average; in 1920–21 they drew 21 of their 42 matches and the following season their defence conceded only 24 League goals.

The reward for consistency was finally earned in 1930 when the Devon club took the title with unmistakable authority, finishing seven points clear.

Probably no League club has travelled more miles *in England* during their history than Argyle. Yet for all the strain which long journeys inevitably impose on players, the club have gone near to winning First Division status on several occasions. They finished fourth in Division Two in 1932 and 1953, and fifth in seasons 1937 and 1962.

In season 1973–74 Plymouth, despite being in the lower half of Division Three, went closer to Wembley than ever before. They lifted West Country hearts with thrilling League Cup victories away to First Division opponents Burnley, Queen's Park Rangers and Birmingham before Manchester City halted their run in the semi-final. The impetus was maintained in 1974–75, when Argyle won back a place in the Second Division.

Division 3 (South) Champions: 1929–30, 1951–52.
Division 3 Champions: 1958–59.
Record attendance: 43,596 v. Aston Villa (League), October 1936.
Modern Capacity: 40,000. **Nickname:** 'Pilgrims.'
Entered Football League: 1920—Div. 3.
Biggest win: 8–1 v. Millwall (Div. 2), January 1932.
Heaviest defeat: 0–9 v. Stoke City (Div. 2), December 1960.
Best in F.A. Cup: 5th Round 1952–53.
Best in League Cup: Semi-final 1964–65, 1973–74.
Pitch measurements: 112 x 75 yd.
Highest League Scorer in Single Season: Jack Cock—32 in 1925–26 (Div. 3 South).
Transfers—
  Highest fee paid: £50,000—John Peddelty (from Ipswich), October 1976; £50,000—Brian Hall (from Liverpool), July 1976.
  Highest fee received: £220,000—Paul Mariner (to Ipswich), October 1976.

PORTSMOUTH

Fratton Park, Portsmouth PO4 8RA, Portsmouth 31204/5

Shirts: dark blue with white collars & cuffs. *Shorts:* white. *Stockings:* red. *Second colours:* red shirts & stockings.

Portsmouth spent 25 consecutive seasons in Division One after gaining promotion in 1927 on the strength of a goal average that was 1/250th of a goal better than Manchester City's. Elevation to football's top flight was to be the launching pad for a catalogue of League and Cup successes. Portsmouth were defeated in the 1929 and 1934 F.A. Cup Finals, but beat hot favourites Wolves 4–1 in the 1939 Final.

The famous 'Pompey Chimes' rang out across Fratton Park as the League title was won in 1949, and Portsmouth successfully defended it the following season, becoming only the eighth club in the history of the game to complete such a double.

Thus Portsmouth were the first former Third Division club to win the Championship, but their star waned dramatically. They dropped to Division Two in 1959 and to the Third two years later, but returned first time as Third Division Champions in 1962.

Between 1946 and 1965 Jimmy Dickinson, England half-back in 48 post-war Internationals, set a British record with 764 League appearances—all for Portsmouth, with whom he is now club secretary. It was beaten by Terry Paine (Hereford) in 1975–76, a season which ended with Portsmouth back in the Third Division and facing grave financial trouble.

League Champions: 1948–49, 1949–50.
Division 3 (South) Champions: 1923–24.
Division 3 Champions: 1961–62.
F.A. Cup Winners: 1938–39.
Record attendance: 51,385 v. Derby County (F.A. Cup), February 1949.
Modern Capacity: 46,000. **Nickname:** 'Pompey.'
Entered Football League: 1920—Div. 3.
Biggest win: 9–1 v. Notts County (Div. 2), April 1927.
Heaviest defeat: 0–10 v. Leicester City (Div. 1), October 1928.
Best in League Cup: 5th Round 1960–61.
Pitch measurements: 116 x 72 yd.
Highest League Scorer in Single Season: Billy Haines—40 in 1926–27 (Div. 2).
Transfers—
  Highest fee paid: £154,000—Paul Went (from Fulham), December 1973.
  Highest fee received: £50,000—George Smith (to Middlesbrough), January 1969.

PORT VALE

Vale Park, Burslem, Stoke-on-Trent ST6 1AW, Stoke-on-Trent 87626

Shirts: white with black & white sleeves. *Shorts:* black with white stripe. *Stockings:* black with white tops. *Second colours:* yellow shirts with green sleeveband, yellow shorts with green seam.

Port Vale nearly wrote a fresh page in the history of the F.A. Cup in 1954. No Third Division club has reached the final, but Vale, caught up on a wave of enthusiasm which spread far beyond the Potteries, beat Queen's Park Rangers away (1–0), Cardiff away (2–0), Blackpool at home (2–0) and Leyton Orient away (1–0) on their way to the semi-finals. Before a crowd of 68,221 at Villa Park, they faced their Staffordshire neighbours and famed Cup fighters, West Bromwich Albion and, incredibly, led them until the second half. Albion triumphed 2–1, but as consolation Port Vale won the Third North title that season by a margin of eleven points.

A number of players have given Vale outstanding service, but none more so than local-born Roy Sproson who made 762 League appearances between 1950 and 1972. He was a member of the sides which won the Third Division (North) in 1953–54, the Fourth Division title in 1958–59 and was still an ever-present defender in the team which again won promotion to the Third Division in 1970.

Division 3 (North) Champions: 1929–30, 1953–54.
Division 4 Champions: 1958–59.
Record attendance: 50,000 v. Aston Villa (F.A. Cup), February 1960.
Modern Capacity: 50,000. **Nickname:** 'Valiants.'
Entered Football League: 1892–Div. 2.
Biggest win: 9–1 v. Chesterfield (Div. 2), September 1932.
Heaviest defeat: 0–10 v. Sheffield United (Div. 2), December 1892; 0–10 v. Notts County (Div. 2), February 1895.
Best in F.A. Cup: Semi-final 1953–54.
Best in League Cup: 5th Round 1976–77.
Pitch measurements: 116 x 76 yd.
Highest League Scorer in Single Season: Wilf Kirkham—38 in 1926–27 (Div. 2).
Transfers—
  Highest fee paid: £15,000—Albert Cheesebrough (from Leicester), July 1963; £15,000—Billy Bingham (from Everton), August 1963; £15,000—Ken Beamish (from Blackburn), September 1976.
  Highest fee received: £30,000—Terry Alcock (to Blackpool), August 1967; £30,000—Brian Horton (to Brighton), March 1976.

PRESTON NORTH END

Deepdale, Preston PR1 6RU, Preston 795919

Shirts: white with blue collar & cuffs. *Shorts:* white with blue stripe. *Stockings:* white. *Second colours:* yellow shirts & shorts.

Preston North End won the first League Championship of all in 1888–89 without losing a match, and the F.A. Cup the same season without conceding a goal—a 'double' without parallel.

Founder members of the League, Preston justified their title 'Invincibles' until they were relegated in 1901. They returned in 1904, continuing to move ten times up and down between the divisions until, for the first time in their history, in 1970, they found themselves in Division Three. A year later they were champions of that section.

After being beaten by Sunderland in the 1937 F.A. Cup Final, Preston carried off the trophy in 1938 when George Mutch gave them a 1–0 victory over Huddersfield from the penalty spot with the last kick of Wembley's first extra-time Final.

Tom Finney, who made 433 League appearances (187 goals) and won 76 England caps, was the outstanding figure in Preston football from 1946–60, and in 1973 another of England's greatest post-war forwards, Bobby Charlton, joined the club as manager after an illustrious career with Manchester United. His first season at Deepdale, however, ended with Preston relegated to Division Three, and at the start of 1975–76 Charlton resigned after differences with the board over a transfer deal.

The Double (League Champions, F.A. Cup Winners): 1888–89.
League Champions: 1888–89, 1889–90.
Division 2 Champions: 1903–04, 1912–13, 1950–51.
Division 3 Champions: 1970–71.
F.A. Cup Winners: 1888–89, 1937–38.
Record attendance: 42,684 v. Arsenal (League), April 1938.
Modern Capacity: 40,000.
Entered Football League: 1888—Div. 1.
Biggest win: 26–0 v. Hyde (F.A. Cup), October 1887.
Heaviest defeat: 0–7 v. Blackpool (Div. 1), May 1948.
Best in League Cup: 4th Round 1962–63, 1965–66, 1971–72.
Pitch measurements: 112 x 78 yd.
Highest League Scorer in Single Season: Ted Harper—37 in 1932–33 (Div. 2).
Transfers—
  Highest fee paid: £70,000—Mike Elwiss (from Doncaster), February 1974.
  Highest fee received: £150,000—Alec Bruce (to Newcastle), January 1974.

QUEEN'S PARK RANGERS

Rangers Stadium, Shepherd's Bush, London W12 7PA,
01-743 2618/2670

Shirts: blue & white hoops with white sleeves. *Shorts:* white with blue stripes. *Stockings:* white with blue rings. *Second colours:* red & white halved shirts, black shorts.

Season 1966–67 will always be recalled as a vintage one by supporters of Queen's Park Rangers. The club not only took the Third Division title by a margin of twelve points, but became the first outside the first two divisions to win the Football League Cup. In a thrilling decider at Wembley—the first time that venue was used for the League Cup—Rangers beat First Division opponents West Bromwich Albion 3–2 after being two down.

The magic continued under Alec Stock's managership and the following year Rangers completed the greatest period in their history by going up into Division One—thus emulating Charlton's feat (1935 and 1936) of moving from Third to First Division in consecutive years. But Rangers immediately found the highest class too much, and were relegated (1969) after just four years down.

But in 1973, managed by Gordon Jago, they swept back to the First Division as the top scorers in the Football League (81 goals) and this time they proved ready to meet top-class opposition. In October 1974 Dave Sexton (ex-Chelsea) took over, and after collecting 27 points from the last 15 games in 1975–76, Q.P.R. spent ten days in the position of League Champions while awaiting Liverpool's remaining fixture. They finished runners-up, with a U.E.F.A. Cup place compensation for some of the season's most stylish football.

Division 3 (South) Champions: 1947–48.
Division 3 Champions: 1966–67.
League Cup Winners: 1966–67.
Record attendance: 35,353 v. Leeds (League), April 1974.
Modern Capacity: 31,000.
Entered Football League: 1920—Div. 3.
Biggest win: 9–2 v. Tranmere Rovers (Div. 3), December 1960.
Heaviest defeat: 1–8 v. Mansfield Town (Div. 3), March 1965 ; 1–8 v. Manchester United (Div. 1), March 1969.
Best in F.A. Cup: 6th Round 1947–48, 1969–70, 1973–74 (also reached last eight—old 4th Round—in 1909–10, 1913–14, 1922–23).
Pitch measurements: 112 x 72 yd.
Highest League Scorer in Single Season: George Goddard— 37 in 1929–30 (Div. 3 South).
Transfers—
  Highest fee paid: £165,000—Dave Thomas (from Burnley), October 1972.
  Highest fee received: £200,000—Rodney Marsh (to Manchester City), March 1972 ; £200,000—Dave Thomas (to Everton), August 1977.

READING

Elm Park, Reading RG3 2EF, Reading 57878/80

Shirts: blue & white hoops. *Shorts:* white. *Stockings:* white with blue rings. *Second colours:* yellow shirts & shorts.

The Berkshire club were 100 years old in 1971, but far from celebrating their centenary in style, they were relegated to Division Four for the first time. In the last eight seasons before the war they never finished lower than sixth in Division Three (South) and twice were runners-up. When the Football League resumed in 1946 they twice more occupied second place, in 1949 and 1952.

Between the wars Reading won the Third Division (South) Championship in 1925–26 and lasted in the Second Division for five seasons.

Many splendid players have served the club, among them Jack Palethorpe, who later scored in Sheffield Wednesday's Cup-winning side at Wembley in 1935; W. H. McConnell, an Ireland cap; Tony McPhee, a clever, goalscoring leader; George Marks, later Arsenal's goalkeeper; Pat McConnell, another Irish international; Maurice Edelston, an England Amateur international; and Ronnie Blackman, whose 156 League goals between 1947—54 stand as a record for the club.

A five-season stay in the Fourth Division ended in 1976, when Reading were promoted with one of the best home records in the country. They went up 50 years after their previous promotion—to the Second Division in 1926.

Division 3 (South) Champions: 1925–26.
Record attendance: 33,042 v. Brentford (F.A. Cup), February 1927.
Modern Capacity: 28,000. **Nickname:** 'Biscuitmen.'
Entered Football League: 1920—Div. 3.
Biggest win: 10–2 v. Crystal Palace (Div. 3 South), September 1946.
Heaviest defeat: 0–18 v. Preston N.E. (F.A. Cup), 1893–94.
Best in F.A. Cup: Semi-final 1926–27.
Best in League Cup: 4th Round 1964–65, 1965–66.
Pitch measurements: 112 x 75 yd.
Highest League Scorer in Single Season: Ronnie Blackman—39 in 1951–52 (Div. 3 South).
Transfers—
    Highest fee paid: £20,000—Steve Death (from West Ham) August 1970.
    Highest fee received: £60,000—Tom Jenkins (to Southampton), December 1969.

ROCHDALE

Spotland, Sandy Lane, Rochdale OL11 5DS, Rochdale 44648/9

Shirts: blue with white stripes. *Shorts:* white with blue stripes. *Stockings:* white with blue rings. *Second colours:* yellow shirts with blue collar & cuffs, blue shorts.

It says much for the resolution and perseverance of those associated with the club that Rochdale have remained in continuous member- ship of the Football League since being elected to the Northern Section in 1921.

In 1931–32 they failed to win a Division Three (North) match after 7 November. They played 26 matches, lost 25 and drew one, and a total of 33 defeats that season is the worst in League football, as is the sequence of 17 consecutive losses they included.

Another lowlight, on Tuesday, 5 February 1974, was the smallest crowd for any post-war League fixture. The club refused to issue an official attendance against Cambridge that afternoon, but the estimate was 450. The season ended with Rochdale relegated to Division Four.

Rochdale made a mark in the Football League Cup as runners-up to Norwich City in 1962 ; no other Division Four team has reached the Final.

A boost to club finances came in November 1974 with the £40,000 transfer of Alan Taylor, and six months later he completed a storybook climb from Fourth Division to First by scoring West Ham's F.A. Cup-winning goals at Wembley.

Record attendance: 24,231 v. Notts County (F.A. Cup) December 1949.
Modern Capacity: 28,000. **Nickname:** 'Dale.'
Entered Football League: 1921—Div. 3 (North).
Biggest win: 8–1 v. Chesterfield (Div. 3 North), December 1926.
Heaviest defeat: 0–8 v. Wrexham (Div. 3 North), December 1929.
Highest final League position: Runners-up Div. 3 (North) 1923–24, 1926–27.
Best in F.A. Cup: 4th Round 1970–71.
Best in League Cup: Runners-up 1961–62.
Pitch measurements: 110 x 72 yd.
Highest League Scorer in Single Season: Albert Whitehurst— 44 in 1926–27 (Div. 3 North).
Transfers—
  Highest fee paid: £15,000—Malcolm Darling (from Norwich), October 1971.
  Highest fee received: £40,000—David Cross (to Norwich), October 1971 ; £40,000—Alan Taylor (to West Ham), November 1974.

ROTHERHAM UNITED

Millmoor, Masbro, Rotherham S60 1HR, Rotherham 2434

Shirts: red, white collar & sleeves. *Shorts:* white. *Stockings:* red. *Second colours:* blue with yellow cuffs & collar, blue shorts with yellow stripe.

Fortune has certainly played some unkind tricks on Rotherham United, none more so than in 1955, when, by winning eight of the last nine games and finally beating Liverpool 6–1, they finished level on points at the top of Division Two with Birmingham City and Luton Town. Yet, despite scoring more goals than their rivals, they missed a First Division place on goal average.

In the three seasons directly after the Second World War they were runners-up in Division Three North (only the Champions gained promotion). Their points totals were 64, 59 and 62, all enough to have won the divisional title in many another season.

Rotherham slipped to sixth the following season (1949–50), but a year later their perseverance paid off. They became Champions by seven points, but 17 seasons in the Second Division ended with relegation in 1968. Five years later they fell into the Fourth for two seasons.

Rotherham, in company with other small clubs, rely heavily on finding their own players. Among the best known have been Danny Williams, a stalwart defender who made 459 League appearances between 1946–60 and Wally Ardron, whose 38 League goals in 1946–47 are still a Rotherham record.

Division 3 (North) Champions: 1950–51.

Record attendance: 25,000 v. Sheffield United (League), December 1952.

Modern Capacity: 24,000. **Nickname:** 'Millers.'

Entered Football League: 1893—Div. 2.

Biggest win: 8–0 v. Oldham Athletic (Div. 3 North), May 1947.

Heaviest defeat: 1–11 v. Bradford City (Div. 3 North), August 1928.

Best in F.A. Cup: 5th Round 1952–53, 1967–68.

Best in League Cup: Runners-up 1960–61.

Pitch measurements: 116 x 76 yd.

Highest League Scorer in Single Season: Wally Ardron—38 in 1946–47 (Div. 3 North).

Transfers—

    Highest fee paid: £27,000—John Quinn (from Sheffield Wednesday), November 1967.

    Highest fee received: £100,000—Dave Watson (to Sunderland), December 1970.

SCUNTHORPE UNITED

Old Show Ground, Scunthorpe DN15 7RH, Scunthorpe 2954

Shirts: red. *Shorts:* red. *Stockings:* red. *Second colours:* yellow shirts & shorts.

Scunthorpe and Lindsey United were themselves surprised by the manner in which they were elected in 1950 at the time the Football League was extending both Northern and Southern Sections of the Third Division by two clubs. When the 'North' vote was taken Scunthorpe were not even placed second. Workington and Wigan tied and there was a fresh vote. At the new count Scunthorpe and Wigan tied, and it needed a third vote before the Midland League club won election. A few years later the name Lindsey was dropped from their title.

Scunthorpe were not long in justifying their place in higher company. After finishing third in 1954, and again in 1955, they won the Northern Section in 1958.

Scunthorpe came close to providing First Division football at their picturesquely-named Old Show Ground in 1961–62, when finishing fourth, but they have since declined, going down to the Third Division in 1964, to the Fourth in 1968, up again in 1972 and back to the Fourth a year later. In 1975 Scunthorpe finished bottom of the Football League.

Their longest-serving player was Jack Brownsword, who made 657 League and Cup appearances between 1950–65, and was the game's first full-back to score 50 League goals. Among modern stars, goalkeeper Ray Clemence and striker Kevin Keegan, both of England and Liverpool, were produced by Scunthorpe.

Division 3 (North) Champions: 1957–58.
Record attendance: 23,935 v. Portsmouth (F.A. Cup), January 1954.
Modern Capacity: 25,000. **Nickname:** 'Irons.'
Entered Football League: 1950—Div. 3 (North).
Biggest win: 9–0 v. Boston United (F.A. Cup), November 1953.
Heaviest defeat: 0–8 v. Carlisle United (Div. 3 North), December 1952.
Best in F.A. Cup: 5th Round 1957–58, 1969–70.
Best in League Cup: 3rd Round 1962–63, 1968–69.
Pitch measurements: 112 x 78 yd.
Highest League Scorer in Single Season: Barrie Thomas—31 in 1961–62 (Div. 2).
Transfers—
    Highest fee paid: £20,000—Barrie Thomas (from Newcastle), November 1964.
    Highest fee received: £50,000—Richard Money (to Fulham), November 1977.

SHEFFIELD UNITED

Bramall Lane, Sheffield S2 4SU, 0742–738955

Shirts: red, white & thin black stripes. *Shorts:* black with red & white seams. *Stockings:* white with red, black & white tops. *Second colours:* yellow & black shirts, black shorts.

For all their long Football League history, Sheffield United achieved their greatest feats in the F.A. Cup, winning the trophy four times by 1925.

In 1925–26 they headed the First Division scorers with 102 goals, beating Cardiff 11–2 and Manchester City 8–3. But after brief moments of glory in the 1920s, 'The Blades' lost their cutting edge and were relegated from the First Division in 1934. Five years later they just beat their neighbours, Wednesday, for second place in the Second Division.

The summer of 1973 marked the end of an era as Yorkshire C.C.C. played at Bramall Lane for the last time, and United erected a magnificent stand on the side where, for 118 years, the cricket square had been situated.

After finishing sixth in the First Division in 1975, United suddenly slumped, and with Wednesday in even worse trouble, Sheffield suffered its deepest gloom as a soccer city in season 1975–76. At the end, United were relegated (for the fourth time since the war) with only six wins and 22 points.

League Champions: 1897–98.
Division 2 Champions: 1952–53.
F.A. Cup Winners: 1898–99, 1901–02, 1914–15, 1924–25.
Record attendance: 68,287 v. Leeds (F.A. Cup), February 1936.
Modern Capacity: 55,000. **Nickname:** 'Blades.'
Entered Football League: 1892—Div. 2.
Biggest win: 11–2 v. Cardiff City (Div. 1), January 1926.
Heaviest defeat: 0–13 v. Bolton Wanderers (F.A. Cup), February 1890.
Best in League Cup: 5th Round 1961–62, 1966–67, 1971–72.
Pitch measurements: 115 x 73 yd.
Highest League Scorer in Single Season: Jimmy Dunne—41 in 1930–31 (Div. 1).
Transfers—
    Highest fee paid: £100,000—Chris Guthrie (from Southend), April 1975.
    Highest fee received: £240,000—Tony Currie (to Leeds), June 1976.

SHEFFIELD WEDNESDAY

Hillsborough, Sheffield S6 1SW, 0742–343123

Shirts: blue & white stripes. *Shorts:* blue. *Stockings:* white. *Second colours:* yellow shirts with blue collar & cuffs, blue shorts.

Sheffield Wednesday reached a success peak between 1929 and 1935, winning the F.A. Cup and two League Championships, and finishing third in the First Division on four other occasions. Those two League title triumphs, inspired by the veteran inside-forward Jimmy Seed, were in 1929 and 1930. It was a repetition of a similar Championship double by them in 1903 and 1904.

Wednesday's lavish ground, with seating for 23,500, was used for World Cup matches in 1966 and is a regular F.A. Cup semi-final venue.

Their most celebrated player for many years was Derek Dooley, who scored 46 goals in season 1951–52 in 30 Division Two matches. A broken leg, which had to be amputated, ended his playing career the following season, and from January 1971 to December 1973 Dooley was team manager of the club for which he had starred so briefly, so spectacularly.

Reflecting the alarming decline of Wednesday is the fact that, from being a First Division club in 1970, they slumped to Division 3 by 1975 and a year later missed the Fourth Division by only one place.

Until they return to the First Division, Hillsborough will be a white elephant—a stately home of soccer in search of a team capable of filling it with football style and football fans as in days gone by.

League Champions: 1902–03, 1903–04, 1928–29, 1929–30.
Division 2 Champions: 1899–1900, 1925–26, 1951–52, 1955–56, 1958–59.
F.A. Cup Winners: 1895–96, 1906–07, 1934–35.
Record attendance: 72,841 v. Manchester City (F.A. Cup), February 1934.
Modern Capacity: 55,000. **Nickname:** 'Owls.'
Entered Football League: 1892—Div. 1.
Biggest win: 12–0 v. Halliwell (F.A. Cup), January 1891.
Heaviest defeat: 0–10 v. Aston Villa (Div. 1), October 1912.
Best in League Cup: 4th Round 1967–68, 1976–77.
Pitch measurements: 115 x 75 yd.
Highest League Scorer in Single Season: Derek Dooley—46 in 1951–52 (Div. 2).
Transfers—
  Highest fee paid: £100,000—Tommy Craig (from Aberdeen), May 1969.
  Highest fee received: £110,000—Tommy Craig (to Newcastle), December 1974.

SHREWSBURY TOWN

Gay Meadow, Shrewsbury SY2 6AB, Shrewsbury 56068

Shirts: blue with amber trim. *Shorts:* amber with blue stripe.
Stockings: amber with blue band. *Second colours:* red or white
shirts, red or white shorts.

For 64 years Shrewsbury had been in existence, but it was not until
1950 that they were elected to membership of the Football League.
They spent the first season in Division Three (North) but then
switched to the Southern section, where they remained until the
League was reorganized in season 1958–59.

Shrewsbury moved into Division Four and immediately won
promotion by finishing fourth. Twice since then the club has missed
going up into the Second Division by one place, being third in 1960
and 1968. By the end of season 1973–74 Town were back in
Division Four, but were immediately promoted as runners-up.

Arthur Rowley's League scoring record of 434 goals included 152
for Shrewsbury and he also holds the club's single-season record
with 38 in Division Four during 1958–59.

When the Football League Cup was launched in season 1960–61,
Shrewsbury reached the semi-final before losing to Rotherham
United 4–3 on aggregate.

Shrewsbury have enjoyed years of comparative success, too, in
the F.A. Cup, progressing to the fifth rounds in 1965 and 1966.

Record attendance: 18,917 v. Walsall (League), April 1961.
Modern Capacity: 20,000.
Entered Football League: 1950—Div. 3 (North).
Biggest win: 7–0 v. Swindon Town (Div. 3 South), May 1955.
Heaviest defeat: 1–8 v. Norwich City (Div. 3 South), September
   1952 ; 1–8 v. Coventry City (Div. 3), October 1963.
Highest final League position: 3rd in Div. 3 1959–60, 1967–68.
Best in F.A. Cup: 5th Round 1964–65, 1965–66.
Best in League Cup: Semi-final 1960–61.
Pitch measurements: 116 x 74 yd.
Highest League Scorer in Single Season: Arthur Rowley—38
   in 1958–59 (Div. 4).
Transfers—
   Highest fee paid: £30,000—Graham Turner (from Chester),
   January 1973.
   Highest fee received: £95,000—Jim Holton (to Manchester
   United), January 1973.

SOUTHAMPTON

The Dell, Southampton SO9 4XX, Southampton 23408/28108

Shirts: red & white stripes. *Shorts:* black with red stripe. *Stockings:* white. *Second colours:* gold shirts, blue shorts.

A new name went on the F.A. Cup in 1976 when Southampton, twice losing Finalists at the beginning of the century, became the third Second Division club to win the trophy at Wembley. (West Bromwich in 1931 and Sunderland in 1973 were the others.) A solitary goal by Bobby Stokes beat 3–1 on favourites Manchester United and brought about one of the biggest shocks in Cup Final history. The players who produced it under the genial Geordie managership of Lawrie McMenemy were: Turner, Rodrigues, Peach, Holmes, Blyth, Steele, Gilchrist, Channon, Osgood, McCalliog, Stokes.

Saints' success added to the romantic story of the competition; so did their 32-year-old Welsh internatonal captain Peter Rodrigues who, only a year before receiving the Cup from the Queen, experienced relegation and a free transfer from Sheffield Wednesday.

Southampton's previous highest peak was in reaching the First Division in 1966. They retained top status until 1974 when they were partners in relegation with Manchester United, the club destined to be the shock victims of Saints' first appearance at Wembley.

F.A. Cup Winners: 1975–76.
Division 3 (South) Champions: 1921–22.
Division 3 Champions: 1959–60.
Record attendance: 31,044 v. Manchester United (League) October 1969.
Modern Capacity: 31,000. **Nickname:** 'Saints.'
Entered Football League: 1920—Div. 3.
Biggest win: 14–0 v. Newbury (F.A. Cup), September 1894.
Heaviest defeat: 0–8 v. Tottenham (Div. 2) March 1936; 0–8 v. Everton (Div. 1), November 1971.
Best in League Cup: 5th Round 1960–61, 1968–69.
Pitch measurements: 110 x 72 yd.
Highest League Scorer in Single Season: Derek Reeves—39 in 1959–60 (Div. 3).
Transfers—
  Highest fee paid: £275,000—Peter Osgood (from Chelsea), March 1974.
  Highest fee received: £300,000—Mick Channon (to Manchester City), July 1977.

SOUTHEND UNITED

Roots Hall ground, Southend-on-Sea SS2 6NQ, Southend 40707

Shirts: royal blue with red & white trim. *Shorts:* white with blue & red trim. *Stockings:* white with blue & red trim. *Second colours:* amber & black shirts & shorts.

A succession of ambitious and dedicated Southend United officials have done their best to bring a higher standard of football to London's nearest seaside resort. In 1955 the club moved from Southend Stadium to a new ground at Roots Hall, Prittlewell, and three years later it looked as though Southend were heading for the Second Division.

But though they gained 54 points, they were still six points behind Brighton, the promoted club. Sammy McCrory, who won Northern Ireland honours, scored 31 of their 90 League goals that season, but by 1966 Southend had dropped to the Fourth Division, from which they climbed again six years later.

Twice in their formative years the club finished runners-up in the Second Division of the Southern League, but there have been few moments of real glory and their highest final League position remains third in Division Three in 1932 and 1950.

The F.A. Cup competition of 1951–52 produced three months of excitement when, drawn at home five times out of five, Southend fought their way into the last 16 before losing 2–1 to Sheffield United. Twenty-four years later a place in the fifth round again, followed by relegation, reflected the ups and downs of Southend in season 1975–76.

Record attendance: 28,059 v. Birmingham City (F.A. Cup), January 1957.

Modern Capacity: 35,000. **Nickname:** 'Shrimpers.'

Entered Football League: 1920—Div. 3.

Biggest win: 10–1 v. Golders Green (F.A. Cup), November 1934 ; 10–1 v. Brentwood (F.A. Cup), December 1968.

Heaviest defeat: 1–11 v. Northampton Town (Southern League), December 1909.

Highest final League position: 3rd in Div. 3 (South) 1931–32, 1949–50.

Best in F.A. Cup: 5th Round 1925–26, 1951–52, 1975–76.

Best in League Cup: 3rd Round 1963–64, 1964–65, 1969–70.

Pitch measurements: 110 x 74 yd.

Highest League Scorer in Single Season: Jim Shankly—31 in 1928–29 (Div. 3 South) ; Sammy McCrory—31 in 1957–58 (Div. 3 South).

Transfers—

    Highest fee paid: £20,000—Tony Taylor (from Crystal Palace), August 1974.

    Highest fee received: £120,000—Peter Taylor (to Crystal Palace), October 1973.

SOUTHPORT

Haig Avenue, Southport, Southport 33422

Shirts: yellow. *Shorts:* royal blue. *Stockings:* yellow. *Second colours:* blue shirts, white shorts.

Formed in 1881 as Southport Central, the club took their present name in 1919, two years before joining the Northern section of the old Third Division.

Twice they finished in fourth place before the Second World War —in 1924–25 and again in 1938–39. In 1958, Southport transferred to the Fourth Division and after a number of indifferent seasons they gained promotion in 1967, winning 23 and drawing 13 of their 46 matches, but they were relegated three seasons later.

Season 1972–73 ended with Southport winning their first title as Fourth Division Champions, but they immediately found themselves struggling and went down again in 1974.

Older supporters still recall Southport's splendid run in the 1931 F.A. Cup. Millwall, Blackpool and Bradford were all beaten at Southport. Then the quaintly nicknamed 'Sandgrounders' were drawn to meet Everton in the sixth round . . . and crashed to a 9–1 defeat. It was a calamitous end to what remains to this day Southport's longest run in the competition.

With gates falling below 1,500, their existence was seriously threatened in season 1975–76, which ended with Southport bottom but one of the Fourth Division—the ninth time they had finished in the re-election zone.

Division 4 Champions: 1972–73.
Record attendance: 20,010 v. Newcastle (F.A. Cup), January 1932.
Modern Capacity: 21,000. **Nickname:** 'Sandgrounders.'
Entered Football League: 1921—Div. 3 (North).
Biggest win: 8–1 v. Nelson (Div. 3 North), January 1931.
Heaviest defeat: 0–11 v. Oldham Athletic (Div. 4). December 1962.
Best in F.A. Cup: 6th Round 1930–31.
Best in League Cup: 2nd Round 1962–63, 1963–64, 1968–69 1969–70, 1971–72, 1972–73, 1975–76.
Pitch measurements: 113 x 77 yd.
Highest League Scorer in Single Season: Archie Waterston— 31 in 1930–31 (Div. 3 North).
Transfers—
  Highest fee paid: £6000—Malcolm Russell (from Halifax), September 1968.
  Highest fee received: £20,000—Tony Field (to Blackburn), October 1971.

STOCKPORT COUNTY

Edgeley Park, Stockport, Cheshire SK3 9DD, 061–480 8888/9

Shirts: white with blue & yellow sleeves. *Shorts:* blue. *Stockings:* white, blue tops. *Second colours:* yellow shirts with blue sleeves, yellow shorts.

Only 13 people paid to watch a Football League match at Old Trafford in May 1921. This stranger-than-fiction event came about because Stockport's own ground was under suspension and the club used the nearby Manchester United venue for their Division Two match against Leicester City.

Nearly 13 years later, on 6 January 1934, Stockport scored 13 times without reply against Halifax Town in a Division Three (North) match. This and Newcastle's 13–0 victory over Newport County on 5 October 1946 are the biggest wins in Football League history.

Alex Herd, who played in Manchester City's 1933 and 1934 Cup Final teams, gave Stockport splendid service. At 39, he and his 17-year-old son, David, provided a rare instance of father and son playing together in the same League side—inside-right and inside-left respectively against Hartlepools at Edgeley Park on 5 May 1951. David scored one of the goals in a 2–0 win.

In November 1975, while struggling for survival, County signed 29-year-old George Best (ex-Manchester United) for a month—his third comeback attempt after two years out of the game. On his Fourth Division debut against Swansea, he more than trebled the gate at 9,240, made two goals and scored the winner (3–2), but Best's appearance was a quickly-passing phase in Stockport history.

Division 3 (North) Champions: 1921–22, 1936–37.
Division 4 Champions: 1966–67.
Record attendance: 27,833 v. Liverpool (F.A. Cup), February 1950.
Modern Capacity: 24,000.
Entered League Football: 1900—Div. 2.
Biggest win: 13–0 v. Halifax Town (Div. 3 North), January 1934.
Heaviest defeat: 1–8 v. Chesterfield (Division 2), April 1902.
Best in F.A. Cup: 5th Round 1934–35, 1949–50.
Best in League Cup: 4th Round 1972–73.
Pitch measurements: 111 x 73 yd.
Highest League Scorer in Single Season: Alf Lythgoe—46 in 1933–34 (Div. 3 North).
Transfers—
  Highest fee paid: £14,000—Alex Young (from Glentoran), November 1968.
  Highest fee received: £25,000—Paul Hart (to Blackpool), June 1973.

STOKE CITY

Victoria Ground, Stoke-on-Trent ST4 4EG, 0782–44660

Shirts: red & white stripes. *Shorts:* white with red & black seams.
Stockings: white. *Second colours:* white shirts with black sash,
black shorts.

Until 1972, what success Stoke achieved in a long tradition of
football had been linked with Stanley Matthews. In 1933, the young
Matthews was a promising winger in the side that brought back
First Division football to the Potteries after ten years.

After relegation in 1953, Stoke spent another ten-year spell in the
Second Division. In 1960 Tony Waddington took over as manager
and he recruited several veterans including Matthews, who returned
from Blackpool, aged 46, at a bargain £3000 fee.

Matthews and company—their average age was the highest in
the four divisions—took the club back to the First Division in 1963,
and Stoke have remained there. They are unique in having had only
three managers since the last war—Bob McGrory, Frank Taylor and
Tony Waddington.

One of the original twelve in 1888, they are the second oldest
League club—formed in 1863, the year after Notts County. Wembley
1972 brought Stoke their long-awaited first prize, the League Cup.

England's Gordon Banks, who played an outstanding part in that
achievement, was Stoke goalkeeper for six seasons from 1967 until
eye injuries received in a car crash ended his career. In January 1974
manager Waddington showed his appreciation of young talent by
paying £240,000 for Chelsea midfield player Alan Hudson, and the
following November, Stoke bought Leicester and England goalkeeper Peter Shilton for £340,000, then a record British cash
transfer.

League Cup Winners: 1971–72.
Division 2 Champions: 1932–33, 1962–63.
Division 3 (North) Champions: 1926–27.
Record attendance: 51,380 v. Arsenal (League), March 1937.
Modern Capacity: 50,000. **Nickname:** 'Potters.'
Entered Football League: 1888—Div. 1.
Biggest win: 10–3 v. W.B.A. (Div. 1), February 1937.
Heaviest defeat: 0–10 v. Preston (Div. 1), September 1889.
Best in F.A. Cup: Semi-final 1898–99, 1970–71, 1971–72.
Pitch measurements: 116½ x 75 yd.
Highest League Scorer in Single Season: Freddie Steele—33
in 1936–37 (Div. 1).

Transfers—
  Highest fee paid: £340,000—Peter Shilton (from Leicester),
  November 1974.

  Highest fee received: £270,000—Peter Shilton (to Nottingham
  Forest), September 1977.

SUNDERLAND

Roker Park, Sunderland SR6 9SW, Sunderland 72077/58638

Shirts: red & white stripes. *Shorts:* black. *Stockings:* red, white tops.
Second colours: blue shirts, red shorts.

When Bob Stokoe was appointed manager in November 1972,
Sunderland were drifting third from bottom of the Second Division.
In the months that followed, glory—and the crowds—returned to
Roker Park, and after thrilling F.A. Cup victories over Manchester
City and, in the semi-final, Arsenal, Sunderland found themselves
participating in Wembley's 50th birthday celebrations.

Having reached the final, they turned back the clock 42 years, for
by their 1–0 triumph over Leeds the Cup went outside the First
Division for the first time since West Bromwich's success in 1931.
Ian Porterfield shot the goal that brought victory to the original
250–1 outsiders.

For Sunderland, six times League Champions, this was the first
prize they had won since their previous F.A. Cup victory in 1937.
Until 1958 they could claim, proudly and exclusively, that they had
never played outside the First Division.

The 1973 Cup triumph was secondary to manager Stokoe's
ambition to bring First Division football back to Roker Park.
Sunderland occupied one of the three promotion places almost
throughout season 1974–75 until the final week, but a year later
they did go up as Champions and the North-east rejoiced at having
three First Division clubs for the first time since 1954.

League Champions: 1891–92, 1892–93, 1894–95, 1901–02,
   1912–13, 1935–36.
Division 2 Champions: 1975–76.
F.A. Cup Winners: 1936–37, 1972–73.
Record attendance: 75,118 v. Derby (F.A. Cup), March 1933.
Modern Capacity: 57,500. **Nickname:** 'Rokerites.'
Entered Football League: 1890—Div. 1.
Biggest win: 11–1 v. Fairfield (F.A. Cup), 1894–95.
Heaviest defeat: 0–8 v. Sheffield Wednesday (Div. 1), December
   1911 ; 0–8 v. West Ham (Div. 1), October 1968.
Best in League Cup: Semi-final 1962–63.
Pitch measurements: 112 x 72 yd.
Highest League Scorer in Single Season: Dave Halliday—43
   in 1928–29 (Div. 1).
Transfers—
   Highest fee paid: £200,000—Bob Lee (from Leicester),
      September 1976.
   Highest fee received: £275,000—Dennis Tueart (to Man-
      chester City), March 1974 ; £275,000—Dave Watson (to
      Manchester City), June 1975.

SWANSEA CITY

Vetch Field, Swansea SA1 3SU, Swansea 42855

Shirts: white with black trim. *Shorts:* white. *Stockings:* white. *Second colours:* red & green striped shirts, red shorts.

When Swansea won the Third Division (South) Championship in 1949 by seven points, they fielded seven Internationals in their side. They were Paul, Richards and Lucas (Wales), Feeney, McCrory, Keane and O'Driscoll (Ireland). This title enabled Irish manager Billy McCandless to complete a remarkable 'hat trick' of successes with Welsh clubs. He had previously guided Newport (1938–39) and Cardiff City (1946–47) into the Second Division.

Swansea has always been a reservoir of great soccer talent. Roy John, Trevor Ford, Ivor and Len Allchurch, Cliff Jones and Jack Kelsey are just a few of many fine players discovered.

In season 1963–64, Swansea only just avoided relegation from Division Two, yet almost reached the F.A. Cup Final. They won their way through to the last four with victories over such formidable First Division opponents as Sheffield United, Stoke City and Liverpool (League Champions that season) before going down 2–1 to Preston in the semi-final.

The 'Swans' changed their title from Town to City in 1970 on winning promotion from Division Four, but were relegated again three years later.

Division 3 (South) Champions: 1924–25, 1948–49.
Record attendance: 32,796 v. Arsenal (F.A. Cup), February 1968.
Modern Capacity: 35,000. **Nickname:** 'Swans.'
Entered Football League: 1920—Div. 3.
Biggest win: 8–1 v. Bristol Rovers (Div. 3 South), April 1922; 8–1 v. Bradford City (Div. 2), February 1926.
Heaviest defeat: 1–8 v. Fulham (Div. 2), January 1938.
Best in F.A. Cup: Semi-final 1925–26, 1963–64.
Best in League Cup: 4th Round 1964–65.
Pitch measurements: 110 x 70 yd.
Highest League Scorer in Single Season: Cyril Pearce—35 in 1931–32 (Div. 2).
Transfers—
  Highest fee paid: £26,000—Ronnie Rees (from Nottingham Forest), January 1972.
  Highest fee received: £45,000—Barrie Jones (to Plymouth), September 1964.

SWINDON TOWN

County Ground, Swindon, Wilts, SN1 1AA, Swindon 22118

Shirts: red with white trimmings. *Shorts:* white. *Stockings:* red. *Second colours:* blue shirts & shorts.

Enthusiasm reached unprecedented heights in the West Country on 6 March 1969, when Swindon Town became League Cup holders by beating Arsenal 3–1 in extra time at Wembley—and at the end of the season also gained promotion to Division Two.

After 43 years as a Third Division club, Swindon gained promotion as runners-up in 1963. They started off well in Second Division football, being undefeated for their first nine games, but finished the season well down the table, and the following year they were back in the Third Division.

One of the club's earliest stars was Harold Fleming, an inside-forward capped nine times for England. His skills played a major part in Swindon's two F.A. Cup semi-final appearances in 1910 and 1912. Others of renown have included Harry Morris, who scored 47 League goals in 1926–27 and a total of 216 in eight seasons (1926–33); Norman Uprichard, Ireland's goalkeeper in the 1950s; England International Mike Summerbee and Under-23 caps Ernie Hunt and Don Rogers; Dave Mackay (ex-Tottenham and Scotland), who was player, then manager from November 1971, before moving to Nottingham Forest and Derby; and full-back John Trollope, who played for the club more than 700 times from 1960 onwards.

League Cup Winners: 1968–69.
Record attendance: 32,000 v. Arsenal (F.A. Cup), January 1972.
Modern Capacity: 32,000. **Nickname:** 'Robins.'
Entered Football League: 1920—Div. 3.
Biggest win: 10–1 v. Farnham United Breweries (F.A. Cup), November 1925.
Heaviest defeat: 1–10 v. Manchester City (F.A. Cup), January 1930.
Highest final League position: Runners-up Div. 3 1962–63, 1968–69.
Best in F.A. Cup: Semi-final 1909–10, 1911–12.
Pitch measurements: 117 x 78 yd.
Highest League Scorer in Single Season: Harry Morris—47 in 1926–27 (Div. 3 South).
Transfers—
    Highest fee paid: £80,000—Peter Eastoe (from Wolves), March 1974.
    Highest fee received: £140,000—Don Rogers (to Crystal Palace), October 1972.

96

LEAGUE CLUBS: COLOUR GUIDE

Aldershot

Arsenal

Aston Villa

Barnsley

Birmingham City

Blackburn Rovers

Blackpool

Bolton Wanderers

LEAGUE CLUBS: COLOUR GUIDE

A.F.C. Bournemouth

Bradford City

Brentford

Brighton &
Hove Albion

Bristol City

Bristol Rovers

Burnley

LEAGUE CLUBS: COLOUR GUIDE

Bury

Cambridge United

Cardiff City

Carlisle United

Charlton Athletic

Chelsea

Chester

Chesterfield

LEAGUE CLUBS: COLOUR GUIDE

Colchester United   Coventry City

Crewe Alexandra   Crystal Palace   Darlington

Derby County   Doncaster Rovers

LEAGUE CLUBS: COLOUR GUIDE

Everton

Exeter City

Fulham

Gillingham

Grimsby Town

Halifax Town

Hartlepool United

Hereford United

LEAGUE CLUBS: COLOUR GUIDE

Huddersfield Town

Hull City

Ipswich Tow

Leeds United

Leicester City

Lincoln City

Liverpool

Luton Tow

LEAGUE CLUBS: COLOUR GUIDE

Manchester City

Manchester United

Mansfield Town

Middlesbrough

Millwall

Newcastle United

Newport County

Northampton Town

LEAGUE CLUBS: COLOUR GUIDE

Norwich City

Nottingham Forest

Notts County

Oldham Athletic

Orient

Oxford United

Peterborough
United

LEAGUE CLUBS : COLOUR GUIDE

Plymouth Argyle

Portsmouth

Port Vale

Preston North End

Queen's Park
Rangers

Reading

Rochdale

Rotherham United

LEAGUE CLUBS: COLOUR GUIDE

Scunthorpe United

Sheffield United

effield Wednesday

Shrewsbury Town

Southampton

Southend United

Southport

LEAGUE CLUBS: COLOUR GUIDE

Stockport County   Stoke City   Sunderland

Swansea City   Swindon Town

Torquay United   Tottenham Hotspur   Tranmere Rovers

LEAGUE CLUBS: COLOUR GUIDE

Walsall

Watford

West Bromwich Albion

West Ham United

Wimbledon

Wolverhampton Wanderers

Wrexham

York City

COLOURS OF SOME WELL-KNOWN SCOTTISH CLUBS

Celtic

Rangers

Hearts

Motherwell

Hibernian

Aberdeen

Dundee

GOALKEEPERS' COLOURS

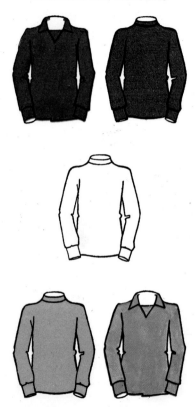

Internationals only

INTERNATIONAL SHIRTS

England

Scotland

Wales

Northern Ireland

Republic of Ireland

INTERNATIONAL BADGES

England

Scotland

Wales

Northern Ireland

Republic of Ireland

TORQUAY UNITED

Plainmoor, Torquay, Devon TQ1 3PS, Torquay 38666/7

Shirts: white with blue & yellow stripe down side. *Shorts:* white. *Stockings:* white with blue & yellow turnover. *Second colours:* yellow shirts with blue collar & cuffs, blue shorts with yellow stripe.

Two local amateur clubs, Torquay Town and Babbacombe, joined forces to form the present club which became professional in 1922. In season 1927–28 the Football League clubs recognized Torquay's promise by electing them to the Southern Section of the old Division Three. Their first season ended disastrously—in bottom place—and in the years before and immediately after the Second World War they rarely rose above half-way in the table.

This applied until 1956, when they finished fifth. The following year they were runners-up, missing promotion to the Second Division only on goal average, but by the time the League was extended in 1958 they found themselves in Division Four.

Since then Torquay have alternated between Third and Fourth Divisions without achieving a title. With little money available, and situated in an area of the country where League football has seldom attracted national attention, Torquay United struggle along on depressingly small attendances, which dropped below 2000 in 1975–76, the lowest level in the club's history.

United appealed to Torbay Council for help with ground rent and interest charges if that was not to be their last season in the Football League.

Record attendance: 21,736 v. Huddersfield Town (F.A. Cup), January 1955.

Modern Capacity: 22,000. **Nickname:** 'Gulls.'

Entered Football League: 1927—Div. 3 (South).

Biggest win: 9–0 v. Swindon Town (Div. 3 South), March 1952.

Heaviest defeat: 2–10 v. Fulham (Div. 3 South), September 1931 ; 2–10 v. Luton Town (Div. 3 South), September 1933.

Highest final League position: Runners-up Div. 3 (South) 1956–57.

Best in F.A. Cup: 4th Round 1948–49, 1954–55, 1970–71.

Best in League Cup: 3rd Round 1967–68, 1971–72, 1975–76, 1976–77.

Pitch measurements: 112 x 74 yd.

Highest League Scorer in Single Season: Sammy Collins—40 in 1955–56 (Div. 3 South).

Transfers—
    Highest fee paid: £15,000—David Tearse (from Leicester), November 1971.
    Highest fee received: £60,000—Colin Lee (to Tottenham), October 1977.

TOTTENHAM HOTSPUR

748 High Road, London NI7 0AP, 01–808 2046

Shirts: white. *Shorts:* navy blue. *Stockings:* white. *Second colours:* yellow shirts with blue trim, yellow shorts.

Since the war there have been two truly great Spurs sides—Arthur Rowe's 'push and run' team, which won the Second and First Division titles in successive years (1950 and 1951) and Bill Nicholson's Tottenham. What happened on 11 October 1958, when Nicholson, former Spurs player and coach, became manager, was a pointer to the future. Tottenham beat Everton 10–4. With Danny Blanchflower, Dave Mackay, Cliff Jones and John White the corner-stones, they did the 'double' in 1960–61.

Over the next decade the club spent more than a million pounds on new players, including Jimmy Greaves, Alan Mullery, Terry Venables, Mike England, Martin Chivers, Martin Peters and Ralph Coates. By the time Spurs took the 1973 League Cup they had contested seven finals in four different competitions under Nicholson's command and won the lot. It was the end of an era and of an unparalleled success record when, in August 1974, he resigned after 38 years with the club.

The Double (League Champions, F.A. Cup Winners): 1960–61.
League Champions: 1950–51, 1960–61.
Division 2 Champions: 1919–20, 1949–50.
F.A. Cup Winners: 1900–01, 1920–21, 1960–61, 1961–62, 1966–67.
Winners of European Cup-Winners' Cup: 1962–63.
League Cup Winners: 1970–71, 1972–73.
U.E.F.A. Cup Winners: 1971–72.
Record attendance: 75,038 v. Sunderland (F.A. Cup), March 1938.
Modern Capacity: 57,000. **Nickname:** 'Spurs.'
Entered Football League: 1908—Div. 2.
Biggest win: 13–2 v. Crewe (F.A. Cup), February 1960.
Heaviest defeat: 2–8 v. Derby (Div. 1), October 1976.
Pitch measurements: 111 x 73 yd.
Highest League Scorer in Single Season: Jimmy Greaves—37 in 1962–63 (Div. 1).
Transfers—
  Highest fee paid: £200,000—Peter Taylor (from Crystal Palace), September 1976.
  Highest fee received: £70,000—Terry Venables (to Q.P.R.), June 1969.

TRANMERE ROVERS

Prenton Park, Birkenhead, Merseyside, 051–608 3677/4194

Shirts: white with blue edging. *Shorts:* royal blue. *Stockings:* white.
Second colours: red shirts & shorts.

Living in the shadows of Merseyside giants Everton and Liverpool
has meant a continual battle for players and supporters for Tranmere
Rovers. League members since 1921, they won the Northern Section
of the Third Division in fine style in 1937–38, only to suffer relegation
the following season.

Devotees of the Birkenhead club fondly recall nine goals by
'Bunny' Bell in a 13–4 Third Division (North) victory over Oldham
Athletic on Boxing Day, 1935, the only time 17 goals have been
scored in a Football League match.

While 'Bunny' Bell is remembered for his goalscoring feats, centre-
half Harold Bell earned a distinguished place in the records for
Tranmere. He was ever-present for nine seasons between 1946 and
1955, playing 401 consecutive matches—the League record—and
altogether made 595 League appearances for the club, the last of
them in 1964.

Tranmere were responsible for one of the biggest shocks in League
Cup history when, on 2 October 1973, they beat Arsenal 1–0 in the
second round at Highbury.

When winning promotion back to the Third Division in 1976, a
year after relegation, Rovers had one of the season's highest League
scorers in Ronnie Moore, whose total of 34 included three 4-goal
performances.

Division 3 (North) Champions: 1937–38.
Record attendance: 24,424 v. Stoke City (F.A. Cup), February
1972.
Modern Capacity: 29,000.
Entered Football League: 1921—Div. 3 (North).
Biggest win: 13–4 v. Oldham Athletic (Div. 3 North), December
1935.
Heaviest defeat: 1–9 v. Tottenham Hotspur (F.A. Cup), January
1953.
Best in F.A. Cup: 5th Round 1967–68.
Best in League Cup: 4th Round 1960–61.
Pitch measurements: 112 x 72 yd.
Highest League Scorer in Single Season: R. ('Bunny') Bell—
35 in 1933–34 (Div. 3 North).
Transfers—
  Highest fee paid: £15,000—George Hudson (from North-
  ampton), January 1967.
  Highest fee received: £60,000—Steve Coppell (to Manchester
  United), March 1975.

WALSALL

Fellows Park, Walsall WS2 9DB, Walsall 22791

Shirts: red. *Shorts:* white. *Stockings:* green with red top and white band. *Second colours:* blue and white striped shirts, black shorts.

Whenever the name of Walsall is mentioned someone is almost certain to remark: 'Do you recall the day they knocked Arsenal out of the F.A. Cup?' Few football events between the two World Wars caused a greater stir than Walsall's famous 2–0 win over Arsenal in the third round on 14 January 1933. The 'Gunners' team, then the most powerful in the land, was packed with internationals; Walsall were a Third Division (North) side of no special skills. Yet they won that afternoon on their merits, Gilbert Alsop, a centre-forward who gave the club wonderful service, getting one of the goals.

The story and the legends of this game will continue to be told until Walsall achieve something more extraordinary. As it is, the rest of their history recounts few achievements, though they won the Division Four title in 1960 convincingly enough with 65 points, five more than their nearest challengers. A year later Walsall again won promotion to the Second Division, but survived there only two seasons.

Perhaps the best known of their 'home produced' players has been Allan Clarke, of Leeds United and England. Walsall transferred him to Fulham for £35,000 in March 1966, and by the time Clarke joined Leeds via Leicester City, his transfer deals had involved £350,000.

Division 4 Champions: 1959–60.
Record attendance: 25,453 v. Newcastle United (League), August 1961.
Modern Capacity: 25,000. **Nickname:** 'Saddlers.'
Entered Football League: 1892—Div. 2.
Biggest win: 10–0 v. Darwen (Div. 2), March 1899.
Heaviest defeat: 0–12 v. Small Heath (Div. 2), December 1892; 0–12 v. Darwen (Div. 2), December 1896.
Best in F.A. Cup: 5th Round 1938–39, 1974–75.
Best in League Cup: 4th Round 1966–67.
Pitch measurements: 113 x 73 yd.
Highest League Scorer in Single Season: Gilbert Alsop—40 in 1933–34 and 40 in 1934–35 (both in Div. 3 North).
Transfers—
    Highest fee paid: £25,000—Mick Bates (from Leeds), June 1976.
    Highest fee received: £60,000—Gary Shelton (to Aston Villa), January 1978.

WATFORD

Vicarage Road, Watford, Herts, WD1 8ER, Watford 21759/24729

Shirts: gold with black & red trim. *Shorts:* black. *Stockings:* black with red & gold tops. *Second colours:* red shirts with black & gold striped sleeves, red shorts with black & gold stripe.

After spending 49 years in lower grade League football, Watford came out of comparative obscurity in 1969 to win promotion to the Second Division and earn a name as F.A. Cup fighters. They became Third Division champions on goal average and in the Cup held Manchester United to a fourth round draw at Old Trafford.

The following season, Watford enjoyed an even better Cup run, beating Bolton, Stoke and Liverpool before losing 5–1 to Chelsea in the semi-final. But Second Division life was hard and the club were relegated back to the Third in 1972.

Watford moved to their present ground at Vicarage Road in 1919. The following year they became founder members of the Third Division. Apart from two seasons (1958–60) in the newly-formed Fourth Division, Watford spent the whole of their League career up to 1969 in the Third Division, but by 1975 they were in Division Four again.

Cliff Holton broke Watford's scoring record for a single season with 42 goals in 1959–60, and defender Duncan Welbourne, with 411 games between 1963–74, set a new League appearances record for the club.

The club's outstanding discovery since the war was Northern Ireland goalkeeper Pat Jennings, sold to Tottenham in June 1964 for £25,000.

Division 3 Champions: 1968–69.
Record attendance: 34,099 v. Manchester United (F.A. Cup), February 1969.
Modern Capacity: 36,500. **Nickname:** 'Hornets.'
Entered Football League: 1920—Div. 3.
Biggest win: 10–1 v. Lowestoft Town (F.A. Cup), November 1926.
Heaviest defeat: 0–10 v. Wolves (F.A. Cup), January 1912.
Best in F.A. Cup: Semi-final 1969–70.
Best in League Cup: 3rd Round 1961–62, 1971–72.
Pitch measurements: 112 x 74 yd.
Highest League Scorer in Single Season: Cliff Holton—42 in 1959–60 (Div. 4).
Transfers—
   Highest fee paid: £30,000—Ross Jenkins (from Crystal Palace), November 1972.
   Highest fee received: £110,000—Billy Jennings (to West Ham), September 1974.

WEST BROMWICH ALBION

The Hawthorns, West Bromwich, West Midlands, B71 4LF,
021–553 0095

Shirts: navy blue & white stripes. *Shorts:* white. *Stockings:* white.
Second colours: yellow & green striped shirts, green shorts.

As F.A. Cup winners five times, West Bromwich Albion have a proud record, but League honours have usually eluded them. They have appeared in ten F.A. Cup Finals and 17 semi-finals.

In 1965–66, West Bromwich made a belated entry into the League Cup and won it; they were also Finalists in 1967 and 1970. In the summer of 1971 they appointed as manager their former full-back Don Howe, under whose coaching Arsenal did the 'double' the previous season, but 1972–73 marked the end of a 24-year stay in Divison One. After a poor start to season 1975–76 they snatched promotion under player-manager Johnny Giles, signed from Leeds.

One of the highlights in Albion's history was their 1931 F.A. Cup Final triumph (as a Second Division team) over Birmingham. They are still the only club to have won the Cup and promotion in the same season.

West Bromwich were among the original 12 members of the Football League in 1888, but have won the Championship only once—in 1920—despite long spells in the First Division. In that Championship season they often fielded seven internationals.

League Champions: 1919–20.
Division 2 Champions: 1901–02, 1910–11.
F.A. Cup Winners: 1887–88, 1891–92, 1930–31, 1953–54, 1967–68.
League Cup Winners: 1965–66.
Record attendance: 64,815 v. Arsenal (F.A. Cup), March 1937.
Modern Capacity: 50,000. **Nickname:** 'Throstles' or 'Baggies'.
Entered Football League: 1888—Div. 1.
Biggest win: 12–0 v. Darwen (Div. 1), April 1892.
Heaviest defeat: 3–10 v. Stoke City (Div. 1), February 1937.
Pitch measurements: 115 x 75 yd.
Highest League Scorer in Single Season: W. ('Ginger') Richardson—39 in 1935–36 (Div. 1).
Transfers—
  Highest fee paid: £140,000—David Cross (from Coventry), November 1976.
  Highest fee received: £240,000—Asa Hartford (to Manchester City), August 1974.

WEST HAM UNITED

Boleyn Ground, Upton Park, London E13, 01–472 0704

Shirts: claret, blue yoke and sleeves. *Shorts:* white with claret & blue seams. *Stockings:* white. *Second colours:* white shirts with claret & blue facings, sky blue shorts.

Victory over Fulham in the 1975 F.A. Cup Final put West Ham back on the honours list after ten years of stylish soccer without reward. The triumph climaxed a season in which Ron Greenwood became overall manager and John Lyall took charge of the team. New forwards from lower divisions contributed to that success— and Alan Taylor (£40,000 from Rochdale) scored twice in the sixth round, semi-final and Final.

When England won the World Cup in 1966, West Ham provided the captain, Bobby Moore, and two other stars—Geoff Hurst and Martin Peters. Upton Park has also produced a galaxy of well-known managers from its former players, among them Frank O'Farrell, Malcolm Allison, Dave Sexton, Noel Cantwell, Jimmy Bloomfield, John Bond, Jimmy Andrews and Andy Nelson.

In 1923, four years after being elected to the Football League, West Ham gained promotion to the First Division and also reached the first Wembley Cup Final, which they lost 2–0 to Bolton.

They have had only six managers in their history, and during Ron Greenwood's reign were among the most attractive sides in Britain, especially during the sixties, when they won the F.A. Cup (1964) and the European Cup-Winners' Cup (1965). In 1976 they were runners-up in the same European competition.

F.A. Cup Winners: 1963–64, 1974–75.
Winners of European Cup-Winners' Cup: 1964–65.
Division 2 Champions: 1957–58.
Record attendance: 42,322 v. Tottenham (League), Oct. 1970.
Modern Capacity: 41,000. **Nickname:** 'Hammers.'
Entered Football League: 1919—Div. 2.
Biggest win: 8–0 v. Rotherham United (Div. 2), March 1958; 8–0 v. Sunderland (Div. 1), October 1968.
Heaviest defeat: 0–10 v. Tottenham (Southern League), 1904–05.
Best in League Cup: Runners-up 1965–66.
Pitch measurements: 110 x 72 yd.
Highest League Scorer in Single Season: Vic Watson—41 in 1929–30 (Div. 1).
Transfers—
  Highest fee paid: £200,000—David Cross (from West Bromwich), December 1977.
  Highest fee received: £200,000 equivalent—Martin Peters (to Tottenham—£146,000 plus Jimmy Greaves in part exchange), March 1970.

WIMBLEDON

Durnsford Road, Wimbledon, London SW19, 01-946 6311

Shirts: white. *Shorts:* white. *Stockings:* white with blue turnover. *Second colours:* blue shirts and blue shorts.

The Football League's newest club was founded as long ago as 1889 when a group of ex-pupils of Central School formed themselves into Wimbledon Old Centrals. They played on common land and used a local pub for changing rooms, but even in those days their colours were blue and white. They moved to their present ground just before the First World War when it was swamp land in use as a rubbish dump.

They were elected to the Athenian League in 1921 and joined the Isthmian League two years later. Forty years on, they had become the most powerful amateur club in the country, many times fielding no fewer than ten internationals. When they had conquered the Isthmian League four years in succession, there was only one way to go. So they became semi-professional, and joined the Southern League. Behind them were two Amateur Cup finals. They lost the first 2–1 to Bishop Auckland at Stamford Bridge after a 0–0 draw at Middlesbrough and won the second when they beat Sutton United 4–2 at Wembley in 1963.

They were Southern League champions in each of the last three seasons before being elected to the Football League in place of Workington in June 1977. Eighteen months earlier, in January 1975, they became the first non-League club to win an F.A. Cup tie on a First Division ground for 54 years when they won 1–0 at Burnley. Then in the next round they held powerful Leeds to 0–0 at Elland Road before being beaten by an own goal in the replay at Crystal Palace. In January 1976, they held Middlesbrough to 0–0 before losing the replay 1–0 at Ayresome Park.

Record attendance: 18,000 v. H.M.S. Victory, F.A. Amateur Cup, 1932–33.
Modern Capacity: 18,000. **Nickname:** 'The Dons.'
Biggest win: 15–2 v. Polytechnic, F.A. Cup 1932–33.
Heaviest defeat: 4–7 v. Hounslow, London Senior Cup, 1950–51.
Best in F.A. Cup: 4th Round replay, 1974–75.
Pitch measurements: 110 x 72 yd.
Highest Scorer in a Single Season: Eddie Reynolds—57 in 1964–65.
Isthmian League Champions: 1930–31, 1934–35, 1935–36, 1958–59, 1960–61, 1961–62, 1962–63, 1963–64.
Southern League Champions: 1974–75, 1975–76, 1976–77.
Transfers—
    Highest fee paid: £16,000—Les Briley (from Hereford), February 1978.
    Highest fee received: £10,000—Billy Holmes (to Hereford), October 1977.

WOLVERHAMPTON WANDERERS

Molineux Grounds, Wolverhampton, 0902–24053

Shirts: gold with black motif. *Shorts:* black. *Stockings:* gold. *Second colours:* white shirts & shorts.

Football fame came back to the Wolves in the fifties. Not only did they challenge for the title of Britain's top club, but they also shone in prestige matches against the best of that era in Europe.

Behind their amazing record of success was the genius of manager Stan Cullis, the captaincy of Billy Wright and an all-star team excelling at the long-ball game.

Wolves began the most glamorous period in their history with a 3–1 Wembley win over Leicester City in the 1949 F.A. Cup Final. They went on to become League Champions in 1954, 1958 and 1959, and won the Cup again in 1960.

Then for Wolves, one of the League's founder clubs in 1888, came 14 years of unsuccessful striving for further glory before they returned to Wembley, under manager Bill McGarry, for the 1974 League Cup Final, in which they defeated Manchester City 2–1.

Billy Wright, first England player to complete a century of Internationals (105 appearances) played more League and Cup games —535 between 1946 and 1959—than anyone in Wolves' history.

League Champions: 1953–54, 1957–58, 1958–59.
Division 2 Champions: 1931–32, 1976–77.
Division 3 (North) Champions: 1923–24.
F.A. Cup Winners: 1892–93, 1907–08, 1948–49, 1959–60.
League Cup Winners: 1973–74.
Record attendance: 61,315 v. Liverpool (F.A. Cup), February 1939.
Modern Capacity: 53,500. **Nickname:** 'Wolves.'
Entered Football League: 1888–Div. 1.
Biggest win: 14–0 v. Crosswell's Brewery (F.A. Cup), 1886–87.
Heaviest defeat: 1–10 v. Newton Heath (Div. 1), October 1892.
Pitch measurements: 115 x 72 yd.
Highest League Scorer in Single Season: Dennis Westcott— 37 in 1946–47 (Div. 1).
Transfers—
  Highest fee paid: £200,000—Alan Sunderland (from Arsenal), November 1977.
  Highest fee received: £150,000—Paul Bradshaw (to Blackburn), September 1977.

WREXHAM

Racecourse Ground, Mold Road, Wrexham LL11 2AN,
Wrexham 2414

Shirts: red, white trim. *Shorts:* white, red seam. *Stockings:* white.
Second colours: white shirts, black shorts.

Wrexham hold the distinction of being the oldest Association
football club in Wales. They were founded in 1873 and have
provided a steady flow of players to the International team. Wrexham
have also won the Welsh Cup more than 20 times, and in the 1975–76
Cup-Winners' Cup they became the first Third Division side to reach
a European quarter-final, beating Djurgardens (Sweden) and Stal
Rzeszow (Poland) before going out to Belgian cracks Anderlecht.

Wrexham's Racecourse Ground is an International venue, and
in November 1975 was the scene of a 1–0 victory over Austria
which took Wales, in their centenary season, into the European
Championship quarter-finals for the first time. The scorer was
34-year-old local hero Arfon Griffiths, who later became manager.

Wrexham provided F.A. Cup sensations in season 1973–74. They
beat Second Division leaders Middlesbrough 1–0 to reach the fifth
round for the first time, and did even better by winning 1–0 away
to First Division Southampton. Then they were drawn away to
another First Division club, Burnley, and went out by the only goal.

Twice in 1975 Wrexham received from Merseyside a new record
transfer fee—£70,000 from Everton for striker David Smallman and,
four months later, £110,000 from Liverpool for full-back Joey Jones.

Record attendance: 34,445 v. Manchester United (F.A. Cup),
  January 1957.
Modern Capacity: 36,000. **Nickname:** 'Robins.'
Entered Football League: 1921—Div. 3 (North).
Biggest win: 10–1 v. Hartlepools United (Div. 4), March 1962.
Heaviest defeat: 0–9 v. Brentford (Div. 3), October 1963.
Highest final League position: Runners-up Div. 3 (North),
  1932–33; runners-up Div. 4 1969–70.
Best in F.A. Cup: 6th Round 1973–74, 1977–78.
Best in League Cup: 5th Round 1960–61.
Pitch measurements: 117 x 75 yd.
Highest League Scorer in Single Season: Tommy Bamford
  44 in 1933–34 (Div. 3 North).
Transfers—
  Highest fee paid: £60,000—Dixie McNeil (from Hereford),
  September 1977.
  Highest fee received: £120,000—Billy Ashcroft (to Middles-
  brough), August 1977.

YORK CITY

Bootham Crescent, York YO3 7AQ, York 24447

Shirts: white with maroon Y. *Shorts:* white. *Stockings:* white with maroon tops. *Second colours:* maroon shirts with white Y, maroon shorts.

York City are one of only five Third Division clubs who have reached the F.A. Cup semi-final. Millwall (1937), Port Vale (1954), Norwich (1959) and C. Palace (1976) are the others. City startled the football world in 1955 with an extraordinary Cup run which actually carried them further than any other Third Division side in history; they took Newcastle United to a replay before losing the semi-final 2–0.

York had reached the last eight in 1938 when their team, said to have cost only £50, defeated teams from all four divisions. Some of the club's best performances have been achieved more recently. Three times since the League was extended in 1958 they have won promotion to the Third Division—in 1959, 1965 and 1971.

Between October–December 1973 York equalled a 47-year-old record (Millwall, Div. 3 South 1926) by playing 11 consecutive Third Division matches without conceding a goal. Such defence played a major part in City finishing third and so reaching the Second Division for the first time in their history.

York finished 15th on their arrival in Division Two, but were relegated a year later, in 1976.

Record attendance: 28,123 v. Huddersfield Town (F.A. Cup), March 1938.
Modern Capacity: 23,500. **Nickname:** 'Minsters.'
Entered Football League: 1929—Div. 3 (North).
Biggest win: 9–1 v. Southport (Div. 3 North), February 1957.
Heaviest defeat: 0–12 v. Chester (Div. 3 North), February 1936.
Highest final League position: 3rd in Div. 4 1958–59, 1964–1965; 3rd in Div. 3 1973–74.
Best in F.A. Cup: Semi-final 1954–55.
Best in League Cup: 5th Round 1961–62.
Pitch measurements: 115 x 75 yd.
Highest League Scorer in Single Season: Bill Fenton—31 in 1951–52 (Div. 3 North); Alf Bottom—31 in 1954–55 (Div. 3 North).
Transfers—
Highest fee paid: £18,000—Micky Cave (from Bournemouth), August 1974.
Highest fee received: £35,000—Cliff Calvert (to Sheffield United), September 1975.

107

The Scottish League

In a controversial move aimed at revitalizing public interest, the Scottish Football League made one of the most revolutionary changes in its history at the start of season 1975–76, regrouping from two to three divisions. The Premier League consisted of ten clubs (meeting four times per season instead of twice as previously), and the First and Second Divisions each comprised 14 teams in the inaugural season.

This system was retained for the 1976–77 and the 1977–78 seasons, but it is doubtful if it will be kept beyond that. Ten teams does not seem to be sufficient for the Premier Division. It is argued that two or three defeats can plunge a team straight into a relegation struggle. There is also the factor that gates in Scotland are dominated by the games against Celtic and Rangers, consequently more clubs want visits from them.

Aberdeen, the principal club in the north-east of Scotland, were founded in 1903 and from the early years they built a reputation for playing attractive football although rarely achieving top honours.

In 1905 they left the North-east Alliance to enter the Scottish League, and although they stayed in the First Division, it took them half a century to become League Champions. After being runners-up in 1911 and 1937, they at last took the title in 1955. They were runners-up the following year and again in 1971 and 1972.

By 1967 Aberdeen had reached the Scottish Cup Final six times but won the trophy only once—when defeating Hibernian 2–1 in 1947. Their second F.A. Cup triumph came in 1970, when they beat Celtic 3–1 in the Final. They took the League Cup in its inaugural season (1945–46) and won it again ten years later. They captured it again in 1976–77.

Since 1969 Aberdeen have been Scotland's biggest exporters of soccer talent to England, transferring several players at six-figure fees—Tommy Craig to Sheffield Wednesday (£100,000), Jim Smith to Newcastle (£100,000), Martin Buchan to Manchester United (£125,000), Joe Harper to Everton (£180,000) and Willie Young to Tottenham (£100,000).

Airdrieonians climbed their highest peaks in the early 1920s when they challenged the supremacy of Rangers and Celtic. They were First Division runners-up in four successive seasons (1923–26) and won the Scottish Cup for the only time in 1924, beating Hibernian 2–0 in the Final. It was half a century before they reached the Final again (1975), and then they lost 3–1 to Celtic.

In the League during that era, Airdrie were unbeaten on their own Broomfield Park pitch for more than three years. They fielded six Scottish Internationalists, the greatest of them Hughie Gallacher.

Airdrie dropped into the Second Division in 1936 and did not get back into the top class until 1947, since when they have fought an almost constant battle to stay up—or go up. As Second Division Champions in 1974, they were the only British club to top a century of League goals (102), and by finishing eleventh in the First Division in 1975, they just missed a place in the newly-formed Premier Division.

Albion Rovers' most memorable year was 1920 when, for the only time, they reached the Scottish Cup Final, after beating mighty Rangers in the semi-final. In that Rovers team beaten 3–2 by Kilmarnock was Jock White, still their only International, who was capped with them before moving on to Hearts and Leeds. Elected to the First Division in 1919, 'Wee Albion' have had at best a see-saw existence, being relegated three times—the last occasion in 1949. One of their most outstanding players was Jock Stein, subsequently the triumphant manager of Celtic and a star defender at Cliftonhill during the 1940s.

For **Alloa Athletic** the proudest achievement came in season 1921–22, when they won the very first Second Division Championship by a margin of 13 points. But a year later they were relegated and have not played in the top division since. They were, however, harshly affected by the outbreak of the Second World War. They were due for promotion at the end of season 1938–39, but the League was disbanded because of the war, and when it was reformed, Alloa were not elected to the First Division.

The small Scottish coastal town of **Arbroath** is famous for kippers —and the club's 36–0 victory over Bon Accord in a first round Cup-tie on 12 September 1885. This stands as the biggest score in a first-class match in Britain. Bon Accord's regular goalkeeper Jimmie Grant was unfit and replaced by wing-half Andrew Lornie. John Petrie scored 13 against him and Arbroath totalled 55 goals in the Cup that season before losing to Hibernian in the fourth round. The previous year Arbroath were robbed of another place in the history books. They beat Rangers in a fourth round Cup-tie, but after protesting that the Gayfield pitch was smaller than regulation size, Rangers won the replayed game 8–1 on their own ground. Arbroath had to wait another 90 years to achieve that first win over Rangers—a stunning 3–2 League victory on 2 February 1974. At Ibrox Park, too!

Ayr United have enjoyed steady support since they entered the Scottish First Division in 1913. They have mostly struggled on the fringe of the First Division. Between 1925 and 1969 they won promotion six times—but since that last elevation they have consolidated, and a final position of seventh in 1975 ensured a place for the Somerset Park club among the giants in the new Premier League.

For as long as football is played in Scotland, **Berwick Rangers** 1, Glasgow Rangers 0 will stand high on the list of 'unbelievable' results. The date was 28 January 1967 in the first round of the Cup, and Shielfield Park, home of the little English border-town team of part-timers who play in the Scottish League, was crammed with a record 13,365 crowd.

Sammy Reid, a former Liverpool player, scored the historic 32nd-minute goal, and for the rest of the game Berwick's 35-year-old goalkeeper-manager Jock Wallace (ex-Airdrie and West Bromwich Albion) and his defence heroically resisted all Rangers' pressure to produce Scotland's greatest 'Jock the giantkiller' story.

Never before had Rangers been knocked out of the Cup by Second Division opposition . . . and it is said that many of the 7000 fans who followed them from Glasgow to Tweedmouth that day still refuse to believe it ever happened. Jock Wallace later became manager of Rangers.

Brechin City has the smallest population (6000) supporting a senior club in Britain. During the 1920s—when Brechin moved to their present ground, Glebe Park—the town was inhabited by more than 10,000 and attendances averaged 3000, but after the war the population fell dramatically, and so did support for Brechin. They have never been seen in top-division football.

Celtic, arch rivals of Rangers as the top club in Scottish football, were formed in 1888 by Irish Catholics living in Glasgow, the first object being to raise money for the poor of the city's East End.

Under former captain Jock Stein (appointed manager in 1965) they have reached astonishing heights, with 1966–67 their greatest season. In an historic clean sweep, they became the first British club to win the European Cup, defeating Inter-Milan 2–1 in the Final; they won the League Championship (scoring 111 goals and losing only one game out of 34) ; they took the Scottish Cup ; and the Scottish League Cup also went to Parkhead.

Celtic's famous green and white strip has long been an emblem of attacking football, and season 1971–72 brought them the Double for the fourth time in six years. A ninth *successive* League Championship (their 29th in all) in 1973–74 equalled a world record by Hungarian club MTK Budapest (1917–25) and the Bulgarians CDNA Sofia (1954–62), a feat celebrated by completion of the Double for the ninth time in their history.

Celtic have won the Scottish Cup a total of 25 times and the League Cup on eight occasions.

Of Celtic's galaxy of star players down the years, Jimmy McGrory was unquestionably the greatest goalscorer. In 378 games between 1922–39 he obtained 397 goals for them—the highest all-time total in the Scottish League—and after a playing career in which his goal aggregate reached 550, he also managed the club.

Clyde were formed in 1877 and took their name from the river and dockyards of Glasgow. Their home, Shawfield Park, is in the East End and they have constantly struggled to keep up with their big city rivals.

Although slipping out of the First Division on six occasions, they always made a rapid return to the top bracket, five times doing so at the first attempt.

Clyde have never been Champions of Scotland, nor have they won the League Cup, but they have triumphed three times in the F.A. Cup.

After defeats in the 1910 and 1912 Finals they at last won the trophy in 1939, when they beat Motherwell 4–0. They were also Cup winners in 1955, defeating Celtic 1–0 in a replay, and in 1958 another single goal gave them victory over Hibernian.

Clydebank, formed in 1967, had played one season in the Second Division under the name of East Stirlingshire Clydebank, but there was a legal dispute and Clydebank became established in their own right.

In the 1920s the original Clydebank FC were a First Division club, but they resigned from the Scottish League in 1931. A team built from their remnants continued under the name of Clydebank Intermediate, but they failed to gain senior status. When the Scottish League was restructured in 1975, Clydebank found themselves in the bottom section, but they won promotion first time to Division One. They spent only one season there before winning promotion to the Premier Division.

After years of Second Division obscurity, **Cowdenbeath** won unexpected promotion in season 1969–70, and within months they were in a League Cup semi-final against Rangers—excitement unheard of at Central Park since the Second Division Championship of 1938–39. But they lasted only one more season in the top class.

Cowdenbeath won the Second Division in 1939 by 12 points, but when League football was resumed seven years later there was no place for them in the First Division.

Season 1972–73 saw **Dumbarton** playing their first match in the First Division for fifty years, while Clyde returned to the Second. It was an ironic twist, for two seasons earlier Dumbarton made a take-over bid for Clyde, but it was rejected as an attempt to buy their way out of the Second Division.

Founded in 1872, Dumbarton were one of the original members of the Scottish League in 1890. They shared the first Championship title with Rangers, and won it outright the following year. They entered the first Scottish Cup in 1873–74 and have done so ever since—a record equalled only by Queen's Park and Kilmarnock. They won the Cup in 1883.

Dundee, a First Division club for most of their history, did not win the League Championship until 1962—after four times being runners-up. That is still their only League title to date, but they were F.A. Cup winners in 1910, and their three League Cup successes were gained in seasons 1951–52, 1952–53 and 1973–74 (when they shocked Celtic 1–0 in the Final).

In 1963 Dundee were close to becoming the first British club to win the European Cup, losing in the semi-finals to AC Milan, who went on to win the competition. In October 1974 the transfer of goalscorer John Duncan to Tottenham brought Dundee a new record fee of £150,000.

Dundee United, founded in 1910, have constantly struggled to emulate the deeds of their next-door neighbours, Dundee—and are still trying to win their first major prize. Originally known as Dundee Hibernian, they changed their name in 1923 on gaining election to the Second Division of the Scottish League. Two years later they won promotion but they led an up-and-down existence (relegated 1927–30–32) until stability was brought to the side at the start of the 1960s, since when United have consistently maintained a place in the Scottish Championship.

In 1974 they reached the F.A. Cup Final for the first time, losing 3–0 to Celtic. The Tannadice Park club received a record £150,000 when they transferred striker Andy Gray to Aston Villa in Sept. 1975.

Dunfermline Athletic did not 'arrive' as a top club in Scotland until the sixties, although they were formed as long ago as 1907. Their real rise began in 1960, when Jock Stein was appointed manager. The following year they reached the Scottish Cup Final for the first time, and after a goalless draw beat Celtic 2–0 in a replay. Their second F.A. Cup victory came in 1968 when they defeated Hearts 3–1 in the Final.

After Stein left, Dunfermline remained strong and were only two points from putting their name on the First Division title in 1964–65, when third to champions Kilmarnock and Hearts. They finished third again in 1968–69.

In 1969, Dunfermline reached the semi-finals of the European Cup-Winners' Cup, eventually losing 1–2 on aggregate to Slovan Bratislava.

112

East Fife are unique in having won the Scottish Cup while members of the old Second Division. That highest peak came in 1938, when they beat Kilmarnock 4–2 in a Final replay after a 1–1 draw.

As a Second Division side, East Fife had sprung a surprise in 1927 by reaching the Final, but were beaten 3–1 by Celtic. In their only other F.A. Cup Final they lost 3–0 to Rangers in 1950.

Third has been their highest final position in the Championship (in 1952 and 1953), and the League Cup has been East Fife's most successful tournament with three triumphs—in 1948, 1950 and 1954.

East Stirling, in their only post-war First Division season, 1963–64, attracted crowds of 10,000 to Firs Park. Then, following relegation, they merged with Clydebank, but after only one season they reverted to their original identity.

Many fine players have begun their careers at Firs Park, and in 1962 Eddie McCreadie, later capped 23 times by Scotland at full-back, Tommy Knox and Jim Mulholland were all transferred to Chelsea.

Falkirk's closest bid for the Scottish League Championship was made at the start of the century, when they finished runners-up to Celtic in 1908 and 1910. Since the last war they have four times been relegated to the Second Division.

In the Scottish F.A. Cup they have had two successes, beating Raith 2–0 in the 1913 Final and then, after a break of 44 years, taking the trophy again in 1957 with a replay victory by 2–1 against Kilmarnock.

Falkirk have produced many star players—for English as well as bigger Scottish clubs—and none better than Scottish International inside-forward John White, who moved to Tottenham for £20,000 in October 1959.

Although **Forfar Athletic** were formed as long ago as 1884, they are not to be found anywhere on the list of League or Cup honours. Indeed, their highest final position remains sixth in the Second Division in season 1967–68, and even then their average gate was less than 1500. Yet the fact that they are approaching their centenary is a tribute to their perseverance despite all the odds . . . and despite winning only one of 38 Second Division matches (7 draws, 30 defeats) in season 1974–75.

Unique in title among first-class clubs in Britain, **Hamilton Academicals** owe their derivation to the local academy at the time of their formation in 1870. No major honours have gone to Douglas Park, but Hamilton were Scottish Cup Finalists in 1911 and 1935.

The club's best period was in the 1930s when, besides reaching the Cup Final—in which Rangers beat them 2–1—they finished in the top eight in the First Division five times in seven seasons.

Over the years Hamilton have often had to transfer star players to help finances, and probably their most famous 'discovery' was forward Alec Herd, who went on to a great career with Hearts, Manchester City and Scotland.

Heart of Midlothian were among the founder-members of the Scottish League in 1890 and had never been out of the Championship Division until 1977—a wonderful record, even if it is more than a decade since they won the last of their four League titles (1895, 1897, 1958 and 1960).

Hearts' Scottish Cup triumphs number five (1891, 1896, 1901, 1906 and 1956) and the League Cup has been won by the famous Maroons of Tynecastle Park, Edinburgh, on four occasions—1955, 1959, 1960 and 1963. The 1960 success gave them a double, because they were League Champions as well that season.

Among more than 50 Scottish Internationals to represent the club, there has been no greater artist than Tommy Walker, ace inside-forward of the thirties and beyond. After a spell with Chelsea just after the war, he returned to Tynecastle and managed Hearts through one of the most spectacular phases in their history.

Other players of truly star quality to serve Hearts with distinction have included Tom Purdie (the club's first captain), Bobby Walker, Charlie Thomson, 'Barney' Battles, Alex Massie, Dave McCulloch, Willie Bauld, Jimmy Wardhaugh and Dave Mackay.

Hibernian form with Hearts the football strength in the city of Edinburgh, and although their combined records do not begin to measure up to those of the Glasgow 'big two', they have nevertheless made an invaluable contribution to the Scottish soccer scene. Hibs' two Scottish F.A. Cup victories were achieved long ago, in 1887 and 1902. The first of four occasions when they have taken the League title was in 1903.

Apart from two seasons at the start of the thirties, they have spent the whole of this century as members of the top division, with the Championship won in 1948, 1951 and 1952. Season 1972–73 marked Hibs' only League Cup success.

The first British team to take part in the European Cup when it was launched in 1955, Hibernian, like most Scottish clubs, have at times been forced for financial reasons to sell star players. Forward 'exports' have been their speciality—Colin Stein was sold to Rangers for £100,000 in October 1968. Peter Marinello went to Arsenal at the same fee in January 1970, and two months later the transfer of Peter Cormack to Nottingham Forest fetched £85,000.

In February 1974 Hibs used the transfer market in the opposite way to make history—they signed Scotland striker Joe Harper from

Everton for £120,000, then the highest Scottish fee ever paid to an English club. The following December they sold profitably again, taking £150,000 from Arsenal for striker Alex Cropley.

No one could say that **Kilmarnock** were winning out of turn when they took the Scottish League title in 1965; they had been runners-up in four of the previous five seasons.

That remains the only League honour to go so far to Rugby Park, and the League Cup has still to be won, but Kilmarnock have had two successes in the Scottish Cup, in 1920 and 1929.

Over the years they have become almost the champion runners-up of Scottish football; besides those four 'seconds' in the League in the early 1960s, they have been beaten F.A. Cup Finalists five times and three times losers of the League Cup Final.

At the start of season 1973–74 they faced the task of winning back a First Division place lost after 19 years—and achieved that objective first time. Kilmarnock were two places short of the Premier League on its inception in 1975, but within twelve months they were promoted from Division One.

In 1974, when the Scottish League decided to elect an additional club to make an even number (38), the extra place surprisingly went to the Edinburgh works side Ferranti Thistle, from the East of Scotland League, by 21 votes to 16 over Highland League club Inverness Thistle. On election, they were required to drop the commercial name and, having rented the 30,000-capacity Meadowbank Stadium from Edinburgh Corporation, the newcomers adopted the title **Meadowbank Thistle.** With a run of 15 consecutive defeats, their start did not match the impressive surroundings in which they played, but by the end of their first season, Meadowbank had achieved comparative revival with nine Second Division victories.

Montrose belong among the Scottish clubs never to have competed in the Championship Division, and between 1947 and 1955 they dropped into Division C. The club's most noteworthy achievements were in reaching the Cup quarter-finals in 1930 and 1948 and they were within one place of promotion to the Premier League in 1976.

The only major honour to come to Greenock **Morton** was the Scottish Cup in 1922 by a shock 1–0 win over Rangers in the Final. But they are very much part of the fabric of Scottish football with their home at Cappielow Park close to the shipyards of Clydeside.

In 1964, Morton became the first Scottish club to recruit Scandinavian players by taking on goalkeeper Erik Sorensen, a Dane. The idea came from director-manager Hal Stewart, who took over in 1962 when they were a dying club—last but one in the

Second Division with only two signed players on the staff.

Under his guidance, they reached the League Cup Final in 1963–1964, and at the end of the season were Second Division Champions by the record margin of 14 points. At one stage that winter Morton won 23 games in a row (a Scottish League record). Three years later in 1967, they were Second Division winners again with 69 points, another record.

Until season 1931–32, Celtic and Rangers had monopolized Scottish League football for 27 years, but then **Motherwell** came upon the scene as new Champions—a reward for the attractive football they had played for many years.

The previous season, Motherwell reached the Scottish Cup Final for the first time and would have won it but for a tragic last-minute own goal allowing Celtic the chance of a replay which they won 4–2.

Motherwell had to wait another 21 years for their F.A. Cup Final victory which came in 1952 (4–0 against Dundee), but the year before they put their name on the League Cup for the first time.

In the 1973 close season Motherwell placed their management in the hands of their former star player, Ian St John, who returned to Fir Park after an illustrious career with Liverpool. His immediate task was to revive interest, but although St John brought Motherwell to life on the field, the Lanarkshire public were still sceptical about giving solid support after more than 20 years without success.

When the Premier League was formed in 1975, Motherwell just qualified—in tenth place. For more than half the season they were challenging for the Championship, but all the time English clubs were casting envious glances at Willie Pettigrew, the hottest goalscoring property in Scottish football.

On 23 October 1971 **Partick Thistle** caused the biggest sensation in Scottish football for years by thrashing odds-on favourites Celtic 4–1 in the League Cup Final. With an average age of 22—and just six months after winning back their First Division place following one season in the Second—Thistle astonished a crowd of 62,740 at Hampden Park by scoring four goals in a 30-minute spell. It was their first major success in 50 years.

Thistle's only other triumph since being formed in the north-west of Glasgow in 1876 was a Cup Final victory in 1921, when they beat Rangers 1–0.

In the League Championship Partick's highest final placing has been third, three times—in 1948, 1954 and 1963. They missed a place in the new Premier League, but qualified a year later.

Queen of the South's most successful period was between 1933 and 1950, when they competed in the First Division. During that period they played in the Cup quarter-finals three times, and in the relegation season of 1949–50 they reached the semi-final. They

116

were formed in 1919 when three local sides, Dumfries, the King's Own Scottish Borderers and Arrol Johnston, amalgamated: Their outstanding discovery was Hughie Gallacher—later to become one of the greatest Scottish forwards—who played two seasons for the Queens' before joining Airdrie on his way to a spectacular career with Newcastle, Chelsea, Derby and Scotland.

Queen's Park, for long the only amateur club competing in Britain's big professional leagues, are unique in many other ways. From their year of formation in 1867 they went unbeaten for seven years (in the first five of which goalkeeper Jock Grant did not have a goal scored against him).

They won the Scottish Cup **ten** times between 1874–93, before the Scottish F.A. legalized professionalism, and in addition Queen's Park were English F.A. Cup finalists in 1884 and 1885.

Except for winning the 1955–56 Second Division championship and the honour of supplying the big majority of Scotland's amateur international players, Queen's Park have had no post-war claims to fame. They were last relegated in 1958 and, though seldom watched nowadays by more than a few hundred spectators, this club of great tradition have gone on playing their home games in Britain's biggest arena, Hampden Park.

Raith Rovers can claim the most goals ever scored in a league season by a British club: 142 in 34 matches when they won the Scottish Second Division championship in 1937–38. It is a record that, short of a tactical revolution within the game, will never be beaten.

Third in 1922, behind Celtic and Rangers, is the closest Raith have ever been to the First Division title; in knockout football they were beaten finalists in the Scottish Cup in 1913 and runners-up in the League Cup in season 1948–49.

Easily the outstanding player produced by the Kirkcaldy club was Alex James, who became a classic inside-forward with Preston, Arsenal and Scotland in the 1920s and 1930s.

Although their great rivals Celtic have dominated Scotland's honours list in modern times, **Rangers** are still ahead in the overall Championship-winners' table with 36 titles. The Scottish F.A. Cup has gone to Ibrox 21 times, and the 'Gers' have won eight League Cups, giving them a grand total of 65 prizes in the three tournaments.

Rangers' richest phase came just after the first war with the appointment of Willie Struth as manager in 1920. In 33 years under his command—until at 79 he went on the board—Rangers won the League 18 times, the Cup ten times and the League Cup twice. Some record !

Under Struth's successor, Scot Symon, Rangers continued triumphantly until in 1967, Celtic became predominant. Davie

Scotland's Gordon McQueen became Britain's first half-million pound footballer when he was transferred from Leeds United to Manchester United. He is being tackled by England rival, Dave Watson of Manchester City.

The man behind the most successful side Nottingham Forest have ever had—England goalkeeper Peter Shilton. Forest manager, Brian Clough, has said that Shilton is worth ten points a season to Forest.

Scenes of jubilation from Nottingham Forest players after their 1—0 victory at the replay, of the League Cup Final against Liverpool.

White followed him, lasted two years and was succeeded in the managerial chair by Willie Waddell, whose first success was of double value in that it came against Celtic in the 1970–71 League Cup Final.

In European campaigns, Rangers are one of Britain's most experienced clubs. In 1961 and 1967 they were runners-up in the Cup-Winners' Cup, but season 1971–72 proved third time lucky in this particular final, with Rangers beating Moscow Dynamo 3–2 to take the trophy. Their triumph was tarnished, however, by the misconduct of Glaswegian supporters who invaded the Barcelona pitch during the final, with the sequel that U.E.F.A. banned Rangers from Europe for the following season.

In 1975, under manager Jock Wallace, Rangers ended the nine-year Championship domination of Celtic. A clean sweep of League Championship, League Cup and F.A. Cup which followed in season 1975–76 gave Rangers a record three 'grand slams'. (Their others were in 1948–49 and 1963–64.)

St Johnstone, one of the sturdy provincials of Scottish football, were formed in 1884 but, apart from three times winning the Second Division championship, they made no mark for 85 years.

Then in season 1969–70, they reached the Final of the League Cup and football fever gripped the picturesque and usually quiet Tayside town of Perth. At Hampden Park, however, the mighty Celtic beat them, though only by the lone goal of a fiercely fought game.

Before being relegated in 1971, **St Mirren** had spent only two seasons outside the First Division (1936–37, 1967–68)—a remarkable record considering the club have only once finished as high as third in the Championship, and that as long ago as 1893. They were Scottish Cup winners in 1926 and 1959.

In modern times English clubs have come to regard St Mirren as something of a source for transfer bargains—such as Jimmy Robertson to Tottenham (£25,000), Archie Gemmill to Preston (£13,000), Gordon McQueen to Leeds (£35,000) and Jim Blair to Norwich (£18,000).

Since their formation in 1884 **Stenhousemuir** have failed to win a major honour and have never moved above the Second Division. But they could claim a part in Scotland's qualification for the 1974 World Cup Finals in Munich, for national team manager Willie Ormond began his playing career at Ochilview Park.

Stirling Albion owed their formation in 1945 to the miscalculations of a German bomb-aimer some five years earlier. In 1940 an enemy aircraft discharged its cargo over the town of Stirling, and the Forth Bank ground—home of King's Park FC—was destroyed. Local feeling demanded the formation of a new club and under the leadership of coal merchant Tom Fergusson, Stirling Albion was born after the war. Their ground became Annfield Park, with the dressing-rooms located in a huge mansion.

In their first season Stirling won the inaugural post-war Scottish Division C Championship. The pattern of an up-and-down existence has continued ever since.

Stranraer, situated on the south-west coast, have the smallest ground capacity (6000) on Scotland's League club circuit. Formed in 1870, they have passed their centenary without achieving a major prize.

Prominent European Clubs

(Details as at 31 May 1977)

Ajax Amsterdam: Formed in 1900 and came to prominence only after professionalism introduced in 1953. Have a tiny ground of their own (22,000) but play their big matches at the Olympic Stadium (capacity 65,000). Dutch Champions 16 times (a record) including a hat-trick between 1966 and 1968, and also F.A. Cup winners 1969–70 (when they completed the double), 1970–71 and 1971–72. Have won the Cup seven times altogether. Finalists in the European Cup in 1969, their open attacking play foundered against the *cattenacio* defence of AC Milan. After crashing 1–4, they were more cautious when they reached the Final again in 1971 and won the trophy 2–0 against Panathinaikos at Wembley. The start of a run of three consecutive European successes. Beat Independiente (Argentina) 4–1 on aggregate to take the World Club crown in 1972. Managed through most of their triumphs by former player Rinus Michels, who rejoined them in 1975 after three years with CF Barcelona. Stars: Wim Suurbier and Ruud Krol (full-backs in the 1974 World Cup Final), Barry Hulshoff, Gerrie Muhren and free-scoring Ruud Geels.

RSC Anderlecht: Formed in 1908, the Royal Sporting Club Anderlecht play at their own Parc Astrid in Brussels (capacity 28,000) with the 60,000 Stade de Heysel reserved for big games. Champions of Belgium 16 times (a record) and Cup winners in 1965, 1972, 1973, 1975 and 1976. Recorded a spectacular success in the sixties when they won the championship five times in a row (another record) between 1964 and 1968. Crashed 0–10 to Manchester United in their first venture into the European Cup (1956–57), but improved later to become one of the few teams to have the distinction of eliminating Real Madrid in Di Stefano's time. Fairs Cup Finalists 1970. Best known players: Jeff Mermans (56 caps) in the fifties; Joseph Jurion (64 caps) in the sixties; in the seventies, Arie Haan and Robbie Rensenbrink, who both played for Holland in the 1974 World Cup Final. Won the Cup-Winners' Cup in 1975–76.

Atletico Madrid: Founded in 1923 and adopted by the Spanish forces in the thirties, when known as Aviaciones Atletico. Champions of Spain eight times and F.A. Cup winners five times. Most recent success—champions in 1976–77 and the Cup in 1976. Built the futuristic Estadio Manzanares in the sixties, intended to rival Real's Chamartin, with a capacity of 70,000. Won the European Cup-Winners' Cup in 1962 and were Finalists again in 1963. By defeating Independiente, of Argentina, Atletico became World Club Champions in 1975 when, as European Cup runners-up, they competed in place

123

of Bayern Munich, who declined to participate. Stars: coloured sweeper Luis Pereira and centre-forward Leivinha, both members of Brazil's 1974 World Cup squad and engaged in the 1975 autumn; Argentinians Ayala and Heredia.

CF Barcelona: Formed in 1899 and today the wealthiest club in Spain with their Nou Camp Stadium (completed in 1968) accommodating 90,000. Spanish champions nine times and F.A. Cup winners 17 times. Most recent successes—Spanish champions in 1973–74 and Spanish Cup winners in 1968 and 1971. Also Latin Cup winners in 1949 and 1951. European Cup Finalists in 1961; Cup-Winners' Cup Finalists in 1969 and the only club to win the Fairs Cup three times—in 1958, 1960 and 1966. Their most successful phase was 1959–61 when, under the guidance of Helenio Herrera, they won the championship two years in succession. Best known stars of the sixties: Luis Suarez, Sandor Kocsis (Hungary), Ladislav Kubala (Hungary). Today: Johan Cruyff and Johan Neeskens, Holland and former Ajax stars, and Hugo Sotil, who played in the 1970 World Cup for Peru.

FC Bayern Munich: The outstanding West German team of recent years but omitted from the Bundesliga when it was formed in 1963, preference being given to neighbours München 1860, who were subsequently relegated. Bayern were promoted in 1965 and quickly established themselves by winning the F.A. Cup in 1966. A year later they added the European Cup-Winners' Cup to their trophies and also retained the F.A. Cup. Champions of West Germany five times, the most recent successes being in 1972, 1973 and 1974, and Cup Winners on five occasions (a record), four of them since 1966. Won the European Cup in 1973–74 and retained it in 1975 and 1976. Managed by the former F.I.F.A. coach Dettmar Cramer. Stars: Gerd Muller, Franz Beckenbauer, Uli Hoeness and Sepp Maier.

Benfica: Champions of Portugal 23 times and F.A. Cup winners 18 times—both records. Also Latin Cup winners 1950. Formed in 1904 and play at the 75,000-capacity Estadio da Luz. Their most successful period was in the sixties when champions eight times in ten seasons. Most recent successes: champions 1974–75 and Cup-winners 1971–72. Rose to international eminence soon after professionalism was introduced and under guidance of Hungarian-born manager Bela Guttman twice won the European Cup—1961 and 1962. Also reached the Final in 1963, 1965 and 1968. Beaten in the World Club Championship by Penarol (1961) and Santos (1962). Mario Coluna (captain) and Jose Aguas best-known stars of their triumphs, with Eusebio their ace striker in his hey-day. Stars: Nene, Jordao and Moinhos.

124

Borussia Moenchengladbach: Like their West German rivals Bayern, they failed to gain a Bundesliga place on its inception in 1963 but won promotion in 1965. Steadily developed since then and at their best are today one of the Continent's strongest teams. Champions of West Germany five times—1970, 1971, 1975, 1976 and 1977—and F.A. Cup winners twice. Thrashed Internazionale-Milan 7–1 in a European Cup-tie in 1971 only to have U.E.F.A. demand a replay in Berlin because of crowd trouble. Completed a double in 1974–75 by winning the U.E.F.A. Cup. Manager Hennes Weisweiler then quit after ten years to take over Barcelona and was replaced by former Bayern coach Udo Lattek. Stars: Berti Vogts and Rainer Bonhof, who helped win the 1974 World Cup, and top scorer Jupp Heynckes, who would have been there, too, but for injury.

C.S.K.A. Sofia: Formed in 1948 as the team of the Bulgarian Army and immediately successful. Champions nineteen times (a record) and Cup winners ten times. Pulled off an incredible run of success when winning the championship nine times in a row between 1954 and 1962. Most recent success—Bulgarian champions in 1975–76. Took part 14 times in European Cup, reaching the semi-finals in 1967 and taking Inter-Milan to a third game. Inside-left Ivan Kolev was the star of the sixties with a record 76 caps. Centre-forward Petar Jekov and inside-left Dimiter Yakimov, each capped more than 50 times, starred later. C.S.K.A. made a name for themselves in 1973 when they ended Ajax's three-year run of unbroken European success.

Dukla Prague: The Sports Club of the Czechoslovak Army, formerly known as U.D.A. and later A.T.K. Prague. Champions nine times (a post-war record) under manager Jaroslav Vejvoda, and Cup winners four times (the competition started only in 1961). Most recent successes, champions in 1965–66 and Cup winners 1968–69, but they slumped when Vejvoda left to take over Legia (Poland). Eight times in European Cup but never progressed beyond the quarter-finals; twice (1961 and 1962) won the International Cup staged in New York. Best-known players of the sixties: wing-halves Josef Masopust and Svatopluk Pluskal, and left-back Ladislav Novak. Vejvoda returned late in 1975 to take over as manager from Masopust. Goalkeeper Ivo Viktor won more than 60 caps.

Dynamo Kiev: Achieved a unique double in being the first provincial club to break the Moscow clubs' stranglehold on the major Russian honours—winning the F.A. Cup for the first time in 1954 and taking the league title in 1961. They have gone on to win seven championships and the F.A. Cup four times. Most recent honours: champions three times in a row (1966 to 1968) and again in 1974 and 1975. The stars who contributed most to those successes were goalkeeper Jevgueni Rudakov, spearhead Anatol Bychevetz and an exceptionally skilful midfield trio—Josif Szabo (Hungarian-born), Viktor Serebrianikov and Vladimir Muntjan. Dynamo won the European Cup-Winners' Cup in 1975, after which they took over the Soviet Union's international fixtures with immediate improvement. Stars: Oleg Blokhin, 1975 European Footballer of the Year, and Victor Kolotov, the captain.

Dynamo Moscow: Formed in 1887 and today the team of the Electrical Trades Union in Moscow. League champions ten times (a Russian record) and F.A. Cup winners four times. Most recent successes—four times champions in the fifties, champions again in 1963 and Cup winners in 1967 and 1970. Gained world-wide fame when, in November 1945, they toured briefly and very successfully in Britain, but 12 years of isolation followed for Russian football. Made their bow in international competition in 1971–72 Cup-Winners' Cup. Most famous player Alexei 'Tiger' Khomich, goalkeeper in the fifties, and they provided another world-class goalkeeper, Lev Yashin, and right-winger Igor Chislenko for the 1966 World Cup.

PSV Eindhoven: Philips Sport Verein are the sports club of the international electrical giants. One innovation at their 22,000 capacity ground is overhead heating for spectators. Formed in 1913, they were amateurs until the mid-fifties, when Dutch soccer began its rise to world standard. Champions in 1929, 1935, 1951 and 1963, they surprised everyone by taking the title in 1974–75, beating the reigning champions Feyenoord at home and away. A year earlier, in the spring of 1974, they lifted the Dutch F.A. Cup, winning the final 6–0. Also won the Cup in 1937, 1950 and 1976. PSV engaged Welsh international centre-forward Trevor Ford in the fifties. Their modern rise is associated with the arrival of the much sought Swedish giant Ralf Edstrom, one of the stars of the 1974 World Cup, in which he played for Sweden with another PSV player Bjorn Nordquist, now back in Sweden. Stars: goalscorer Willy van der Kuylen, Jan van Beveren (goalkeeper), the Van der Kerkhoff brothers, Rene and Willy—all Dutch internationals—and Edstrom. In June 1975 Nick Deacy, Hereford United's 21-year-old striker, joined PSV in a £17,500 transfer on the eve of Britain's Common Market referendum.

Ferencvaros: Formed in 1899 as an athletics and gymnastic club. Champions of Hungary 22 times (a record) and winners of the F.A. Cup 13 times, the most recent triumph being in 1975. Also Mitropa Cup winners in 1928 and 1937. Most recent successes: champions in 1968 and league runners-up in 1973. The first East European club to win a modern international tournament when they won the Fairs Cup in 1965—beating AS Roma, Bilbao, Manchester United and Juventus (in the Final). Finalists again in 1968. Best known stars of the sixties: Florian Albert (centre-forward); Mate Fenyvesi (left wing) and Sandor Matrai (stopper), who all gained more than 70 caps.

Feyenoord: Founded 1908 and established as top club in Holland during the thirties, they built a superb 64,000-capacity stadium in Rotterdam in 1938. Champions eleven times and F.A. Cup winners four times (the Cup was abandoned in the fifties because of lack of public interest). Most recent successes: a double in 1968–69 and champions 1973–74. Surprised everyone by winning the European Cup in 1970, beating Celtic 2–1 in the Final in Milan after extra time, and followed that success with an even greater achievement—the World Club Championship, beating Argentina's Estudiantes 1–0 in Rotterdam after a 2–2 draw in Buenos Aires. Star of that team, Swedish centre-forward Ove Kindvall. Pre-war, Puck Van Heel was their big name, winning a record 64 caps. Stars of the sixties: Coen Moulijn and Rinus Israel. Won the U.E.F.A. Cup in 1974, with key players Wim Van Hanegem and Wim Jansen, both 1974 World Cup finalists. Other stars include Austrian international centre-forward Willi Kreuz and Danish left-winger Jorgen Kristensen.

Fiorentina: Formed relatively late in 1926 and champions of Italy three times. Also Cup winners four times. Most recent successes: F.A. Cup winners 1974–75 and champions in 1968–69. Won the European Cup-Winners' Cup in 1961 and were Finalists in 1962. Their most distinguished performances came when they ran away with the 1955–56 Italian championship—they were unbeaten until the last day of the season—and the following year (1956–57) when they reached the European Cup Final, only to meet Real Madrid playing on their home ground and lost 0–2. Best known stars: Julinho (Brazil), Michelangelo Montuori (Argentina), and Italy's Giancarlo Antognoni.

Gornik Zabrze: Gornik, meaning 'Miners', have established themselves as the leading club in Poland since the war and built something of an international reputation, too. Champions nine times and Cup winners six times, they have been consistently successful in recent years, winning the league five times in a row (1963–67) and five consecutive F.A. Cups (1968–72). In the European Cup reached the quarter-final in 1968, falling to Manchester United (1–2 on aggregate) directly after their three-month winter lay-off. Responded better to this challenge in 1970 and reached the 1970 Cup-Winners' Cup Final, losing 1–2 to Manchester City. In the sixties their stars were Ernst Pohl (inside-forward) and Stanislas Oslizlo (stopper), who both earned 60 caps. Gornik's best-ever player was probably centre-forward Wlodzimierz Lubanski, who helped Poland beat

England in the 1974 World Cup qualifying rounds, but a knee injury reduced his effectiveness. Other stars: Jerzy Gorgon (stopper) and centre-forward Andrzej Szarmach, who both played in the 1974 World Cup.

Internazionale FC: Formed in 1909 as a breakaway from AC Milan and known before the war as Ambrosiana-Inter. Champions of Italy 11 times (including three successes in the sixties). Most recent success: champions 1970–71. Reached international prominence under manager Helenio Herrera, winning the European Cup in 1964 and 1965. Also finalists in 1967 and 1972. Their peak achievement came in 1964, when they won the Italian championship, the European Cup and the World Club Championship—and they retained the World title in 1965 by beating Independiente (Argentina) a second time. Modern stars: Sandro Mazzola, Roberto Boninsegna and Giacinto Facchetti, who all appeared for Italy in the 1970 World Cup Final.

Juventus: Founded in 1897 and share the Stadio Communale in Turin (75,000) with AC Torino. Known affectionately throughout Italy as the 'Old Lady', they have been champions of Italy 17 times and F.A. Cup winners five times (both records). Most recent successes: champions in 1975 and 1977. Also reached the Cup Final and European Cup Final in 1973. F.A. Cup winners 1964–65. Fairs Cup Finalists in 1965 and 1971, and winners in 1976–77. Rarely outside the top four in the Italian league, they have imported some of the world's outstanding players over the years. Their best period was perhaps in the early sixties, when John Charles (Wales) and Enrico Sivori (Argentina) spearheaded their attack. Stars: Pietro Anastasi, goalkeeper Dino Zoff and Italy's right wing pair Fabio Capello and Franco Causio.

AC Milan: Formed in 1899 as Milan Cricket and Football Club they play at the 90,000-capacity San Siro stadium. Italian champions nine times and F.A. Cup-winners three times—they went on to win the European Cup-Winners' Cup the following season (1967–68). Most recent successes: European Cup 1963, 1969 and in 1973 won a double: European Cup-Winners' Cup and Italian F.A. Cup. Won the World Club title in 1969 against Estudiantes (Argentina) 4–2 on aggregate. Also won the now defunct Latin Cup in 1951 and 1956. Best-ever team was probably in 1955. Studded with stars, their line-up included Nils Liedholm and Gunnar Nordahl (Sweden), Eduardo Ricagni (Argentina), Arne Soerensen (Denmark) and Juan Schiaffino (Uruguay). Recent stars: Gianni Rivera, right-back Giuseppe Sabadini and left-winger Luciano Chiarugi.

Partizan Belgrade: The team of the Yugoslav Army who took over Belgrade S.K. (five times pre-war champions) in 1946. Play at the Partizan Stadium, capacity 60,000. Champions 11 times and F.A. Cup winners on five occasions. Won the league title four times in five seasons in the sixties. Their best side of recent years was probably that of 1965–66 which eliminated Manchester United in the European Cup semi-final with a superb rearguard action. They were then beaten in the Final 1–2 by Real Madrid after leading. Stars of the sixties: goalkeeper Milutin Soskic and full-back Fahrudin Jusufi and centre-half Velibor Vasovic, who retired after helping Ajax Amsterdam win the European Cup in 1971 and is now manager. Current star: Nenad Bjekovic.

SC Rapid: Vienna's traditional masters of the Austrian game, formed in 1898 and champions 25 times (a record). Also F.A. Cup winners seven times. Champions four times in the sixties. Cup winners in 1969 and did the Cup and League double in 1967–68. Also had the unique distinction of winning the German Championship and Cup during the war when Austria was annexed. Eliminated Real Madrid from the European Cup in 1969. Gerhardt Hanappi, a play-anywhere type, has been their greatest post-war star with 92 caps. Most recent success: F.A. Cup winners in 1971 and 1976.

Real Madrid: Founded in 1898 and rose to world eminence under chairmanship of Santiago Bernabeu, who built the 120,000-capacity Chamartin Stadium and signed Alfredo Di Stefano in the fifties. Champions of Spain 17 times (a record) and F.A. Cup winners 13 times. Champions five times in succession (1961–65), a record, and again in 1967, 1968 and 1969. Also Cup winners 1969–70, they went on to reach the European Cup-Winners' Cup Final in 1971. Latin Cup Winners 1955 and 1957, but best known for their fabulous team of the fifties which won the first five European Cup tournaments (1956 to 1960) with Di Stefano, Ferenc Puskas and Jose Santamaria the stars. Won the European Cup again in 1966 and Finalists in 1962 and 1964. First World Club Champions in 1960. Most recent success: Cup and league double in 1974–75 under Yugoslav manager Miljan Miljanic. Recent stars: Paul Breitner and Gunter Netzer, from West Germany; Roberto Martinez, from Argentina, and a galaxy of Spanish caps including goalkeeper Miguel Angel, Benito, Camacho, Pirri and Santillana.

Red Star Belgrade: Known pre-war as Jugoslawija FK, they were reformed in 1945 as the sports club of Belgrade University. Champions of Yugoslavia 12 times (a record) and F.A. Cup winners nine times (all in the post-war period). Most recent successes in seasons 1967–68, 1968–69 and 1969–70, when they achieved a league title hat-trick, adding the F.A. Cup to their honours in 1968 and 1970 to pull off two 'doubles': Champions again in 1973 and beaten Cup finalists. Best known players: Vladimir Beara (goalkeeper) and Rajko Mitic (inside-forward) in the fifties; Dragoslav Sekularec (inside-forward) in the sixties. Lost a string of stars to professional clubs after the 1974 World Cup.

A.S. St Etienne: Association Sportive St Etienne have taken over as pace-makers in the French game from Reims, and a link between the two is provided by Albert Batteux, coach of Reims in two European Cup Finals and of France when they took third place in the 1958 World Cup. Batteux joined the club in the sixties and led them to many successes before resigning and handing over to the current manager, former captain and international star Robert Herbin. Formed in 1920, they were a Division II club until 1938. They first won the championship in 1957 and the Cup in 1962, and it was Batteux's work in the 1960s that took them to the top. Champions nine times (including four in a row): 1957, 1964, 1967, 1968, 1969, 1970, 1974, 1975 and 1976. French Cup winners in 1962, 1968, 1970, 1974, 1975 and 1977, they have achieved cup and league double four times. Stars: 1975 French Footballer of the Year Jean-Michel Larque, the club captain; strikers Patrick and Hervé Revelli (brothers) and 20-year-old right-winger Dominique Rocheteau, who was capped in his first season of top-class football.

Slovan Bratislava: Known before the last war as S.K. Bratislava and after it as NV Bratislava, they adopted their current title in the 1950s. Their ground, the Tehelne Pole, accommodates 55,000 and is frequently used for international matches. A few hundred yards away is the home of Internacional Bratislava, formerly known as Red Star, with whom Slovan should not be confused. Slovan first became a force in Czech football when taking the championship (for the first time) in 1949 and repeating the feat in 1950 and 1951. Since then they have increased the number of championship successes to seven, including 1970 and the last two seasons, 1973–74 (when they completed a cup and league double) and 1974–75. Slovan surprised everyone by winning the European Cup-Winners' Cup in 1969, beating Barcelona 3–2 in the Final and taking a major trophy to Eastern Europe for the first time. They are managed by Jozef Venglos, a former international who played for the club in the fifties and is also assistant manager to the Czech national team, of which Slovan provides the backbone. Stars: Jan Pivarnik (captain and right-back of Czechoslovakia), Anton Ondrus, Marian Masny and the Capkovic twins, Jan and Jozef.

Spartak Moscow: Founded in 1922 and over the years one of the most consistent Russian clubs. Champions nine times and F.A. Cup winners on ten occasions. Most recent honours: Cup winners 1965, champions in 1969 and Cup winners again in 1971. Took the championship four times in the fifties (and the Cup three times) with star centre-forward Nikita Simonian the key man. His career record of 156 league goals for Spartak seems unassailable in the defence-dominated game played in Russia today.

Spartak Trnava: Firmly established as a Division II club, Trnava, a small town team in Slovakia, leapt into prominence in the 1960s. Under the guidance of former player Anton Malatinsky they won promotion and went on to dominate Czech football. Their first honour was the Czech F.A. Cup in 1967 and the Mitropa Cup. They took the F.A. Cup again in 1971 to complete a cup and league double. From 1967–68 they took the championship five times in six seasons. In 1970, when they failed in the league, Malatinsky was in Austria, working for Admira but returned to lead them to a double in 1971. Cup winners again in 1975, although struggling to replace veterans Ladislav Kuna, Jozef Adamec, Karol Dobias and Vladimir Hagara (now retired).

Sporting Lisbon: Eternal rivals of Benfica, they play at the 45,000 Estadio Jose Alvalade. Champions of Portugal 14 times and F.A. Cup winners on nine occasions. Champions in 1969–70 and after Benfica had overshadowed them in the 1970–71 title race, they had the satisfaction of crushing their neighbours 4–1 in the 1971 Cup Final. Also won the Cup in 1973 and the Cup and League double in 1974. In the international arena their best performance was to win the European Cup-Winners' Cup in 1964, beating Atalanta (Italy), Manchester United, Lyon (France) and, in the Final, MTK (Hungary). After losing 1–4 at Old Trafford that year, they produced an astonishing 5–0 victory over Manchester United in Lisbon. Provided seven men for Portugal's 1966 World Cup squad.

Standard Liège: Playing at the Stade de Sclessin (capacity 40,000), they have been pace-makers in the Belgian game since professionalism came into the open. Champions six times and F.A. Cup winners three times. In recent years have won the Cup in 1967, and the championship in successive seasons 1969, 1970 and 1971. The only Belgian club to reach the European Cup semi-finals, they did so in 1962, beating Real Madrid 2–0 in their home leg but losing 0–4 in Madrid. Best-known players of the sixties were Paul Bonga Bonga (Congo), Johnny Crossan (N. Ireland) and Istvan Sztani (Hungary). Recent teams included six Belgian internationals headed by goalkeeper Christian Piot, stopper Nico Dewalque and midfield dynamo Wilfried Van Moer.

Ujpest Dozsa: Founded in 1899 and now the team of the Hungarian Ministry of the Interior. The Dozsa Stadium, which holds

40,000, is probably the best-equipped club ground in Budapest. Champions 16 times and F.A. Cup winners four times. Most recent successes: 1969—Cup and League double; 1970—Cup and League double, 1970–71 (changeover season)—champions. League winners seven times in succession 1969 to 1975. Also winners of the Mitropa Cup in 1929 and 1939. Ujpest reached the Fairs Cup Final in 1969, losing 2–6 on aggregate to Newcastle United.

The World Cup

THE ORIGINAL WORLD CUP
Jules Rimet Trophy

THE F.I.F.A. WORLD CUP
First contested in 1974

The greatest football show on earth, the most prized possession in the soccer universe, is the World Cup, staged every four years. For the first 40 years of its existence it was known as the Jules Rimet trophy, after the French lawyer who aired the idea of a world football championship among nations when he became president of F.I.F.A. in 1920.

Ten years later the dream turned to reality with the launching of the World Cup in Montevideo, Uruguay . . . but when the tenth tournament was staged in West Germany in 1974, the prize at stake was of new design and titled not the Jules Rimet Cup but the F.I.F.A. World Cup.

The reason for the change of trophy dates from the time the rules were framed for the very first tournament in 1930. Included was a clause to the effect that if any country won the Jules Rimet Cup three times, it would become theirs permanently—and Brazil's success in Mexico in 1970 was their third world conquest in the last four series. Amid unprecedented scenes of welcome and celebration, they took home to Rio the original World Cup—made of solid gold and weighing nine pounds, though standing only a foot high—to keep for ever.

In Britain the tournament was not regarded as truly representative of world football until 1950 when, having rejoined F.I.F.A. after lengthy disagreement over amateurism and broken-time payments, the Home Countries became eligible to compete for the first time. The prize remained beyond British reach for another 16 years ; then, in 1966, England became the third host country to triumph, the first since 1934. They took it from Brazil with football that was functional, disciplined and supremely efficient. In Mexico four years later Brazil, committed to all-out attack to cover their suspect defence and weakness in goal, won it back with the magic and flair of Pele, Gerson, Jairzinho and Rivelino. No country could more worthily have won the World Cup outright.

The 1930 World Cup: Uruguay staged and won the first World Cup. Only 13 countries took part, and all 17 matches were played in Montevideo. Because of travelling difficulties and the lengthy absence involved in a trip by sea to South America and back, Europe's representatives were restricted to France, Yugoslavia, Rumania and Belgium. Uruguay, who had trained their players in isolation for two months, and Argentina each won their semi-final by 6–1 (against U.S.A. and Yugoslavia respectively), and in the first World Cup Final, played on 30 July 1930, the host country rallied from 2–1 down at half-time to triumph 4–2, to the delight of a 90,000 crowd.

The 1934 World Cup: The holders, Uruguay, refused to go to Italy to defend their title, as so few European countries had participated in the first tournament. Of the 16 nations who qualified from an entry of 29, 12 were from Europe. The 'group qualifying' method up to the semi-finals was replaced by an unsatisfactory knock-out system throughout—defeat at the first attempt meant that Brazil, Argentina and U.S.A. travelled halfway across the world for only one match each. Italy kicked off with the 7–1 thrashing of U.S.A., then beat Spain and Austria, both 1–0, to reach the Final against Czechoslovakia in Rome. There the unfancied Czechs took a surprise lead with 20 minutes left, but Italy scored a late equalizer and in extra time they squeezed home 2–1 to emulate Uruguay's feat as the second successive host nation to take the World Cup.

The 1938 World Cup: Now it was Argentina's turn to stay out, in protest over their request to stage the tournament being rejected. Instead, the series was held in Europe for the second successive series, this time in France, and Italy impressively retained the trophy. Victories over Norway, France and Brazil carried them to the Final, in which Hungary were well beaten by 4–2. Once again Italy, under the managership of Vittorio Pozzo, had done it, and with the Second World War soon to break out, they were to hold the Cup longer than anyone before or after—until 1950.

The 1950 World Cup: After an interval of 12 years, the war having erased two tournaments, the world football championship was resumed in Brazil. The British Association had rejoined F.I.F.A. in 1946, so were eligible for the first time, but only England entered; Scotland could have done so as runners-up in the Home Championship, but all along they had declared they would take part only if they were British Champions. In their first World Cup, England suffered their greatest-ever humiliation, for after beating Chile 2–0 in their opening match in Rio, they took the same eleven to Belo Horizonte on Sunday, 25 June, and ludicrously lost one–nil to the United States' part-timers. America won by a 30th-minute goal by their centre-forward Gaetjens, miraculously surviving a rearguard action that lasted all the second half. England contributed an equal part to their own destruction by missing so many chances. The team was: Williams; Ramsey, Aston, Wright, Hughes, Dickinson, Finney, Mannion, Bentley, Mortensen, Mullen. England's elimination was complete when Spain beat them 1–0 in Rio. This was the only time that the competition was based on four qualifying groups, whose winners went into a final pool which comprised Brazil, Spain, Sweden and Uruguay (participating for the first time since the inaugural tournament). After magnificent wins against Sweden (7–1) and Spain (6–1) in the final pool, Brazil needed only to draw with Uruguay in the grand finale to be crowned World Champions for the first time, and in anticipation the all-time world record attendance of 200,000 filled the Maracana Stadium. Brazil began brilliantly and scored first, directly after half-time, but with a superbly marshalled defence Uruguay gradually wore them down, then hit them with two smoothly taken goals to triumph 2–1 and bring their World Cup record to two conquests in two attempts spanning 20 years.

The 1954 World Cup: The fifth World Championship, in Switzerland, established the tournament format that was to be used until 1974, with four groups each providing two qualifiers to contest the quarter-finals and beyond on a knock-out system. Hungary, with Puskas, Hidegkuti and Kocsis superb in attack, were rated 'unbeatable'. In the previous six months they had shattered England's unbeaten home record against foreign countries with an astonishing 6–3 victory at Wembley and completed the double by 7–1 in Budapest. So England were hardly in better shape to face the world than when they had left Brazil demoralized four years earlier, and after topping their group with little conviction, they went out in the quarter-final 4–2 to Uruguay, who had still to be beaten in the World Cup after 24 years! Scotland's entry meant that Britain was doubly represented for the first time, but theirs was no more than a token appearance. In the qualifying group they failed to register a goal or a point, being humbled 7–0 by Uruguay and losing 1–0 to Austria. Meanwhile, Hungary clinched their group by slamming Korea 9–0 and Germany 8–3, and went through to the Final with

4–2 victories over both Brazil and Uruguay; but Germany countered their mastery with guile off the field and then deprived them of the World Cup on it. In their group match against Hungary, the Germans purposely fielded a weak team and did not mind losing 8–3 because they were confident that they could still qualify for the quarter-finals by beating Turkey in a play-off—and did so 7–2. Thus the easier passage to the Final was open to them, and they took it with wins by 2–0 against Yugoslavia and 6–1 against Austria. Yet, for all their strategy, Germany seemed to be heading for defeat in the Final as Puskas (playing for the first time since being injured in the group match against Germany) and Czibor gave Hungary a 2–0 lead. But skipper Fritz Walter rallied his side magnificently, and goals by Morlock and Rahn (2) earned Germany an extraordinary victory by 3–2, which made them the only country in World Cup history to win the trophy after being beaten during the final series.

The 1958 World Cup: In Sweden, Britain was represented for the only time by all four Home Countries, but England (apart from holding Brazil 0–0) and Scotland made no show. Surprisingly, it was the outsiders. Northern Ireland and Wales, who reached the quarter-finals. There, however, a catalogue of injuries proved insurmountable to Ireland, who lost 4–0 to France, and Brazil's one goal was too much for Wales. Hosts Sweden delighted their supporters by reaching the Final, then sent them almost delirious by scoring the first goal, but Brazil answered with one of the greatest exhibitions ever seen in a World Cup Final, devastatingly using 4–2–4 to stamp their mark on the tournament. Garrincha, Didi, Vava and a 17-year-old named Pele showed the world a new conception of attacking play, which brought them the biggest-ever World Cup victory by 5–2—Vava and Pele each scored twice—and a spectacular first success in the competition.

The 1962 World Cup: In contrast to Sweden, Chile staged the least memorable contest for the Jules Rimet Cup since it became a truly world-wide tournament. There was a saturation of negative, defence-ridden football and England, Britain's lone representatives, went out 3–1 to Brazil in the quarter-finals. Pele was lost to Brazil through injury early in the competition but, although now an ageing side and far less impressive than four years previously, they retained the trophy, beating Czechoslovakia in the Final 3–1 after being a goal down.

The 1966 World Cup: Four months before they staged and won the World Cup, England literally lost it. For 36 years the solid gold cup had been in existence. While in Italy's possession it had survived the war years hidden under the bed of Italian F.A. vice-president Dr Ottorino Barassi. Since 1958 it had been in the safe keeping of Brazil, and London saw it ceremonially for the first time in January

1966, at the making of the draw for the qualifying rounds of the final series. Two months later, at about midday on Sunday, 20 March, it vanished in a daring daylight theft from a padlocked cabinet while on display at a £3-million stamp exhibition at the Central Hall, Westminster. For seven days the football world was held spellbound with conjecture that the game's greatest trophy—like the F.A. Cup stolen in 1895—might never be seen again. Then a black and white mongrel dog named Pickles sniffed at a parcel lying under a laurel bush in the garden of his home in Upper Norwood, London—and the World Cup was found intact! The motive for the theft had been a ransom demand for £15,000 to Football Association chairman Joe Mears. One of the accomplices, a London dock labourer, was jailed for two years, while Pickles earned some £6000 in rewards for his owner and a medal for himself. And England, having lost and found the Jules Rimet Cup, won it at Wembley on 30 July in the most sensational World Cup Final of all.

The start of their march to glory, a 0–0 draw against Uruguay, could hardly have been less exciting for Wembley's 75,000 crowd. Then came two 2–0 wins to stir the blood a little, against Mexico (scorers Bobby Charlton and Roger Hunt) and France (Hunt 2). Argentina in the quarter-final posed the toughest problem yet, and England's World Cup hopes might have ended there had not Antonio Rattin, captain of the Argentinians, got himself sent off towards half-time for rough play and arguing with West German referee Rudolf Kreitlein. During a seven-minute hold-up before Rattin finally departed, the entire Argentine team threatened to walk off. The ten who eventually decided to stay stepped up their spoiling tactics and England struggled through 1–0 with a 77th-minute header by Geoff Hurst, replacing the injured Jimmy Greaves.

Brazil's hopes of a World Cup hat-trick dived when Pele was injured in the opening game against Bulgaria, and they failed to survive the qualifying stage. While England were playing that nasty quarter-final with Argentina at Wembley, up at Goodison Park, Portugal and rank outsiders North Korea produced a match straight out of the realms of fiction. Having shocked Italy 1–0 at Middlesbrough to qualify, Pak Doo Ik and his happy-go-lucky Korean teammates went one . . . two . . . three up against Portugal. But they lacked the tactical know-how to hold such an advantage, and Eusebio, striking irresistible form, scored the first four goals (two of them penalties) in Portugal's eventual victory by 5–3. At Hillsborough, Sheffield, West Germany comprehensively beat Uruguay 4–0, and in the other quarter-final at Sunderland Russia defeated Hungary 2–1.

The semi-finals provided an enormous contrast. At Goodison, West Germany scored a laborious 2–1 win against Russia (who were quickly reduced to ten fit men by injury to Sabo, and to nine when Chislenko was sent off for retaliation after a foul that injured him, too). At Wembley the following night the score was also 2–1, but this game between England and Portugal put the seal of world stature back on the competition. In terms of technique it was the finest match of the whole series in England. Bobby Charlton cracked both England goals; late on, brother Jack handled from the spot Eusebio explosively took his only chance of the game—the first time Banks's net had been stretched in the tournament.

For only the second time, the first since 1934, the Final went to an extra half-hour. Haller shot West Germany ahead after 13 minutes, but Hurst equalized six minutes later with a splendid header from Bobby Moore's free-kick and, with 13 minutes left, victory seemed assured as Martin Peters scored at close range after Hurst's shot had been blocked. But in the last seconds Weber slammed Germany level from a disputed free-kick by Emmerich, and at two-all the match went into extra-time. England found the inspiration they needed to win the game all over again in the ceaseless running of Ball. His was the centre which Hurst hammered in off the crossbar for the third goal—Swiss referee Gottfried Dienst awarded it after what seemed a timeless consultation with his Russian linesman Tofik Bakhramov—and through to the closing seconds Moore and his men clung desperately to their lead. Then, in a last-fling attack, West Germany left themselves uncovered at the back and Hurst pounded away down the left flank from halfway and finished with a lashing left-foot shot past Tilkowski from 20 yards. Moments later, England fans in their thousands swept across the Wembley pitch to acclaim the incongruously unemotional Alf Ramsey, who had fashioned the triumph with his wingless, 4–3–3 tactics; to mob the three-goal hero Hurst, first man to score a hat-trick in the World Cup Final; and to salute the whole team with chants of 'Eng-land! Eng-land!' that billowed across the vast arena as Bobby Moore collected the world's greatest soccer prize.

The 1970 World Cup: By winning all six matches they were required to play in Mexico, Brazil worthily became the first country to take the World Cup three times and, in doing so, they won the trophy outright. Compared with the lowest-ever aggregate of 89 goals in each of the two previous tournaments, the 32-match programme now produced 95, with Brazil responsible for 19 of them. It mattered not that they had a suspect defence; their game was based on creation in midfield and a flair for all-out attack in which Pele, kicked out of the two previous World Cups, once again touched his spectacular best in this his fourth tournament. England, as indeed most of the European countries did, overcame the problems of altitude and heat better than expected. They were based at Guadalajara, and Hurst began as he had finished in 1966 —on the scoresheet. England's three group qualifying matches each produced a 1–0 result, with wins against Rumania and Czecho-slovakia and defeat by Jairzinho's goal against Brazil. It was enough to take them through to the quarter-finals as group runners-up to Brazil. Then, with the venue switching to Leon, they were paired with West Germany. For an hour England played as splendidly as they had done against them in the 1966 Final, and when Martin Peters added to Alan Mullery's first-half goal directly after half-time, a lead of 2–0 looked unassailable. But Beckenbauer put Germany back in the game with a diagonal shot that flashed under Bonetti (Banks was in bed, the victim of a stomach bug) and England were shaken again as Seeler scored with a back-header. So, again as in the Wembley Final, the sides went into extra time at 2–2, and in the second period Muller, right in front of the target, smashed in the goal that gave Germany victory by 3–2 and avenged 1966. There were inevitable question-marks—over the tactical substitution of Bobby Charlton (in his record-breaking 106th International) and Norman Hunter, as well as over two of the German goals—but nothing could alter the fact that the World Champions had been dethroned.

In the other quarter-finals Brazil overcame some difficult moments to beat Peru 4–2 in Guadalajara; Uruguay dismissed Russia 1–0 on a disputed goal in the last minute of extra time in Mexico City; and Italy, having scored only one goal in three matches to head their qualifying group, threw away caution, when a goal down, to the hosts Mexico in Toluca, and won 4–1.

Goals were cheap, in extra time, anyway, in the Mexico City semi-final between Italy and West Germany. Boninsegna gave Italy an early lead, and that was still the only goal as the match went into injury time. Then Schnellinger equalized, and West Germany went ahead with the first of five goals scored in the extra half-hour, which finished with Italy winners of an extraordinary match by 4–3. In the other semi-final in Guadalajara, Uruguay took a shock lead, but Brazil, albeit belatedly, turned on the full range of talents and won 3–1, with goals by Clodoaldo, Jairzinho and Rivelino.

The Azteca Stadium, home of Mexican football, did not see Brazil until the Final itself. Their performance in beating Italy 4–1 was well worth the wait. It started with Pele heading in Rivelino's cross after 18 minutes, and although Italy were level by half-time, Boninsegna punishing one of those defensive mistakes to which Brazil were prone, midfield general Gerson restored the lead with a magnificent shot from outside the penalty-area. Gerson and Pele combined to set up the third goal for Jairzinho, and the final scene was stolen by Brazil's captain, Carlos Alberto. He shot a stunning last goal from Pele's perfect pass, and three minutes later he stepped forward to receive the Jules Rimet Cup that was to be Brazil's to keep. Their hat-trick was an incredible achievement for Mario Zagalo, a member of the winning teams in 1958 and 1962, and now triumphant again only a few months after succeeding Joao Saldanha as Brazil's manager.

The 1974 World Cup: Helmut Schoen's West Germany, fourth host nation to win the title, also became the first country to hold the World and European Championships simultaneously. Unimpressive through the group stage, in which they were beaten 1–0 by East Germany in Hamburg, they then showed improving blend with each match and reached a peak when it mattered most—in the Final against the stylists of Holland.

For the third consecutive World Cup, the Finals opened with a goalless match, on this occasion Brazil v. Yugoslavia, and by the time the competition was completed its total of 97 goals in 38 matches represented the lowest scoring average (2.55 per game) in history. The presence of unknowns such as Australia, Haiti and Zaire provided new faces; combined with the absence of such as England, Hungary, Belgium and Portugal, it ridiculed any suggestion that the world's sixteen strongest countries were competing in West Germany.

England, finishing with Wales behind Poland, failed to qualify for the first time, and Scotland were left to carry Britain's banner in the Finals. If there were times when Willie Ormond's players earned less than full marks for discipline off the field, they 'distinguished' themselves as the only country not to lose a game in West Germany. In retrospect, however, their opening match, a 2–0 win against Zaire, was their undoing. One more goal in the last hour would have taken them on; instead Brazil, who failed to replace sufficient stars of the triumphant 1970 side, qualified at Scotland's expense with Yugoslavia from Group 2.

East and West Germany went through from Group 1; Holland topped Group 3 by a point from Sweden; and in Group 4 Poland (conquerors of England on the way to Germany) took maximum points and most goals (12) by beating Argentine, Haiti and Italy. Two goals against both Argentina and Haiti set Polish striker Lato on the way to becoming the tournament's top scorer with a total of seven.

With quarter-finals and semi-finals discontinued, the last eight played in two groups on a league basis. More matches produced more revenue, but the knock-out element was missing. In Group A, Holland gave the most scintillating display of the whole tournament when beating Argentina 4–0 with goals by Cruyff (2), Krol and Rep. After defeating East Germany 2–0, Holland needed only to draw with the holders Brazil in their remaining qualifier to reach the Final, and they answered tough tactics that were unworthy of the reigning Champions with goals by Neeskens and Cruyff to win the group with a 100 per cent record.

On a rain-ruined pitch at Frankfurt, West Germany beat Poland by Muller's lone goal to clinch Group B with another 100 per cent record . . . and so to a dramatic Final in Munich on 7 July. Direct from the kick-off and before even one German had touched the ball, Cruyff was brought down by Hoeness. English referee Jack

Taylor awarded the first penalty in the history of World Cup Finals, and Neeskens scored the fastest World Cup Final goal on record.

Twenty-five minutes later the ball was on the penalty spot again after left-winger Holzenbein was floored. Breitner scored the equalizer, and two minutes before half-time Bonhof's right-wing run led to the winner by Muller—his last goal before announcing his retirement from international football. What a farewell!

Individual style within the framework of brilliant team play had made Holland the most attractive team in the tournament under the management of Rinus Michels, Barcelona and former Ajax coach. They still made second-half chances, but could not put them away. So the new F.I.F.A. World Cup was presented to Franz Beckenbauer, and West Germany, twenty years after their first success, were World Champions again. For their eighth time in ten Finals the winners had come from behind to take the crown.

WORLD CUP SUMMARIES

1930 World Cup—First Tournament—in Uruguay

Winners: Uruguay. **Runners-up:** Argentina. **Third:** U.S.A. **Entries:** 13.

Other countries taking part: Belgium, Bolivia, Brazil, Chile, France, Mexico, Paraguay, Peru, Rumania, Yugoslavia.

All matches played in Montevideo.

Top scorer in tournament: Stabile (Argentina) 8 goals.

Final:

Uruguay 4 (Dorado, Cea, Iriarte, Castro), *Argentina* 2 (Peucelle, Stabile).

Half-time: Uruguay 1, Argentina 2. *Attendance:* 90,000.

Uruguay: Ballesteros; Nasazzi, Mascheroni, Andrade, Fernandez, Gestido, Dorado, Scarone, Castro, Cea, Iriarte.

Argentina: Botasso; Della Torre, Paternoster, Evaristo (J), Monti, Suarez, Eucelle, Varallo, Stabile, Ferreira, Evaristo (M).

1934 World Cup—Second Tournament—in Italy

Winners: Italy. **Runners-up:** Czechoslovakia. **Third:** Germany. **Entries:** 29 (16 qualifiers).

Other countries taking part in final series: Argentina, Austria, Belgium, Brazil, Egypt, France, Holland, Hungary, Rumania, Spain, Sweden, Switzerland, U.S.A.

Venues: Rome, Naples, Milan, Turin, Florence, Bologna, Genoa, Trieste.

Top scorers in tournament: Schiavio (Italy), Nejedly (Czechoslovakia), Conen (Germany) each 4 goals.

Final (Rome):
Italy 2 (Orsi, Schiavio), *Czechoslovakia* 1 (Puc). After extra time.
Half-time: Italy 0, Czechoslovakia 1. *Score after 90 minutes:* 1–1.
    Attendance: 50,000.
Italy: Combi; Monzeglio, Allemandi, Ferraris, Monti, Bertolini,
    Guaita, Meazza, Schiavio, Ferrari, Orsi.
Czechoslovakia: Planicka; Zenisek, Ctyroky, Kostalek, Cambal,
    Krcil, Junek, Svoboda, Sobotka, Nejedly, Puc.

1938 World Cup—Third Tournament—in France

Winners: Italy. **Runners-up:** Hungary. **Third:** Brazil. **Entries:**
    25 (15 qualifiers).
Other countries taking part in final series: Belgium, Cuba,
    Czechoslovakia, Dutch East Indies, France, Germany, Holland,
    Norway, Poland, Rumania, Sweden, Switzerland.
Venues: Paris, Marseilles, Bordeaux, Lille, Antibes, Strasbourg,
    Le Havre, Reims, Toulouse.
Top scorer in tournament: Leonidas (Brazil) 8 goals.

Final (Paris):
Italy 4 (Colaussi 2, Piola 2), *Hungary* 2 (Titkos, Sarosi).
Half-time: Italy 3, Hungary 1. *Attendance:* 45,000.
Italy: Olivieri; Foni, Rava, Serantoni, Andreolo, Locatelli, Biavati,
    Meazza, Piola, Ferrari, Colaussi.
Hungary: Szabo; Polgar, Biro, Szalay, Szucs, Lazar, Sas, Vincze,
    Sarosi, Szengeller, Titkos.

1950 World Cup—Fourth Tournament—in Brazil

Winners: Uruguay. **Runners-up:** Brazil. **Third:** Sweden.
    Entries: 29 (13 qualifiers).
Other countries taking part in final series: Bolivia, Chile
    England, Italy, Mexico, Paraguay, Spain, Switzerland, U.S.A.,
    Yugoslavia.
Venues: Rio de Janeiro, São Paulo, Recife, Curitiba, Belo Horizonte,
    Porto Alegre.
Top scorer in tournament: Ademir (Brazil) 7 goals.

* Deciding Match (Rio de Janeiro):
Uruguay 2 (Schiaffino, Ghiggia), *Brazil* 1 (Friaca).
Half-time: 0–0. *Attendance:* 200,000.
Uruguay: Maspoli; Gonzales, Tejera, Gambetta, Varela, Andrade,
    Ghiggia, Perez, Miguez, Schiaffino, Moran.
Brazil: Barbosa; Augusto, Juvenal, Bauer, Danilo, Bigode, Friaca,
    Zizinho, Ademir, Jair, Chico.
* For the only time, the World Cup was decided on a Final Pool
system, in which the winners of the four qualifying groups met in a
six-match series. So, unlike previous and subsequent tournaments,

there was no official Final as such, but Uruguay v. Brazil was the deciding final match in the Final Pool.

1954 World Cup—Fifth Tournament—in Switzerland

Winners: Germany. **Runners-up:** Hungary. **Third:** Austria. **Entries:** 35 (16 qualifiers).
Other countries taking part in final series: Belgium. Brazil, Czechoslovakia, England, France, Italy, Korea, Mexico, Scotland, Switzerland, Turkey, Uruguay, Yugoslavia.
Venues: Berne, Zürich, Lausanne, Basle, Geneva, Lugano.
Top scorer in tournament: Kocsis (Hungary) 11 goals.

Final (Berne)
Germany 3 (Morlock, Rahn 2), *Hungary* 2 (Puskas, Czibor).
Half-time: 2–2. *Attendance:* 60,000.
Germany: Turek ; Posipal, Kohlmeyer, Eckel, Liebrich, Mai, Rahn, Morlock, Walter (O), Walter (F), Schaefer.
Hungary: Grosics ; Buzansky, Lantos, Boszik, Lorant, Zakarias, Czibor, Kocsis, Hidegkuti, Puskas, Toth.

1958 World Cup—Sixth Tournament—in Sweden

Winners: Brazil. **Runners-up:** Sweden. **Third:** France. **Entries:** 47 (16 qualifiers).
Other countries taking part in final series: Argentina, Austria, Czechoslovakia, England, Hungary, Mexico, Northern Ireland, Paraguay, Russia, Scotland, Wales, West Germany, Yugoslavia.
Venues: Stockholm, Gothenburg, Malmö, Norrköping, Borås, Sandviken, Eskilstuna, Cerebro, Västeras, Hälsingborg, Halmstad.
Top scorer in tournament: Fontaine (France) 13 goals.

Final (Stockholm):
Brazil 5 (Vava 2, Pele 2, Zagalo), *Sweden* 2 (Liedholm, Simonsson)
Half-time: Brazil 2, Sweden 1. *Attendance:* 50,000.
Brazil: Gilmar ; Santos (D), Santos (N), Zito, Bellini, Orlando, Garrincha, Didi, Vava, Pele, Zagalo.
Sweden: Svensson ; Bergmark, Axbom, Boerjesson, Gustavsson, Parling, Hamrin, Gren, Simonsson, Liedholm, Skoglund.

1962 World Cup—Seventh Tournament—in Chile

Winners: Brazil. **Runners-up:** Czechoslovakia. **Third:** Chile. **Entries:** 53 (16 qualifiers).
Other countries taking part in final series: Argentina, Bulgaria, Colombia, England, Hungary, Italy, Mexico, Russia, Spain, Switzerland, Uruguay, West Germany, Yugoslavia.
Venues: Santiago, Vina del Mar, Rancagua, Arica.
Top scorers in tournament: Garrincha (Brazil), Vava (Brazil),

Sanchez (Chile), Albert (Hungary), Ivanov (Russia), Jerkovic (Yugoslavia) each 4 goals.

Final (Santiago):
Brazil 3 (Amarildo, Zito, Vava), *Czechoslovakia* 1 (Masopust).
Half-time: 1–1. *Attendance:* 69,000.
Brazil: Gilmar; Santos (D), Mauro, Zozimo, Santos (N), Zito, Didi, Garrincha, Vava, Amarildo, Zagalo.
Czechoslovakia: Schroiff; Tichy, Novak, Pluskal, Popluhar, Masopust, Pospichal, Scherer, Kvasniak, Kadraba, Jelinek.

1966 World Cup—Eighth Tournament—in England

Winners: England. **Runners-up:** West Germany. **Third:** Portugal.
Entries: 53 (16 qualifiers).
Other countries taking part in final series: Argentina, Brazil, Bulgaria, Chile, France, Hungary, Italy, Mexico, North Korea, Russia, Spain, Switzerland, Uruguay.
Venues: London (Wembley and White City), Sheffield (Hillsborough), Liverpool (Goodison Park), Sunderland, Middlesbrough, Manchester (Old Trafford), Birmingham (Villa Park).
Top scorer in tournament: Eusebio (Portugal) 9 goals.

Final (Wembley):
England 4 (Hurst 3, Peters), *West Germany* 2 (Haller, Weber). After extra time.
Half-time: 1–1. *Score after 90 minutes:* 2–2. *Attendance:* 100,000.
England: Banks; Cohen, Wilson, Stiles, Charlton (J), Moore, Ball, Hurst, Hunt, Charlton (R), Peters.
West Germany: Tilkowski; Hottges, Schnellinger, Beckenbauer, Schulz, Weber, Haller, Held, Seeler, Overath, Emmerich.

1970 World Cup—Ninth Tournament—in Mexico

Winners: Brazil. **Runners-up:** Italy. **Third:** West Germany.
Entries: 68 (16 qualifiers).
Other countries taking part in final series: Belgium, Bulgaria, Czechoslovakia, El Salvador, England, Israel, Mexico, Morocco, Peru, Rumania, Russia, Sweden, Uruguay.
Venues: Mexico City, Guadalajara, Leon, Puebla, Toluca.
Top scorer in tournament: Muller (West Germany) 10 goals.

Final (Mexico City):
Brazil 4 (Pele, Gerson, Jairzinho, Carlos Alberto), *Italy* 1 (Boninsegna).
Half-time: 1–1. *Attendance:* 107,000.
Brazil: Felix; Carlos Alberto, Brito, Piazza, Everaldo, Clodoaldo, Gerson, Jairzinho, Tostao, Pele, Rivelino.
Italy: Albertosi; Burgnich, Facchetti, Cera, Rosato, Bertini (substitute Juliano), Domenghini, De Sisti, Mazzola, Boninsegna (substitute Rivera), Riva.

1974 World Cup—Tenth Tournament—in West Germany

Winners: West Germany. **Runners-up:** Holland. **Third:** Poland.
  Entries: 98 (16 qualifiers).
Other countries taking part in final series: Argentina,
  Australia, Brazil, Bulgaria, Chile, East Germany, Haiti, Italy,
  Scotland, Sweden, Uruguay, Yugoslavia, Zaire.
Venues: Berlin, Hamburg, Frankfurt, Dortmund, Gelsenkirchen,
  Hanover, Dusseldorf, Stuttgart, Munich.
Top scorer in tournament: Lato (Poland) 7 goals.

Final (Munich):
West Germany 2 (Breitner—penalty, Muller), *Holland* 1 (Neeskens—
penalty).
Half-time: 2–1. *Attendance:* 77,833.
West Germany: Maier; Vogts, Schwarzenbeck, Beckenbauer,
Breitner, Bonhof, Hoeness, Overath, Grabowski, Muller, Holzen-
bein.
Holland: Jongbloed; Suurbier, Rijsbergen (substitute De Jong),
Haan, Krol, Jansen, Van Hanegem, Neeskens, Rep, Cruyff,
Rensenbrink (substitute R. Van der Kerkhof).

OTHER WORLD CUP FACTS

The F.I.F.A. World Cup, replacing the Jules Rimet trophy which
Brazil won outright in 1970, is made of 18 carat gold, stands 20 in.
high and weighs 11 lb. Designed in Italy, it depicts two figures holding up the world and was valued at £17,000 when made.

The individual goalscoring record for a World Cup final series
is 13 by Just Fontaine (France) in the 1958 tournament in Sweden.
Two other players have reached a double-figure total: Sandor
Kocsis with 11 goals for Hungary (Switzerland, 1954 tournament)
and Gerd Muller with 10 for West Germany (Mexico, 1970).

Host countries have won four of the ten World Cup tournaments:
Uruguay in 1930, Italy in 1934, England in 1966 and West Germany
in 1974. This is how the other host nations have fared: 1938—
France, unplaced; 1950—Brazil, runners-up; 1954—Switzerland,
unplaced; 1958—Sweden, runners-up; 1962—Chile, third;
1970—Mexico, unplaced.

Hungary set two records that still stand when they were
runners-up to West Germany in the 1954 World Cup in Switzerland.
Their 9–0 win against Korea was the highest score in any Final series
(equalled by Yugoslavia 9, Zaire 0 in West Germany, 1974), and

their total of 27 goals remains the most ever scored by one country in any series of the World Cup proper.

Highest match aggregates in World Cup Final series: 12—Austria 7, Switzerland 5 (Switzerland, 1954); 11—Brazil 6, Poland 5 (France, 1938) and Hungary 8, Germany 3 (Switzerland, 1954).

Mexican goalkeeper Antonio Carbajal holds a World Cup record that may never be equalled. He represented his country in *five* tournaments: in Brazil 1950, Switzerland 1954, Sweden 1958, Chile 1962 and, finally, at Wembley in 1966.

England did not enter the first three World Cup tournaments (1930, 1934 and 1938). This is how they have fared in the competition:
1950 finished second in qualifying group; 1954 beaten in quarter-final; 1958 beaten in play-off for quarter-final place; 1962 beaten in quarter-final; 1966 Winners; 1970 beaten in quarter-final. 1974 failed to qualify for first time.
Scotland's record: 1954 bottom in qualifying group; 1958 bottom in qualifying group. 1974 Britain's only qualifiers—third (unbeaten) in qualifying group.
Northern Ireland's record: 1958 beaten in quarter-final.
Wales's record: 1958 beaten in quarter-final.
Britain has only twice been represented by more than one country in the World Cup Final series—in 1954, when England and Scotland participated in Switzerland, and in 1958, when England, Scotland, Northern Ireland and Wales all qualified for the tournament held in Sweden.

In eight of the ten World Cup Finals the eventual winners have been behind at one stage of the match. The exceptions: Italy 1938 and Brazil 1970.

World Cup Final Results

1930	(Montevideo)	Uruguay	4	Argentina	2
1934	(Rome)	Italy	2	Czechoslovakia	1
		(after extra time)			
1938	(Paris)	Italy	4	Hungary	2
1950	(Rio de Janeiro)	Uruguay	2	Brazil	1
1954	(Berne)	Germany	3	Hungary	2
1958	(Stockholm)	Brazil	5	Sweden	2
1962	(Santiago)	Brazil	3	Czechoslovakia	1
1966	(Wembley)	England	4	West Germany	2
		(after extra time)			
1970	(Mexico City)	Brazil	4	Italy	1
1974	(Munich)	West Germany	2	Holland	1

Venues for the World Cup tournaments after Argentina in 1978 have been arranged as follows: 1982 Spain, 1986 Yugoslavia.

THE 1978 WORLD CUP

The draw for the qualifying round of the eleventh World Cup tournament—scheduled for Argentina from June 1 1978—was made in Guatemala City on 20 November 1975. There were 102 entries, from which the following 16 countries qualified: West Germany (holders), Argentina (hosts), Poland, Italy, Austria, Holland, France, Sweden, Scotland, Spain, Hungary, Iran, Mexico, Tunisia, Brazil, Peru. This is how the groups finished:

GROUP 1

	P	W	D	L	F	A	Pts
Poland	6	5	1	0	17	4	11
Portugal	6	4	1	1	12	6	9
Denmark	6	2	0	4	14	12	4
Cyprus	6	0	0	6	3	24	0

GROUP 2

	P	W	D	L	F	A	Pts
Italy	6	5	0	1	18	4	10
England	6	5	0	1	15	4	10
Finland	6	2	0	4	11	16	4
Luxembourg	6	0	0	6	2	22	0

GROUP 3

	P	W	D	L	F	A	Pts
Austria	6	4	2	0	14	2	10
East Germany	6	3	3	0	15	4	9
Turkey	6	2	1	3	9	5	5
Malta	6	0	0	6	0	27	0

GROUP 4

	P	W	D	L	F	A	Pts
Holland	6	5	1	0	11	3	11
Belgium	6	3	0	3	8	6	6
N. Ireland	6	2	1	3	7	7	5
Iceland	6	1	0	5	2	12	2

GROUP 5

	P	W	D	L	F	A	Pts
France	4	2	1	1	7	4	5
Bulgaria	4	1	2	1	5	6	4
Rep. of Ireland	4	1	1	2	2	4	3

GROUP 6

	P	W	D	L	F	A	Pts
Sweden	4	3	0	1	7	4	6
Norway	4	2	0	2	3	4	4
Switzerland	4	1	0	3	3	5	2

GROUP 7

	P	W	D	L	F	A	Pts
Scotland	4	3	0	1	6	3	6
Czechoslovakia	4	2	0	2	4	6	4
Wales	4	1	0	3	3	4	2

GROUP 8

	P	W	D	L	F	A	Pts
Spain	4	3	0	1	4	1	6
Romania	4	2	0	2	7	8	4
Yugoslavia	4	1	0	3	6	8	2

GROUP 9

	P	W	D	L	F	A	Pts
Hungary	4	2	1	1	6	4	5
Russia	4	2	0	2	5	3	4
Greece	4	1	1	2	2	6	3

* Hungary beat Bolivia 9–2 on aggregate in play-off for place in finals with third-placed country in the South American group

ASIA/OCEANIA GROUP (Final Pool)

	P	W	D	L	F	A	Pts
Iran	8	6	2	0	12	3	14
Korea	8	3	4	1	10	6	10
Kuwait	8	3	2	3	13	9	8
Australia	8	3	2	3	12	8	8
Hong Kong	8	0	0	8	3	24	0

CENTRAL/NORTH AMERICA GROUP

	P	W	D	L	F	A	Pts
Mexico	5	5	0	0	20	5	10
Haiti	5	3	1	1	6	6	7
Canada	5	2	1	2	8	9	5
Salvador	5	2	1	2	9	10	5
Guatemala	5	1	1	3	8	10	3
Surinam	5	0	0	5	6	17	0

AFRICA GROUP (Final Pool)

	P	W	D	L	F	A	Pts
Tunisia	4	2	1	1	7	4	5
Egypt	4	2	0	2	7	11	4
Nigeria	4	1	1	2	5	4	3

SOUTH AMERICA (Final Pool)

	P	W	D	L	F	A	Pts
Brazil	2	2	0	0	9	0	4
Peru	2	1	0	1	5	1	2
Bolivia	2	0	0	2	0	13	0

Brazil and Peru qualify. Bolivia lost play-off with Hungary.

The European Championship

Originally known as the Henri Delaunay Cup, after its French founder, later as the Nations Cup, and now as the European Championship, it was introduced in 1958. The tournament takes two years to complete, with the Final scheduled to take place exactly halfway between one World Cup and the next. The qualifying competition is divided into eight groups, with quarter-final ties decided on a home-and-away basis. The semi-finals and Final are staged in one of the last four surviving countries. Semi-final and Final results:

1958–60: in France
Semi-finals: Yugoslavia 5, France 4 (Paris) ; Russia 3, Czechoslovakia 0 (Marseilles).
Final (Paris) : *Russia* 2, Yugoslavia 1 (after extra time).

1962–64: in Spain
Semi-finals: Russia 3, Denmark 0 (Barcelona) ; Spain 2, Hungary 1 (Madrid).
Final (Madrid) : *Spain* 2, Russia 1.

1966–68: in Italy
Semi-finals: Yugoslavia 1, England 0 (Florence) ; Italy 0, Russia 0 (Naples) after extra time—Italy won on toss.
Final (Rome) : *Italy* 2, Yugoslavia 0 in replay after 1–1 draw.

1970–72: in Belgium
Semi-finals: Russia 1, Hungary 0 (Brussels) ; West Germany 2, Belgium 1 (Antwerp).
Final (Brussels) : *West Germany* 3, Russia 0.

1974–76: in Yugoslavia
Semi-finals: Czechoslovakia 3, Holland 1 (Zagreb) ; West Germany 4, Yugoslavia 2 (Belgrade).
Final (Belgrade) : *Czechoslovakia* 2, West Germany 2 (Czechoslovakia won 5–3 on penalties).

The European Cup

In its 21-year history, the European Cup has presented a standard of international club football that could hardly have been imagined when it was launched in 1955. The idea was conceived by French soccer journalist Gabriel Hanot, a former international player, and developed rapidly after a meeting which he and the proprietors of his newspaper, *L'Equipe*, called in Paris in the spring of 1955 among all the leading European clubs. Six months later the dream became reality, and so began a contest bringing together the champion clubs of all the European countries and now long-established as football's greatest tournament outside the World Cup.

In 1949 Hanot had been a prominent figure in the introduction of the Latin Cup, featuring the champion clubs of France, Spain, Italy and Portugal. As long ago as 1927 a similar competition, the Mitropa Cup, had been started in Central Europe among the principal clubs of Austria, Czechoslovakia, Hungary, Italy and Yugoslavia. By combining these two tournaments, and inviting the champion teams of North and Western Europe to participate, Hanot found the formula for the European Cup.

The champions of 17 countries entered the opening tournament in season 1955–56, but Chelsea subsequently withdrew under pressure from the Football League, who saw the new venture as a threat to their own competition. A year later Manchester United, disregarding the Establishment, took part. Fittingly, in 1968, they became the first English club to win the trophy—ten years after a European Cup journey had decimated the Old Trafford club with the Munich air disaster.

Ironically, although France was the birthplace of the European Cup and the first final was staged in Paris, no French club has taken the prize.

With bewildering football, Spanish champions Real Madrid made the competition their own 'spectacular', winning it for the first five years (1956–60). In the last of that astonishing sequence of finals, they beat the German champions, Eintracht Frankfurt, by 7–3 at Hampden Park, Glasgow, with one of the most dazzling displays in the game's history. Outshining all others in a magnificent team performance were Real's legendary strikers Ferenc Puskas, who scored four goals, and Alfredo di Stefano, who got the other three.

Real Madrid appeared in eight of the first eleven European Cup finals and won the trophy on six of those occasions. Either as its holders or as champions of Spain, they took part in the first 15 seasons of the competition and the following year (1970–71) reached the final of the European Cup-Winners' Cup.

Until the inception of the European Cup, Real Madrid were little known outside Spain. Suddenly they found themselves the centre of world-wide acclaim—and if Real Madrid made the European Cup, it can also be said that the 'European Coupe des Clubs Champions' made Real. Their vast profits from the competition were invested in a permanent monument to their triumphs with the construction of the 120,000-capacity Bernabeu Stadium in the Chamartin suburb of Madrid.

For the first 11 years the European Cup was the 'Latins' Cup', with Spanish, Portuguese and Italian clubs dominating the tournament. During that period its winners came exclusively from three cities: Madrid, Lisbon and Milan.

Britain, through the medium of Glasgow Celtic, finally broke the Latin grip in 1967. Entering the competition for the first time, they had a comfortable passage through the rounds against Zürich, Nantes, Vojvodina and Dukla. The final, in Lisbon, brought them opposition of the strongest calibre in Inter-Milan, and after falling behind to an early penalty, Celtic saved the tie with Gemmell's second-half equalizer and, five minutes from the end, won it with a goal by Chalmers.

Thus Jock Stein's magnificent Celtic put Britain's hand on the European Cup for the first time. At Wembley a year later England took possession of it from Scotland with a wonderful extra-time victory by Manchester United against Benfica. Three times before —in 1957, 1958 and 1966—Matt Busby's men had been foiled at the semi-final stage. Now, in 1968, they beat their bogey, winning the first leg against Real Madrid by Best's only goal at Old Trafford and storming back from 3–1 down with 18 minutes left to draw the return match in Madrid 3–3, so winning the tie 4–3 on aggregate.

The Final, on 29 May 1968, produced at Wembley an emotional occasion which approached England's 1966 World Cup triumph. Remembering how close Manchester United had been to European success in the past, unable to forget how the European Cup had destroyed the famous 'Busby Babes' in the snows of Munich Airport in 1958, everyone, it seemed, was willing them to victory over Benfica, the Eagles of Lisbon.

Charlton's dipping header early in the second half looked to be sufficient when, with 11 minutes left, that was still the only goal. Then Graca smashed Benfica level, and Stepney miraculously held Eusebio's shot to earn extra time. It was a save that lifted the hearts of United and, with fresh wind in their sails, they moved majestically to victory. Aston demoralized Benfica's right defensive flank, and from the moment Best beat one man, then dribbled the 'keeper, to put United back in front, the European Cup was destined for Old Trafford, the margin stretching to 4–1 as Kidd celebrated his 19th birthday by heading in a crossbar rebound and Charlton himself, shooting the final goal.

A year later AC Milan took the European Cup back to Italy, thus sharing four successes in the competition for that country equally with Inter-Milan. In 1970 Celtic were finalists again, and following Arsenal's victory in the Fairs Cup and Manchester City's success in the Cup-Winners' Cup, there was the prospect of a clean sweep by Britain in all three European tournaments.

In anticipation, 25,000 fanatical Celtic supporters travelled to Milan—the biggest following any British team has ever had abroad —for the final against Dutch 'outsiders' Feyenoord. In the semi-final Celtic had twice beaten Leeds United; in Milan full-back Gemmell shot them ahead after half an hour and the Cup seemed to be heading for Glasgow again. But Feyenoord equalized, dominated the second half, and deservedly triumphed.

In 1971 Wembley staged its third European Champion Clubs' Final, in which Ajax (Amsterdam) kept the prize in Dutch possession by beating Panathinaikos, of Greece, 2–0. Ajax retained the trophy in 1972 and 1973, again without conceding a goal in either Final, and so became the first club to win the European Cup in three successive seasons since Real Madrid in the competition's early years.

Ajax's reign as European Champions ended with the departure of ace forward Johan Cruyff to Barcelona, and in 1974 Bayern Munich earned West Germany the trophy for the first time. Yet with barely a minute left in the final in Brussels, the prize seemed destined for Atletico Madrid (who had dealt brutally with Celtic in a goalless semi-final first leg in Glasgow and won the return 2–0). Justice was done, however, when Bayern centre-back Schwarzenbeck equalized in the closing seconds, and in the first replayed final in European Cup history the German champions switched to all-out attack and triumphed 4–0, with two goals apiece from Hoeness and Muller.

In 1975 Leeds United became only the second English club to reach the final—a remarkable end to a season which began with Don Revie gone from Elland Road to manage England, his successor Brian Clough lasting for only 44 turbulent days, and Jimmy Armfield arriving from Bolton to restore calm and stability to the camp.

En route to the final at the Parc des Princes, Leeds beat Zürich 5–3 on aggregate, Hungary's Ujpest Dozsa 5–1, Belgian Champions Anderlecht 4–0 and, in the semi-final, Barcelona (Cruyff, Neeskens and all) 3–2. Then, in Paris, Leeds faced the holders, Bayern Munich, who were also under new management, Udo Lattek having been replaced by Dettmar Cramer.

But a final rich in promise was, in reality, one of the poorest in the history of the competition. A contributing factor was the first Leeds tackle, which put defender Andersson out of the match, and the necessary team reshuffle heightened Bayern's defensive resolve. Leeds had two first-half penalty claims against Beckenbauer rejected, and what looked a perfectly valid goal by Lorimer after

67 minutes was disallowed for offside by French referee Kitabdjian.

When Roth and Muller scored late goals for Bayern, it was too much for Leeds' followers behind Maier's goal. They smashed seats and hurled the wreckage over the wire fencing onto the pitch, then greeted Bayern's lap of honour with a further barrage of cushions and debris. The riot disgraced British football in the eyes of the world, and brought a European ban on Leeds. Their team in the Final was : Stewart ; Reaney, Gray (F), Bremner, Madeley, Hunter, Lorimer, Clarke, Jordan, Giles, Yorath (Gray, E).

By defeating French club St Etienne 1–0 in a splendid 1976 final at Hampden Park, Bayern Munich emulated European Cup hat-tricks previously performed by Real Madrid and Ajax Amsterdam.

Britain's prestige was restored in Rome in May 1977 when Liverpool's fans behaved impeccably and their favourites became only the second English club to win the trophy, beating Moenchengladbach by three goals to one. Liverpool played superbly with goals coming from Terry McDermott, Tommy Smith and a Phil Neal penalty. But without doubt the star of the match was Kevin Keegan, subsequently transferred to S.V. Hamburg for £500,000 and runner-up in the 1977 European footballer of the year Poll.

Results of European Cup Finals

Year	Venue	Winners	Runners-up	Score
1956	Paris	Real Madrid	Reims	4–3
1957	Madrid	Real Madrid	Fiorentina	2–0
1958	Brussels	Real Madrid	AC Milan	3–2
1959	Stuttgart	Real Madrid	Reims	2–0
1960	Glasgow	Real Madrid	Eintracht	7–3
1961	Berne	Benfica	CF Barcelona	3–2
1962	Amsterdam	Benfica	Real Madrid	5–3
1963	Wembley	AC Milan	Benfica	2–1
1964	Vienna	Inter-Milan	Real Madrid	3–1
1965	Milan	Inter-Milan	Benfica	1–0
1966	Brussels	Real Madrid	Partizan	2–1
1967	Lisbon	Celtic	Inter-Milan	2–1
1968	Wembley	Manchester United	Benfica	4–1
1969	Madrid	AC Milan	Ajax Amsterdam	4–1
1970	Milan	Feyenoord	Celtic	2–1
1971	Wembley	Ajax Amsterdam	Panathinaikos	2–0
1972	Rotterdam	Ajax Amsterdam	Inter-Milan	2–0
1973	Belgrade	Ajax Amsterdam	Juventus	1–0
1974	Brussels	Bayern Munich (After 1–1 draw)	Atletico Madrid	4–0
1975	Paris	Bayern Munich	Leeds United	2–0
1976	Glasgow	Bayern Munich	St Etienne	1–0
1977	Rome	Liverpool	M'Gladbach	3–1
1978	Wembley	Liverpool	Bruges	1–0

The European Cup-Winners' Cup

Staged for the first time in season 1960–61, the Cup-Winners' Cup is the youngest of the three European club tournaments, but in prestige it stands second to the Champions' Cup and British teams have done much to popularize it. In nine seasons between 1963 and 1971 the Cup of Cups was won by Football League clubs no fewer than four times, with Tottenham, West Ham, Manchester City and Chelsea all using victory in the F.A. Cup one year as the passport to European success the following season, and in 1972 Rangers became the first Scottish name on the list of winners—compensation for being beaten finalists in 1961 and 1967.

The enormous success of the Champions' Cup clearly indicated scope for another European competition, and in 1959 the organizers of the Mitropa Cup succeeded in their campaign to launch a knock-out competition for national cup-winners.

It started the following year with only ten entries, the initial problem being that in few Continental countries was the domestic cup greeted with the same enthusiasm and regarded with the same seriousness as the F.A. and Scottish Cups. For instance, Spain played their F.A. Cup at the end of the season, Italy in midweek (like the Football League Cup), France on neutral grounds and Portugal on a home-and-away basis.

By the third season (1962–63), however, 24 clubs took part in the Cup-Winners' Cup and there is now a regular entry of 32 teams. Not only has the Cup of Cups grown to full maturity; its development boosted the national cup competitions in many countries, because success brought prospects of a lucrative campaign in Europe.

After the first final, in which Fiorentina triumphed for Italy by beating Rangers home and away, U.E.F.A. took over the competition and one of their first decisions was to do away with two-leg finals. But two matches were still needed to decide the 1962 winners—Atletico Madrid, who held the holders Fiorentina 1–1 in Glasgow and, four months later, triumphed 3–0 in Stuttgart.

In 1963 Tottenham Hotspur put themselves, and the Cup-Winners' Cup, truly on the European map. At the Feyenoord Stadium in Rotterdam a capacity 65,000 crowd saw them take the trophy from Atletico in tremendous style by 5–1, scorers Greaves (2), Dyson (2) and White.

The following year Sporting Lisbon won the cup for Portugal, but in 1965 it was back in England, with Wembley housing the first 100,000 crowd in the history of the competition and West Ham celebrating the occasion by 2–0 against TSV Munich (scorer Sealey, 2).

Britain also supplied a finalist in each of the next two seasons but twice West German opposition proved too powerful, Liverpool losing 2–1 to Borussia Dortmund in Glasgow in 1966 and a year later Rangers going down by the only goal to Bayern Munich in Nuremberg.

Season 1965–66, the year following West Ham's success, may not have retained the trophy for Britain, but a record was established by providing three of the semi-finalists: Liverpool, West Ham and Celtic. But in 1970 the Cup-Winners' Cup did return to England . . . and stayed for two seasons.

Manchester City's 2–1 victory over the Polish mining team Gornik Zabrze in Vienna was earned with goals from Young and Lee, who celebrated his 25th birthday with what proved to be the winner from the penalty spot. Thus City completed a spectacular cup double, for they had already won the Football League Cup that season.

On the night they lifted the Cup-Winners' Cup in the rain-lashed Prater Stadium in Vienna, Chelsea were in Manchester, winning the F.A. Cup in the replayed final against Leeds United—a success that paved the way for them to take over the Cup of Cups from Manchester City in 1971.

Some 4000 supporters journeyed to Athens to cheer Chelsea in the final against the old masters of Europe, Real Madrid. Osgood's lone goal looked all over the winner until, in the most dramatic climax to any European final, Zoco equalized with the last kick of normal time. Webb's goal-line clearance kept Chelsea alive in extra time, and two nights later in the same Karaiskaki Stadium it began all over again.

This time Chelsea, putting the emphasis on attack from the start, took a two-goal lead through Dempsey and Osgood, and although Real Madrid replied 15 minutes from the end, the experience and tradition of eight previous European finals was not enough to save them. So Chelsea won their first European prize.

That 1971–72 tournament ended with Rangers giving Scotland its first sight of the Cup-Winners' Cup. They beat Moscow Dynamo 3–2 in the final in Barcelona, but the Russians protested that their players had been handicapped by the pitch invasions of supporters from Glasgow. It was several weeks before Rangers' victory was confirmed by U.E.F.A., but because of their supporters' misconduct they were barred from European football for two years—a ban subsequently reduced to one season.

Leeds United justifiably claimed that local Greek referee Michas cost them the 1973 final against AC Milan, who were themselves beaten in the final a year later, when FC Magdeburg put East Germany's name on a European trophy for the first time. In 1975 Dynamo Kiev did likewise for Russia. Their team was also chosen to represent the Soviet Union internationally in the European Championship.

In 1976 West Ham became England's seventh finalists in this tournament. As in the earlier rounds, they left behind dismal League form and scored first against Anderlecht in Brussels, but in a fine match were defeated 4–2. It was Belgium's first success in a European competition.

Results of European Cup-Winners' Cup Finals

Year	Venue	Winners	Runners-up	Score
1961	—	Fiorentina	Rangers	4–1
				aggregate

(Fiorentina won first leg 2–0 in Glasgow, second leg 2–1 in Florence)

Year	Venue	Winners	Runners-up	Score
1962	Stuttgart	Atletico Madrid	Fiorentina	3–0

(In replay after 1–1 draw in Glasgow)

1963	Rotterdam	Tottenham Hotspur	Atletico Madrid	5–1
1964	Antwerp	Sporting Lisbon	MTK Budapest	1–0

(In replay after 3–3 draw in Brussels)

1965	Wembley	West Ham United	TSV Munich	2–0
1966	Glasgow	Borussia Dortmund	Liverpool	2–1
1967	Nuremberg	Bayern Munich	Rangers	1–0
1968	Rotterdam	AC Milan	Hamburg	2–0
1969	Basle	Slovan Bratislava	CF Barcelona	3–2
1970	Vienna	Manchester City	Gornik Zabrze	2–1
1971	Athens	Chelsea	Real Madrid	2–1

(In replay after 1–1 draw, also in Athens)

1972	Barcelona	Rangers	Dynamo Moscow	3–2
1973	Salonika	AC Milan	Leeds United	1–0
1974	Rotterdam	FC Magdeburg	AC Milan	2–0
1975	Basle	Dynamo Kiev	Ferencvaros	3–0
1976	Brussels	Anderlecht	West Ham	4–2
1977	Amsterdam	S.V. Hamburg	Anderlecht	2–0

The U.E.F.A. Cup

Season 1971–72 marked the innovation of the U.E.F.A. Cup in succession to the European Fairs Cup, which was originally known as the European Inter-City Industrial Fairs Cup. This was the forerunner of the three major European football competitions, although in Britain at least it is ranked No. 3 behind the European Cup and Cup-Winners' Cup.

For many years before the Fairs Cup was launched in 1955 matches were played between cities on the Continent, but it was not until 1950 that Ernst B. Thommen, of Switzerland, suggested a tournament for cities regularly holding industrial and trade fairs.

The competition got off the ground largely through the initiative of F.I.F.A. president Sir Stanley Rous, and until 1971 it ran independently of U.E.F.A. under an organizing committee.

Some cities (e.g. London) at first entered representative teams but others preferred to nominate club sides, and as the competition grew in prestige and popularity, club sides took over.

Although the first Fairs Cup tournament was begun in 1955 it was not completed until 1958. The reason for staggering the schedule was to avoid a clash with long-standing domestic fixtures. But interest could not be sustained over such a long period, and the competition almost ground to a halt.

The organizers, recognizing this weakness, staged the second series over two years, and since season 1960–61 it has been an annual event.

Spain provided five of the first six winners, starting with two triumphs for Barcelona. They won the drawn-out 1955–58 series, beating a representative London side 6–0 in Barcelona and by what was to remain the record aggregate of 8–2. In the 1958–60 series Barcelona went through to the finals without losing a single game and won the trophy again by defeating Birmingham City 5–2 on aggregate.

Birmingham were also the losing finalists in the 1960–61 series, when they held AS Roma to a 2–2 draw in Birmingham, but lost 2–0 in Rome.

Valencia were the high-scoring winners in 1961–62, defeating Barcelona 7–3 on aggregate. They won the trophy again the following season and went close to completing a hat-trick in

1963–64, when for the first time it was decided to play a one-match final on a neutral ground. In an all-Spanish decider they lost 2–1 to Real Zaragoza in Barcelona.

But single-leg finals were not a success and after Ferencvaros had beaten Juventus 1–0 in Turin in 1965—Hungary's first Fairs Cup conquest—the 1965–66 final reverted to two matches. It was held over until the following season and when it was eventually played Barcelona became the only team to win the Fairs Cup three times, beating their Spanish rivals Real Zaragoza after losing the home leg.

Leeds went down 2–0 on aggregate to Dynamo Zagreb in the 1967 final, but a year later they became the first British winners of the trophy. In the first leg they gained a slender 1–0 lead and then held Ferencvaros to a goalless draw in Budapest.

In the last competition under the original title of Inter-Cities Fairs Cup, another British team took the prize—Newcastle United in season 1968–69. It was Newcastle's first venture into Europe, and the Geordies' theme song, 'Blaydon Races', rang out as the crowds thronged St James's Park to see the Tynesiders beat crack Continental clubs Feyenoord, Sporting Lisbon, Real Zaragoza and Vitoria Setubal.

There was an all-British semi-final between Newcastle and Rangers. United fought a rearguard action to hold Rangers 0–0 at Ibrox and then won 2–0 at St James's Park. With their team two down in the second leg, Rangers followers invaded the field intent on getting the game abandoned and play was held up for 18 minutes. There were 31 arrests, 60 spectators were taken to hospital and the match was played out with 1000 police surrounding the pitch.

In the final, Newcastle beat the Hungarians Ujpest Dozsa 3–0 in the home leg, but even that advantage began to look inadequate when Ujpest quickly pulled back two goals in the return game in Budapest. A storming rally by Newcastle, however, produced three goals and an impressive 6–2 victory on aggregate.

In 1970 Arsenal scored a dramatic victory over Belgium's Anderlecht which kept the Fairs Cup in England for the third successive season. They lost the first leg of the final 3–1 in Brussels, but the second match was won 3–0, and a 51,000 Highbury crowd went wild at Arsenal's first success of any sort for 17 years.

A year later Leeds United became the first British club to win the competition twice. In what was the last European Fairs Cup tournament, they were its first winners on the 'away goals' rule, drawing 2–2 against Juventus in Turin and 1–1 at Elland Road.

Season 1971–72 produced the first all-British final in any European contest, Tottenham beating Wolves 3–2 on aggregate, and by the same score Liverpool defeated Borussia Moenchengladbach in the 1973 final.

Spurs were finalists in 1974, losing this time to Feyenoord, who thus ended England's six-year grip on the competition. Borussia Moenchengladbach's success in 1975 meant that, combined with Bayern Munich's European Cup, West German clubs held two European trophies, but a year later Liverpool brought England the prize again, defeating Bruges after conceding two early goals in the home leg of the final and then clinging on for a draw in Belgium to repeat their League Championship–U.E.F.A. Cup double of 1973.

Results of Fairs Cup/U.E.F.A. Cup Finals

1955–58 **Barcelona** beat *London* 8–2 on aggregate
(London 2, Barcelona 2 ; Barcelona 6, London 0)

1958–60 **Barcelona** beat *Birmingham* 5–2 on aggregate
(Birmingham 1, Barcelona 1 ; Barcelona 4, Birmingham 1)

1961 **AS Roma** beat *Birmingham City* 4–2 on aggregate
(Birmingham 2, AS Roma 2 ; AS Roma 2, Birmingham 0)

1962 **Valencia** beat *Barcelona* 7–3 on aggregate
(Valencia 6, Barcelona 2 ; Barcelona 1, Valencia 1)

1963 **Valencia** beat *Dynamo Zagreb* 4–1 on aggregate
(Dynamo Zagreb 1, Valencia 2 ; Valencia 2, Dynamo Zagreb 0)

1964 **Real Zaragoza** 2, *Valencia* 1 (in Barcelona)

1965 **Ferencvaros** 1, *Juventus* 0 (in Turin)

1966 **Barcelona** beat *Real Zaragoza* 4–3 on aggregate
(Barcelona 0, Real Zaragoza 1 ; Real Zaragoza 2, Barcelona 4)

1967 **Dynamo Zagreb** beat *Leeds United* 2–0 on aggregate
(Dynamo Zagreb 2, Leeds 0 ; Leeds 0, Dynamo Zagreb 0)

1968 **Leeds United** beat *Ferencvaros* 1–0 on aggregate
(Leeds 1, Ferencvaros 0 ; Ferencvaros 0, Leeds 0)

1969 **Newcastle United** beat *Ujpest Dozsa* 6–2 on aggregate (Newcastle 3, Ujpest Dozsa 0 ; Ujpest Dozsa 2, Newcastle 3)

1970 **Arsenal** beat *Anderlecht* 4–3 on aggregate
(Anderlecht 3, Arsenal 1 ; Arsenal 3, Anderlecht 0)

1971 **Leeds United** beat *Juventus* on away goals after 3–3 draw on aggregate (Juventus 0, Leeds 0—abandoned 51 min., rain ; Juventus 2, Leeds 2 ; Leeds 1, Juventus 1)

1972 **Tottenham Hotspur** beat *Wolverhampton Wanderers* 3–2 on aggregate (Wolves 1, Tottenham 2 ; Tottenham 1, Wolves 1)

1973 **Liverpool** beat *Borussia Moenchengladbach* 3–2 on aggregate (Liverpool 3, Borussia 0 ; Borussia 2, Liverpool 0)

1974	**Feyenoord** beat _Tottenham Hotspur_ 4–2 on aggregate (Tottenham 2, Feyenoord 2; Feyenoord 2, Tottenham 0)
1975	**Borussia Moenchengladbach** beat _Twente Enschede_ 5–1 on aggregate (Borussia 0, Twente 0; Twente 1, Borussia 5)
1976	**Liverpool** beat _Bruges_ 4–3 on aggregate (Liverpool 3, Bruges 2; Bruges 1, Liverpool 1)
1977	**Juventus** beat _Athletic Bilbao_ on away goals (Juventus 1, Bilbao 0; Bilbao 2, Juventus 1)

The World Club Championship

This unofficial inter-continental tournament was originally played between the winners of the European Cup and the winners of the South American Cup, but in recent years there have been instances when the European Cup-holders have withdrawn and been replaced by the runners-up.

1960 Real Madrid (Spain) beat _Penarol_ (Uruguay). (In Montevideo—Penarol 0, Real Madrid 0; in Madrid—Real Madrid 5, Penarol 1).

1961 Penarol (Uruguay) beat _Benfica_ (Portugal). (In Lisbon —Benfica 1, Penarol 0; in Montevideo—Penarol 5, Benfica 0; play-off in Montevideo—Penarol 2, Benfica 1).

1962 Santos (Brazil) beat _Benfica_ (Portugal). (In Rio de Janeiro—Santos 3, Benfica 2; in Lisbon—Benfica 2, Santos 5).

1963 Santos (Brazil) beat _AC Milan_ (Italy). (In Milan—AC Milan 4, Santos 2; in Rio de Janeiro—Santos 4, AC Milan 2; play-off in Rio—Santos 1, AC Milan 0).

1964 Internazionale Milan (Italy) beat _Independiente_ (Argentina). (In Buenos Aires—Independiente 1, Internazionale 0; in Milan—Internazionale 2, Independiente 0; play-off in Madrid —Internazionale 1, Independiente 0, after extra time).

1965 Internazionale Milan (Italy) beat _Independiente_ (Argentina). (In Milan—Internazionale 3, Independiente 0; in Buenos Aires—Independiente 0, Internazionale 0).

1966 Penarol (Uruguay) beat _Real Madrid_ (Spain). (In Montevideo—Penarol 2, Real Madrid 0; in Madrid—Real Madrid 0, Penarol 2).

1967 **Racing Club** (Argentina) beat *Celtic* (Scotland). (In Glasgow—Celtic 1, Racing Club 0; in Buenos Aires—Racing Club 2, Celtic 1; play-off, Montevideo—Racing Club 1, Celtic 0).

1968 **Estudiantes** (Argentina) beat *Manchester United* (England). (In Buenos Aires—Estudiantes 1, Manchester United 0; in Manchester—Manchester United 1, Estudiantes 1).

1969 **AC Milan** (Italy) beat *Estudiantes* (Argentina) 4–2 on aggregate. (In Milan—AC Milan 3, Estudiantes 0; in Buenos Aires—Estudiantes 2, AC Milan 1).

1970 **Feyenoord** (Holland) beat *Estudiantes* (Argentina) 3–2 on aggregate. (In Buenos Aires—Estudiantes 2, Feyenoord 2; in Rotterdam—Feyenoord 1, Estudiantes 0).

1971 **Nacional** (Uruguay) beat *Panathinaikos* (Greece) 3–2 on aggregate. European Champions Ajax (Holland) declined to take part and were replaced by runners-up Panathinaikos. (In Athens—Panathinaikos 1, Nacional 1; in Montevideo—Nacional 2, Panathinaikos 1).

1972 **Ajax Amsterdam** (Holland) beat *Independiente* (Argentina) 4–1 on aggregate. (In Buenos Aires—Independiente 1, Ajax 1; in Amsterdam—Ajax 3, Independiente 0).

1973 **Independiente** (Argentina) beat *Juventus* (Italy) 1–0 in Rome—one match only. European Champions Ajax (Holland) declined to play, and runners-up Juventus substituted.

1975 **Atletico Madrid** (Spain) beat *Independiente* (Argentina) 2–1 on aggregate. (In Buenos Aires—Independiente 1, Atletico 0; in Madrid—Atletico 2, Independiente 0). European Champions Bayern Munich (W. Germany) declined to play, and runners-up Atletico substituted.

1976 **Bayern Munich** (West Germany) beat *Cruzeiro* (Brazil) 2–0 on aggregate. (In Munich—Bayern 2, Cruzeiro 0; in Cruzeiro—Cruzeiro 0, Bayern 0.)

Records Section
ENGLAND'S COMPLETE RECORD
IN FULL INTERNATIONALS

Key: WC = World Cup proper; WCQ = World Cup qualifying round; EC = European Championship proper; ECQ = European Championship qualifying round.

Date	Opponents	Venue	Result
		Season 1872–73	
Nov. 30	Scotland	Glasgow	D 0–0
Mar. 8	Scotland	Oval	W 4–2
		Season 1873–74	
Mar. 7	Scotland	Glasgow	L 1–2
		Season 1874–75	
Mar. 6	Scotland	Oval	D 2–2
		Season 1875–76	
Mar. 4	Scotland	Glasgow	L 0–3
		Season 1876–77	
Mar. 3	Scotland	Oval	L 1–3
		Season 1877–78	
Mar. 2	Scotland	Glasgow	L 2–7
		Season 1878–79	
Jan. 18	Wales	Oval	W 2–1
Apr. 5	Scotland	Oval	W 5–4
		Season 1879–80	
Mar. 13	Scotland	Glasgow	L 4–5
Mar. 15	Wales	Wrexham	W 3–2
		Season 1880–81	
Feb. 26	Wales	Blackburn	L 0–1
Mar. 12	Scotland	Oval	L 1–6
		Season 1881–82	
Feb. 18	Ireland	Belfast	W 13–0
Mar. 11	Scotland	Glasgow	L 1–5
Mar. 13	Wales	Wrexham	L 3–5
		Season 1882–83	
Feb. 3	Wales	Oval	W 5–0
Feb. 24	Ireland	Liverpool	W 7–0
Mar. 10	Scotland	Sheffield	L 2–3
		Season 1883–84	
Feb. 23	Ireland	Belfast	W 8–1
Mar. 15	Scotland	Glasgow	L 0–1
Mar. 17	Wales	Wrexham	W 4–0

Date	Opponents	Venue	Result
Season 1884–85			
Feb. 28	Ireland	Manchester	W 4–0
Mar. 14	Wales	Blackburn	D 1–1
Mar. 21	Scotland	Oval	D 1–1
Season 1885–86			
Mar. 13	Ireland	Belfast	W 6–1
Mar. 29	Wales	Wrexham	W 3–1
Mar. 31	Scotland	Glasgow	D 1–1
Season 1886–87			
Feb. 5	Ireland	Sheffield	W 7–0
Feb. 26	Wales	Oval	W 4–0
Mar. 19	Scotland	Blackburn	L 2–3
Season 1887–88			
Feb. 4	Wales	Crewe	W 5–1
Mar. 17	Scotland	Glasgow	W 5–0
Mar. 31	Ireland	Belfast	W 5–1
Season 1888–89			
Feb. 23	Wales	Stoke	W 4–1
Mar. 2	Ireland	Everton	W 6–1
Apr. 13	Scotland	Oval	L 2–3
Season 1889–90			
Mar. 15	Wales	Wrexham	W 3–1
Mar. 15	Ireland	Belfast	W 9–1
Apr. 5	Scotland	Glasgow	D 1–1
Season 1890–91			
Mar. 7	Wales	Sunderland	W 4–1
Mar. 7	Ireland	Wolverhampton	W 6–1
Apr. 6	Scotland	Blackburn	W 2–1
Season 1891–92			
Mar. 5	Ireland	Belfast	W 2–0
Mar. 5	Wales	Wrexham	W 2–0
Apr. 2	Scotland	Glasgow	W 4–1
Season 1892–93			
Feb. 25	Ireland	Birmingham	W 6–1
Mar. 13	Wales	Stoke	W 6–0
Apr. 1	Scotland	Richmond	W 5–2
Season 1893–94			
Mar. 3	Ireland	Belfast	D 2–2
Mar. 12	Wales	Wrexham	W 5–1
Apr. 7	Scotland	Glasgow	D 2–2
Season 1894–95			
Mar. 9	Ireland	Derby	W 9–0
Mar. 18	Wales	Kensington	D 1–1
Apr. 6	Scotland	Everton	W 3–0

Date	Opponents	Venue	Result
		Season 1895–96	
Mar. 7	Ireland	Belfast	W 2–0
Mar. 16	Wales	Cardiff	W 9–1
Apr. 4	Scotland	Glasgow	L 1–2
		Season 1896–97	
Feb. 20	Ireland	Nottingham	W 6–0
Mar. 29	Wales	Sheffield	W 4–0
Apr. 3	Scotland	Crystal Palace	L 1–2
		Season 1897–98	
Mar. 5	Ireland	Belfast	W 3–2
Mar. 28	Wales	Wrexham	W 3–0
Apr. 2	Scotland	Glasgow	W 3–1
		Season 1898–99	
Feb. 18	Ireland	Sunderland	W 13–2
Mar. 20	Wales	Bristol	W 4–0
Apr. 8	Scotland	Birmingham	W 2–1
		Season 1899–1900	
Mar. 17	Ireland	Dublin	W 2–0
Mar. 26	Wales	Cardiff	D 1–1
Apr. 7	Scotland	Glasgow	L 1–4
		Season 1900–01	
Mar. 9	Ireland	Southampton	W 3–0
Mar. 18	Wales	Newcastle	W 6–0
Mar. 30	Scotland	Crystal Palace	D 2–2
		Season 1901–02	
Mar. 3	Wales	Wrexham	D 0–0
Mar. 22	Ireland	Belfast	W 1–0
May 3	Scotland	Birmingham	D 2–2
		Season 1902–03	
Feb. 14	Ireland	Wolverhampton	W 4–0
Mar. 2	Wales	Portsmouth	W 2–1
Apr. 4	Scotland	Sheffield	L 1–2
		Season 1903–04	
Feb. 29	Wales	Wrexham	D 2–2
Mar. 12	Ireland	Belfast	W 3–1
Apr. 9	Scotland	Glasgow	W 1–0
		Season 1904–05	
Feb. 25	Ireland	Middlesbrough	D 1–1
Mar. 27	Wales	Liverpool	W 3–1
Apr. 1	Scotland	Crystal Palace	W 1–0
		Season 1905–06	
Feb. 17	Ireland	Belfast	W 5–0
Mar. 19	Wales	Cardiff	W 1–0
Apr. 7	Scotland	Glasgow	L 1–2

Date	Opponents	Venue	Result
		Season 1906–07	
Feb. 16	Ireland	Everton	W 1–0
Mar. 18	Wales	Fulham	D 1–1
Apr. 6	Scotland	Newcastle	D 1–1
		Season 1907–08	
Feb. 15	Ireland	Belfast	W 3–1
Mar. 16	Wales	Wrexham	W 7–1
Apr. 4	Scotland	Glasgow	D 1–1
June 6	Austria	Vienna	W 6–1
June 8	Austria	Vienna	W 11–1
June 10	Hungary	Budapest	W 7–0
June 13	Bohemia	Prague	W 4–0
		Season 1908–09	
Feb. 13	Ireland	Bradford	W 4–0
Mar. 15	Wales	Nottingham	W 2–0
Apr. 3	Scotland	Crystal Palace	W 2–0
May 29	Hungary	Budapest	W 4–2
May 31	Hungary	Budapest	W 8–2
June 1	Austria	Vienna	W 8–1
		Season 1909–10	
Feb. 12	Ireland	Belfast	D 1–1
Mar. 14	Wales	Cardiff	W 1–0
Apr. 2	Scotland	Glasgow	L 0–2
		Season 1910–11	
Feb. 11	Ireland	Derby	W 2–1
Mar. 13	Wales	Millwall	W 3–0
Apr. 1	Scotland	Everton	D 1–1
		Season 1911–12	
Feb. 10	Ireland	Dublin	W 6–1
Mar. 11	Wales	Wrexham	W 2–0
Mar. 23	Scotland	Glasgow	D 1–1
		Season 1912–13	
Feb. 15	Ireland	Belfast	L 1–2
Mar. 17	Wales	Bristol	W 4–3
Apr. 5	Scotland	Chelsea	W 1–0
		Season 1913–14	
Feb. 14	Ireland	Middlesbrough	L 0–3
Mar. 16	Wales	Cardiff	W 2–0
Apr. 4	Scotland	Glasgow	L 1–3
		Season 1919–20	
Oct. 25	Ireland	Belfast	D 1–1
Mar. 15	Wales	Highbury	L 1–2
Apr. 10	Scotland	Sheffield	W 5–4

Date	Opponents	Venue	Result
		Season 1920–21	
Oct. 23	Ireland	Sunderland	W 2–0
Mar. 14	Wales	Cardiff	D 0–0
Apr. 9	Scotland	Glasgow	L 0–3
May 21	Belgium	Brussels	W 2–0
		Season 1921–22	
Oct. 22	Ireland	Belfast	D 1–1
Mar. 13	Wales	Liverpool	W 1–0
Apr. 8	Scotland	Aston Villa	L 0–1
		Season 1922–23	
Oct. 21	Ireland	West Bromwich	W 2–0
Mar. 5	Wales	Cardiff	D 2–2
Mar. 19	Belgium	Highbury	W 6–1
Apr. 14	Scotland	Glasgow	D 2–2
May 10	France	Paris	W 4–1
May 21	Sweden	Stockholm	W 4–2
May 24	Sweden	Stockholm	W 3–1
		Season 1923–24	
Oct. 20	Ireland	Belfast	L 1–2
Nov. 1	Belgium	Antwerp	D 2–2
Mar. 3	Wales	Blackburn	L 1–2
Apr. 12	Scotland	Wembley	D 1–1
May 17	France	Paris	W 3–1
		Season 1924–25	
Oct. 22	Ireland	Everton	W 3–1
Dec. 8	Belgium	West Bromwich	W 4–0
Feb. 28	Wales	Swansea	W 2–1
Apr. 4	Scotland	Glasgow	L 0–2
May 21	France	Paris	W 3–2
		Season 1925–26	
Oct. 24	Ireland	Belfast	D 0–0
Mar. 1	Wales	Crystal Palace	L 1–3
Apr. 17	Scotland	Manchester	L 0–1
May 24	Belgium	Antwerp	W 5–3
		Season 1926–27	
Oct. 20	Ireland	Liverpool	D 3–3
Feb. 12	Wales	Wrexham	D 3–3
Apr. 2	Scotland	Glasgow	W 2–1
May 11	Belgium	Brussels	W 9–1
May 21	Luxembourg	Luxembourg	W 5–2
May 26	France	Paris	W 6–0
		Season 1927–28	
Oct. 22	Ireland	Belfast	L 0–2
Nov. 28	Wales	Burnley	L 1–2
Mar. 31	Scotland	Wembley	L 1–5

166

Date	Opponents	Venue	Result
May 17	France	Paris	W 5–1
May 19	Belgium	Antwerp	W 3–1

Season 1928–29

Date	Opponents	Venue	Result
Oct. 22	Ireland	Everton	W 2–1
Nov. 17	Wales	Swansea	W 3–2
Apr. 13	Scotland	Glasgow	L 0–1
May 9	France	Paris	W 4–1
May 11	Belgium	Brussels	W 5–1
May 15	Spain	Madrid	L 3–4

Season 1929–30

Date	Opponents	Venue	Result
Oct. 19	Ireland	Belfast	W 3–0
Nov. 20	Wales	Chelsea	W 6–0
Apr. 5	Scotland	Wembley	W 5–2
May 10	Germany	Berlin	D 3–3
May 14	Austria	Vienna	D 0–0

Season 1930–31

Date	Opponents	Venue	Result
Oct. 20	Ireland	Sheffield	W 5–1
Nov. 22	Wales	Wrexham	W 4–0
Mar. 31	Scotland	Glasgow	L 0–2
May 14	France	Paris	L 2–5
May 16	Belgium	Brussels	W 4–1

Season 1931–32

Date	Opponents	Venue	Result
Oct. 17	Ireland	Belfast	W 6–2
Nov. 18	Wales	Liverpool	W 3–1
Dec. 9	Spain	Highbury	W 7–1
Apr. 9	Scotland	Wembley	W 3–0

Season 1932–33

Date	Opponents	Venue	Result
Oct. 17	Ireland	Blackpool	W 1–0
Nov. 16	Wales	Wrexham	D 0–0
Dec. 7	Austria	Chelsea	W 4–3
Apr. 1	Scotland	Glasgow	L 1–2
May 13	Italy	Rome	D 1–1
May 20	Switzerland	Berne	W 4–0

Season 1933–34

Date	Opponents	Venue	Result
Oct. 14	Ireland	Belfast	W 3–0
Nov. 15	Wales	Newcastle	L 1–2
Dec. 6	France	Tottenham	W 4–1
Feb. 6	Ireland	Everton	W 2–1
Apr. 14	Scotland	Wembley	W 3–0
May 10	Hungary	Budapest	L 1–2
May 16	Czechoslovakia	Prague	L 1–2

Season 1934–35

Date	Opponents	Venue	Result
Sept. 29	Wales	Cardiff	W 4–0
Nov. 14	Italy	Highbury	W 3–2
Apr. 6	Scotland	Glasgow	L 0–2

Date		Opponents	Venue	Result
		Season 1935–36		
Oct.	19	Ireland	Belfast	W 3–1
Dec.	4	Germany	Tottenham	W 3–0
Feb.	5	Wales	Wolverhampton	L 1–2
Apr.	4	Scotland	Wembley	D 1–1
May	6	Austria	Vienna	L 1–2
May	9	Belgium	Brussels	L 2–3
May	18	Holland	Amsterdam	W 1–0
		Season 1936–37		
Oct.	17	Wales	Cardiff	L 1–2
Nov.	18	Ireland	Stoke	W 3–1
Dec.	2	Hungary	Highbury	W 6–2
Apr.	17	Scotland	Glasgow	L 1–3
May	14	Norway	Oslo	W 6–0
May	17	Sweden	Stockholm	W 4–0
May	20	Finland	Helsinki	W 8–0
		Season 1937–38		
Oct.	23	Ireland	Belfast	W 5–1
Nov.	17	Wales	Middlesbrough	W 2–1
Dec.	1	Czechoslovakia	Tottenham	W 5–4
Apr.	9	Scotland	Wembley	L 0–1
May	14	Germany	Berlin	W 6–3
May	21	Switzerland	Zürich	L 1–2
May	26	France	Paris	W 4–2
		Season 1938–39		
Oct.	22	Wales	Cardiff	L 2–4
Oct.	26	F.I.F.A.	Highbury	W 3–0
Nov.	9	Norway	Newcastle	W 4–0
Nov.	16	Ireland	Manchester	W 7–0
Apr.	15	Scotland	Glasgow	W 2–1
May	13	Italy	Milan	D 2–2
May	18	Yugoslavia	Belgrade	L 1–2
May	24	Rumania	Bucharest	W 2–0
		Season 1946–47		
Sept.	28	Ireland	Belfast	W 7–2
Sept.	30	Rep. Ireland	Dublin	W 1–0
Nov.	13	Wales	Manchester	W 3–0
Nov.	27	Holland	Huddersfield	W 8–2
Apr.	12	Scotland	Wembley	D 1–1
May	3	France	Highbury	W 3–0
May	18	Switzerland	Zürich	L 0–1
May	25	Portugal	Lisbon	W 10–0
		Season 1947–48		
Sept.	21	Belgium	Brussels	W 5–2
Oct.	18	Wales	Cardiff	W 3–0

Date	Opponents	Venue	Result
Nov. 5	Ireland	Everton	D 2–2
Nov. 19	Sweden	Highbury	W 4–2
Apr. 10	Scotland	Glasgow	W 2–0
May 16	Italy	Turin	W 4–0

Season 1948–49

Date	Opponents	Venue	Result
Sept. 26	Denmark	Copenhagen	D 0–0
Oct. 9	Ireland	Belfast	W 6–2
Nov. 10	Wales	Villa Park	W 1–0
Dec. 2	Switzerland	Highbury	W 6–0
Apr. 9	Scotland	Wembley	L 1–3
May 13	Sweden	Stockholm	L 1–3
May 18	Norway	Oslo	W 4–1
May 22	France	Paris	W 3–1

Season 1949–50

Date	Opponents	Venue	Result
Sept. 21	Rep. Ireland	Everton	L 0–2
Oct. 15	Wales	Cardiff	W 4–1 WCQ
Nov. 16	Ireland	Manchester	W 9–2 WCQ
Nov. 30	Italy	Tottenham	W 2–0
Apr. 15	Scotland	Glasgow	W 1–0 WCQ
May 14	Portugal	Lisbon	W 5–3
May 18	Belgium	Brussels	W 4–1
June 25	Chile	Rio de Janeiro	W 2–0 WC
June 29	U.S.A.	Belo Horizonte	L 0–1 WC
July 2	Spain	Rio de Janeiro	L 0–1 WC

Season 1950–51

Date	Opponents	Venue	Result
Oct. 7	Ireland	Belfast	W 4–1
Nov. 15	Wales	Sunderland	W 4–2
Nov. 22	Yugoslavia	Highbury	D 2–2
Apr. 14	Scotland	Wembley	L 2–3
May 9	Argentina	Wembley	W 2–1
May 19	Portugal	Everton	W 5–2

Season 1951–52

Date	Opponents	Venue	Result
Oct. 3	France	Highbury	D 2–2
Oct. 20	Wales	Cardiff	D 1–1
Nov. 14	Ireland	Villa Park	W 2–0
Nov. 28	Austria	Wembley	D 2–2
Apr. 5	Scotland	Glasgow	W 2–1
May 18	Italy	Florence	D 1–1
May 25	Austria	Vienna	W 3–2
May 28	Switzerland	Zürich	W 3–0

Season 1952–53

Date	Opponents	Venue	Result
Oct. 4	Ireland	Belfast	D 2–2
Nov. 12	Wales	Wembley	W 5–2
Nov. 26	Belgium	Wembley	W 5–0
Apr. 18	Scotland	Wembley	D 2–2

Date	Opponents	Venue	Result
May 17	Argentina	Buenos Aires	0–0
	(Abandoned after 23 min.—rain)		
May 24	Chile	Santiago	W 2–1
May 31	Uruguay	Montevideo	L 1–2
June 8	U.S.A.	New York	W 6–3

Season 1953–54

Oct. 10	Wales	Cardiff	W 4–1 WCQ
Oct. 21	F.I.F.A.	Wembley	D 4–4
Nov. 11	Ireland	Everton	W 3–1 WCQ
Nov. 25	Hungary	Wembley	L 3–6
Apr. 3	Scotland	Glasgow	W 4–2 WCQ
May 16	Yugoslavia	Belgrade	L 0–1
May 23	Hungary	Budapest	L 1–7
June 17	Belgium	Basle	D 4–4 WC
June 20	Switzerland	Berne	W 2–0 WC
June 26	Uruguay	Basle	L 2–4 WC

Season 1954–55

Oct. 2	Ireland	Belfast	W 2–0
Nov. 10	Wales	Wembley	W 3–2
Dec. 1	Germany	Wembley	W 3–1
Apr. 2	Scotland	Wembley	W 7–2
May 15	France	Paris	L 0–1
May 18	Spain	Madrid	D 1–1
May 22	Portugal	Oporto	L 1–3

Season 1955–56

Oct. 2	Denmark	Copenhagen	W 5–1
Oct. 22	Wales	Cardiff	L 1–2
Nov. 2	Ireland	Wembley	W 3–0
Nov. 30	Spain	Wembley	W 4–1
Apr. 14	Scotland	Glasgow	D 1–1
May 9	Brazil	Wembley	W 4–2
May 16	Sweden	Stockholm	D 0–0
May 20	Finland	Helsinki	W 5–1
May 26	Germany	Berlin	W 3–1

Season 1956–57

Oct. 6	Ireland	Belfast	D 1–1
Nov. 14	Wales	Wembley	W 3–1
Nov. 28	Yugoslavia	Wembley	W 3–0
Dec. 5	Denmark	Wolverhampton	W 5–2 WCQ
Apr. 6	Scotland	Wembley	W 2–1
May 8	Rep. Ireland	Wembley	W 5–1 WCQ
May 15	Denmark	Copenhagen	W 4–1 WCQ
May 19	Rep. Ireland	Dublin	D 1–1 WCQ

Season 1957–58

Oct. 19	Wales	Cardiff	W 4–0

Date	Opponents	Venue	Result
Nov. 6	Ireland	Wembley	L 2–3
Nov. 27	France	Wembley	W 4–0
Apr. 19	Scotland	Glasgow	W 4–0
May 7	Portugal	Wembley	W 2–1
May 11	Yugoslavia	Belgrade	L 0–5
May 18	Russia	Moscow	D 1–1
June 8	Russia	Gothenburg	D 2–2 WC
June 11	Brazil	Gothenburg	D 0–0 WC
June 15	Austria	Boras	D 2–2 WC
June 17	Russia	Gothenburg	L 0–1 WC
Season 1958–59			
Oct. 4	Ireland	Belfast	D 3–3
Oct. 22	Russia	Wembley	W 5–0
Nov. 26	Wales	Villa Park	D 2–2
Apr. 11	Scotland	Wembley	W 1–0
May 6	Italy	Wembley	D 2–2
May 13	Brazil	Rio de Janeiro	L 0–2
May 17	Peru	Lima	L 1–4
May 24	Mexico	Mexico City	L 1–2
May 28	U.S.A.	Los Angeles	W 8–1
Season 1959–60			
Oct. 17	Wales	Cardiff	D 1–1
Oct. 28	Sweden	Wembley	L 2–3
Nov. 18	Ireland	Wembley	W 2–1
Apr. 9	Scotland	Glasgow	D 1–1
May 11	Yugoslavia	Wembley	D 3–3
May 15	Spain	Madrid	L 0–3
May 22	Hungary	Budapest	L 0–2
Season 1960–61			
Oct. 8	Ireland	Belfast	W 5–2
Oct. 19	Luxembourg	Luxembourg	W 9–0 WCQ
Oct. 26	Spain	Wembley	W 4–2
Nov. 23	Wales	Wembley	W 5–1
Apr. 15	Scotland	Wembley	W 9–3
May 10	Mexico	Wembley	W 8–0
May 21	Portugal	Lisbon	D 1–1 WCQ
May 24	Italy	Rome	W 3–2
May 27	Austria	Vienna	L 1–3
Season 1961–62			
Sept. 28	Luxembourg	Highbury	W 4–1 WCQ
Oct. 14	Wales	Cardiff	D 1–1
Oct. 25	Portugal	Wembley	W 2–0 WCQ
Nov. 22	Ireland	Wembley	D 1–1
Apr. 4	Austria	Wembley	W 3–1
Apr. 14	Scotland	Glasgow	L 0–2
May 9	Switzerland	Wembley	W 3–1

Date	Opponents	Venue	Result
May 20	Peru	Lima	W 4–0
May 31	Hungary	Rancagua	L 1–2 WC
June 2	Argentina	Rancagua	W 3–1 WC
June 7	Bulgaria	Rancagua	D 0–0 WC
June 10	Brazil	Vina del Mar	L 1–3 WC

Season 1962–63

Date	Opponents	Venue	Result
Oct. 3	France	Sheffield	D 1–1 ECQ
Oct. 20	Ireland	Belfast	W 3–1
Nov. 21	Wales	Wembley	W 4–0
Feb. 27	France	Paris	L 2–5 ECQ
Apr. 6	Scotland	Wembley	L 1–2
May 8	Brazil	Wembley	D 1–1
May 29.	Czechoslovakia	Bratislava	W 4–2
June 2	East Germany	Leipzig	W 2–1
June 5	Switzerland	Basle	W 8–1

Season 1963–64

Date	Opponents	Venue	Result
Oct. 12	Wales	Cardiff	W 4–0
Oct. 23	F.I.F.A.	Wembley	W 2–1
Nov. 20	Ireland	Wembley	W 8–3
Apr. 11	Scotland	Glasgow	L 0–1
May 6	Uruguay	Wembley	W 2–1
May 17	Portugal	Lisbon	W 4–3
May 24	Rep. Ireland	Dublin	W 3–1
May 27	U.S.A.	New York	W 10–0
May 30	Brazil	Rio de Janeiro	L 1–5
June 4	Portugal	São Paulo	D 1–1
June 6	Argentina	Rio de Janeiro	L 0–1

Season 1964–65

Date	Opponents	Venue	Result
Oct. 3	Ireland	Belfast	W 4–3
Oct. 21	Belgium	Wembley	D 2–2
Nov. 18	Wales	Wembley	W 2–1
Dec. 9	Holland	Amsterdam	D 1–1
Apr. 10	Scotland	Wembley	D 2–2
May 5	Hungary	Wembley	W 1–0
May 9	Yugoslavia	Belgrade	D 1–1
May 12	West Germany	Nuremberg	W 1–0
May 16	Sweden	Gothenburg	W 2–1

Season 1965–66

Date	Opponents	Venue	Result
Oct. 2	Wales	Cardiff	D 0–0
Oct. 20	Austria	Wembley	L 2–3
Nov. 10	Ireland	Wembley	W 2–1
Dec. 8	Spain	Madrid	W 2–0
Jan. 5	Poland	Everton	D 1–1
Feb. 23	West Germany	Wembley	W 1–0
Apr. 2	Scotland	Glasgow	W 4–3

172

Date	Opponents	Venue	Result
May 4	Yugoslavia	Wembley	W 2–0
June 26	Finland	Helsinki	W 3–0
June 29	Norway	Oslo	W 6–1
July 3	Denmark	Copenhagen	W 2–0
July 5	Poland	Chorzow	W 1–0
July 11	Uruguay	Wembley	D 0–0 WC
July 16	Mexico	Wembley	W 2–0 WC
July 20	France	Wembley	W 2–0 WC
July 23	Argentina	Wembley	W 1–0 WC
July 26	Portugal	Wembley	W 2–1 WC
July 30	West Germany	Wembley	W 4–2 WC

Season 1966–67

Oct. 22	Ireland	Belfast	W 2–0 ECQ
Nov. 2	Czechoslovakia	Wembley	D 0–0
Nov. 16	Wales	Wembley	W 5–1 ECQ
Apr. 15	Scotland	Wembley	L 2–3 ECQ
May 24	Spain	Wembley	W 2–0
May 27	Austria	Vienna	W 1–0

Season 1967–68

Oct. 21	Wales	Cardiff	W 3–0 ECQ
Nov. 22	Ireland	Wembley	W 2–0 ECQ
Dec. 6	Russia	Wembley	D 2–2
Feb. 24	Scotland	Glasgow	D 1–1 ECQ
Apr. 3	Spain	Wembley	W 1–0 EC
May 8	Spain	Madrid	W 2–1 EC
May 22	Sweden	Wembley	W 3–1
June 1	West Germany	Hanover	L 0–1
June 5	Yugoslavia	Florence	L 0–1 EC
June 8	Russia	Rome	W 2–0 EC

Season 1968–69

Nov. 6	Rumania	Bucharest	D 0–0
Dec. 11	Bulgaria	Wembley	D 1–1
Jan. 15	Rumania	Wembley	D 1–1
Mar. 12	France	Wembley	W 5–0
May 3	Ireland	Belfast	W 3–1
May 7	Wales	Wembley	W 2–1
May 10	Scotland	Wembley	W 4–1
June 1	Mexico	Mexico City	D 0–0
June 8	Uruguay	Montevideo	W 2–1
June 12	Brazil	Rio de Janeiro	L 1–2

Season 1969–70

Nov. 5	Holland	Amsterdam	W 1–0
Dec. 10	Portugal	Wembley	W 1–0
Jan. 14	Holland	Wembley	D 0–0
Feb. 25	Belgium	Brussels	W 3–1

Date	Opponents	Venue	Result
Apr. 18	Wales	Cardiff	D 1-1
Apr. 21	Ireland	Wembley	W 3-1
Apr. 25	Scotland	Glasgow	D 0-0
May 20	Colombia	Bogota	W 4-0
May 24	Ecuador	Quito	W 2-0
June 2	Rumania	Guadalajara	W 1-0 WC
June 7	Brazil	Guadalajara	L 0-1 WC
June 11	Czechoslovakia	Guadalajara	W 1-0 WC
June 14	West Germany	Leon	L 2-3 WC

Season 1970-71

Date	Opponents	Venue	Result
Nov. 25	East Germany	Wembley	W 3-1
Feb. 3	Malta	Valletta	W 1-0 ECQ
Apr. 21	Greece	Wembley	W 3-0 ECQ
May 12	Malta	Wembley	W 5-0 ECQ
May 15	Ireland	Belfast	W 1-0
May 19	Wales	Wembley	D 0-0
May 22	Scotland	Wembley	W 3-1

Season 1971-72

Date	Opponents	Venue	Result
Oct. 13	Switzerland	Basle	W 3-2 ECQ
Nov. 10	Switzerland	Wembley	D 1-1 ECQ
Dec. 1	Greece	Athens	W 2-0 ECQ
Apr. 29	West Germany	Wembley	L 1-3 EC
May 13	West Germany	Berlin	D 0-0 EC
May 20	Wales	Cardiff	W 3-0
May 23	Ireland	Wembley	L 0-1
May 27	Scotland	Glasgow	W 1-0

Season 1972-73

Date	Opponents	Venue	Result
Oct. 11	Yugoslavia	Wembley	D 1-1
Nov. 15	Wales	Cardiff	W 1-0 WCQ
Jan. 24	Wales	Wembley	D 1-1 WCQ
Feb. 14	Scotland	Glasgow	W 5-0
May 12	Ireland	Everton	W 2-1
May 15	Wales	Wembley	W 3-0
May 19	Scotland	Wembley	W 1-0
May 27	Czechoslovakia	Prague	D 1-1
June 6	Poland	Chorzow	L 0-2 WCQ
June 10	Russia	Moscow	W 2-1
June 14	Italy	Turin	L 0-2

Season 1973-74

Date	Opponents	Venue	Result
Sept. 26	Austria	Wembley	W 7-0
Oct. 17	Poland	Wembley	D 1-1 WCQ
Nov. 14	Italy	Wembley	L 0-1
Apr. 3	Portugal	Lisbon	D 0-0
May 11	Wales	Cardiff	W 2-0
May 15	Ireland	Wembley	W 1-0

Date	Opponents	Venue	Result
May 18	Scotland	Glasgow	L 0–2
May 22	Argentina	Wembley	D 2–2
May 29	East Germany	Leipzig	D 1–1
June 1	Bulgaria	Sofia	W 1–0
June 5	Yugoslavia	Belgrade	D 2–2

Season 1974–75

Date	Opponents	Venue	Result
Oct. 30	Czechoslovakia	Wembley	W 3–0 ECQ
Nov. 20	Portugal	Wembley	D 0–0 ECQ
Mar. 12	West Germany	Wembley	W 2–0
Apr. 16	Cyprus	Wembley	W 5–0 ECQ
May 11	Cyprus	Limassol	W 1–0 ECQ
May 17	Ireland	Belfast	D 0–0
May 21	Wales	Wembley	D 2–2
May 24	Scotland	Wembley	W 5–1

Season 1975–76

Date	Opponents	Venue	Result
Sept. 3	Switzerland	Basle	W 2–1
Oct. 29	Czechoslovakia	Bratislava	0–0 ECQ
	(Abandoned after 17 min.—fog)		
Oct. 30	Czechoslovakia	Bratislava	L 1–2 ECQ
Nov. 19	Portugal	Lisbon	D 1–1 ECQ
Mar. 24	Wales	Wrexham	W 2–1
May 8	Wales	Cardiff	W 1–0
May 11	Ireland	Wembley	W 4–0
May 15	Scotland	Glasgow	L 1–2
May 23	Brazil	Los Angeles	L 0–1
May 28	Italy	New York	W 3–2
June 13	Finland	Helsinki	W 4–1 WCQ

Season 1976–77

Date	Opponents	Venue	Result
Sept. 8	Rep. Ireland	Wembley	D 1–1
Oct. 13	Finland	Wembley	W 2–1 WCQ
Nov. 17	Italy	Rome	L 0–2 WCQ
Feb. 9	Holland	Wembley	L 0–2
Mar. 30	Luxembourg	Wembley	W 5–0 WCQ
May 28	Ireland	Belfast	W 2–1
May 31	Wales	Wembley	L 0–1
June 4	Scotland	Wembley	L 1–2
June 8	Brazil	Rio de Janeiro	D 0–0
June 12	Argentina	Buenos Aires	D 1–1
June 15	Uruguay	Montevideo	D 0–0

Season 1977–78

Date	Opponents	Venue	Result
Sept. 7	Switzerland	Wembley	D 0–0
Oct. 12	Luxembourg	Luxembourg	W 2–0 WCQ
Nov. 16	Italy	Wembley	W 2–0 WCQ
Feb. 22	W. Germany	Munich	L 1–2

FOOTBALL LEAGUE CHAMPIONS
AND THEIR RECORDS

Season	Champions	P	W	D	L	F	A	Pts
1888–89	Preston N.E.	22	18	4	0	74	15	40
1889–90	Preston N.E.	22	15	3	4	71	30	33
1890–91	Everton	22	14	1	7	63	29	29
1891–92	Sunderland	26	21	0	5	93	36	42
1892–93	Sunderland	30	22	4	4	100	36	48
1893–94	Aston Villa	30	19	6	5	84	42	44
1894–95	Sunderland	30	21	5	4	80	37	47
1895–96	Aston Villa	30	20	5	5	78	45	45
1896–97	Aston Villa	30	21	5	4	73	38	47
1897–98	Sheffield Utd.	30	17	8	5	56	31	42
1898–99	Aston Villa	34	19	7	8	76	40	45
1899–1900	Aston Villa	34	22	6	6	77	35	50
1900–01	Liverpool	34	19	7	8	59	35	45
1901–02	Sunderland	34	19	6	9	50	35	44
1902–03	Sheffield Wed.	34	19	4	11	54	36	42
1903–04	Sheffield Wed.	34	20	7	7	48	28	47
1904–05	Newcastle Utd.	34	23	2	9	72	33	48
1905–06	Liverpool	38	23	5	10	79	46	51
1906–07	Newcastle Utd.	38	22	7	9	74	46	51
1907–08	Manchester Utd.	38	23	6	9	81	48	52
1908–09	Newcastle Utd.	38	24	5	9	65	41	53
1909–10	Aston Villa	38	23	7	8	84	42	53
1910–11	Manchester Utd.	38	22	8	8	72	40	52
1911–12	Blackburn Rov.	38	20	9	9	60	43	49
1912–13	Sunderland	38	25	4	9	86	43	54
1913–14	Blackburn Rov.	38	20	11	7	78	42	51
1914–15	Everton	38	19	8	11	76	47	46
1915–19	No competition—First World War							
1919–20	West Brom. Albion	42	28	4	10	104	47	60
1920–21	Burnley	42	23	13	6	79	36	59
1921–22	Liverpool	42	22	13	7	63	36	57
1922–23	Liverpool	42	26	8	8	70	31	60
1923–24	Huddersfield Town	42	23	11	8	60	33	57
1924–25	Huddersfield Town	42	21	16	5	69	28	58
1925–26	Huddersfield Town	42	23	11	8	92	60	57
1926–27	Newcastle Utd.	42	25	6	11	96	58	56
1927–28	Everton	42	20	13	9	102	66	53
1928–29	Sheffield Wed.	42	21	10	11	86	62	52
1929–30	Sheffield Wed.	42	26	8	8	105	57	60
1930–31	Arsenal	42	28	10	4	127	59	66
1931–32	Everton	42	26	4	12	116	64	56
1932–33	Arsenal	42	25	8	9	118	61	58
1933–34	Arsenal	42	25	9	8	75	47	59
1934–35	Arsenal	42	23	12	7	115	46	58

Season	Champions	P	W	D	L	F	A	Pts
1935–36	Sunderland	42	25	6	11	109	74	56
1936–37	Manchester City	42	22	13	7	107	61	57
1937–38	Arsenal	42	21	10	11	77	44	52
1938–39	Everton	42	27	5	10	88	52	59
1939–46	No competition—Second World War							
1946–47	Liverpool	42	25	7	10	84	52	57
1947–48	Arsenal	42	23	13	6	81	32	59
1948–49	Portsmouth	42	25	8	9	84	42	58
1949–50	Portsmouth	42	22	9	11	74	38	53
1950–51	Tottenham Hotspur	42	25	10	7	82	44	60
1951–52	Manchester Utd.	42	23	11	8	95	52	57
1952–53	Arsenal	42	21	12	9	97	64	54
1953–54	Wolverhampton W.	42	25	7	10	96	56	57
1954–55	Chelsea	42	20	12	10	81	57	52
1955–56	Manchester Utd.	42	25	10	7	83	51	60
1956–57	Manchester Utd.	42	28	8	6	103	54	64
1957–58	Wolverhampton W.	42	28	8	6	103	47	64
1958–59	Wolverhampton W.	42	28	5	9	110	49	61
1959–60	Burnley	42	24	7	11	85	61	55
1960–61	Tottenham Hotspur	42	31	4	7	115	55	66
1961–62	Ipswich Town	42	24	8	10	93	67	56
1962–63	Everton	42	25	11	6	84	42	61
1963–64	Liverpool	42	26	5	11	92	45	57
1964–65	Manchester Utd.	42	26	9	7	89	39	61
1965–66	Liverpool	42	26	9	7	79	34	61
1966–67	Manchester Utd.	42	24	12	6	84	45	60
1967–68	Manchester City	42	26	6	10	86	43	58
1968–69	Leeds United	42	27	13	2	66	26	67
1969–70	Everton	42	29	8	5	72	34	66
1970–71	Arsenal	42	29	7	6	71	29	65
1971–72	Derby County	42	24	10	8	69	33	58
1972–73	Liverpool	42	25	10	7	72	42	60
1973–74	Leeds United	42	24	14	4	66	31	62
1974–75	Derby County	42	21	11	10	67	49	53
1975–76	Liverpool	42	23	14	5	66	31	60
1976–77	Liverpool	42	23	11	8	62	33	57
1977–78	Notts Forest	42	25	14	3	69	24	64

Summary of Champions

Liverpool	10	Huddersfield	3	Preston	2
Arsenal	8	Wolves	3	Tottenham	2
Everton	7	Blackburn	2	Chelsea	1
Manchester Utd.	7	Burnley	2	Ipswich	1
Aston Villa	6	Derby County	2	Notts Forest	1
Sunderland	6	Leeds	2	Sheffield Utd.	1
Newcastle	4	Manchester City	2	West Bromwich	1
Sheffield Wed.	4	Portsmouth	2		

F.A. CUP WINNERS

Cup Final venues:

1872–92	Kennington Oval (except 1873—at Lillie Bridge, London)	1895–1914	Crystal Palace
		1915	Old Trafford, Manchester
1893	Fallowfield, Manchester	1920–22	Stamford Bridge
1894	Anfield, Liverpool	1923 to date	Wembley

* = Replay; † = After extra time

Season	Winners	Runners-up	Result	Attendance
1871–72	Wanderers	Royal Engineers	1–0	2,000
1872–73	Wanderers	Oxford University	2–0	3,000
1873–74	Oxford University	Royal Engineers	2–0	2,500
1874–75	Royal Engineers	Old Etonians	*2–0 (after 1–1 draw)	3,000
1875–76	Wanderers	Old Etonians	*3–0 (after 0–0 draw)	4,000
1876–77	Wanderers	Oxford University	†2–0	3,000
1877–78	Wanderers	Royal Engineers	3–1	5,000
1878–79	Old Etonians	Clapham Rovers	1–0	5,000
1879–80	Clapham Rovers	Oxford University	1–0	6,000
1880–81	Old Carthusians	Old Etonians	3–0	4,000
1881–82	Old Etonians	Blackburn R.	1–0	7,000
1882–83	Blackburn Olympic	Old Etonians	†2–1	8,000
1883–84	Blackburn R.	Queen's Park, Glasgow	2–1	4,000
1884–85	Blackburn R.	Queen's Park, Glasgow	2–0	12,500
1885–86	Blackburn R.	W.B.A.	*2–0	15,000
	(Replay at Derby—after 0–0 draw)			
1886–87	Aston Villa	W.B.A.	2–0	16,000
1887–88	W.B.A.	Preston N.E.	2–1	19,000
1888–89	Preston N.E.	Wolves	3–0	22,000
1889–90	Blackburn R.	Sheffield Wed.	6–1	20,000
1890–91	Blackburn R.	Notts County	3–1	23,000
1891–92	W.B.A.	Aston Villa	3–0	25,000
1892–93	Wolves	Everton	1–0	45,000
1893–94	Notts County	Bolton W.	4–1	37,000
1894–95	Aston Villa	W.B.A.	1–0	42,500

Season	Winners	Runners-up	Result	Attend. ance
1895–96	Sheffield Wed.	Wolves	2–1	49,000
1896–97	Aston Villa	Everton	3–2	66,000
1897–98	Nott'm Forest	Derby County	3–1	62,000
1898–99	Sheffield Utd.	Derby County	4–1	74,000
1899– 1900	Bury	Southampton	4–0	69,000
1900–01	Tottenham H.	Sheffield Utd.	*3–1	30,000

(Replay at Bolton—after 2–2 draw, att: 110,820)

1901–02	Sheffield Utd.	Southampton	*2–1	33,000

(Replay at Crystal Palace—after 1–1 draw, att: 77,000)

1902–03	Bury	Derby County	6–0	63,000
1903–04	Manchester C.	Bolton W.	1–0	61,000
1904–05	Aston Villa	Newcastle U.	2–0	101,000
1905–06	Everton	Newcastle U.	1–0	76,000
1906–07	Sheffield Wed.	Everton	2–1	84,500
1907–08	Wolves	Newcastle U.	3–1	75,000
1908–09	Manchester U.	Bristol City	1–0	68,000
1909–10	Newcastle U.	Barnsley	*2–0	69,000

(Replay at Goodison Park, Everton—after 1–1 draw, att: 78,000)

1910–11	Bradford City	Newcastle U.	*1–0	58,000

(Replay at Old Trafford, Manchester—after 0–0 draw, att: 69,000)

1911–12	Barnsley	W.B.A.	*1–0	38,500

(Replay at Bramall Lane, Sheffield—after 0–0 draw, att: 54,500)

1912–13	Aston Villa	Sunderland	1–0	120,000
1913–14	Burnley	Liverpool	1–0	73,000
1914–15	Sheffield U.	Chelsea	3–0	50,000
1915–19	No competition—First World War			
1919–20	Aston Villa	Huddersfield T.	†1–0	50,000
1920–21	Tottenham H.	Wolves	1–0	73,000
1921–22	Huddersfield T.	Preston N.E.	1–0	53,000

Results, with scorers, since the F.A. Cup Final has been played at Wembley

Season	Winners	Runners-up	Result	Attend. ance
1922–23	Bolton W. (Jack, J. R. Smith)	West Ham U.	2–0	126,047
1923–24	Newcastle U. (Harris, Seymour)	Aston Villa	2–0	92,000
1924–25	Sheffield Utd. (Tunstall)	Cardiff City	1–0	92,000
1925–26	Bolton W. (Jack)	Manchester C.	1–0	91,500
1926–27	Cardiff City (Ferguson)	Arsenal	1–0	91,000
1927–28	Blackburn R. (Roscamp 2, McLean)	Huddersfield T. (Jackson)	3–1	92,000

Season	Winners	Runners-up	Result	Attend-ance
1928–29	Bolton W. (*Butler, Blackmore*)	Portsmouth	2–0	92,500
1929–30	Arsenal (*James, Lambert*)	Huddersfield T.	2–0	92,500
1930–31	W.B.A. (*W. G. Richardson 2*)	Birmingham (*Bradford*)	2–1	92,500
1931–32	Newcastle U. (*Allen 2*)	Arsenal (*John*)	2–1	92,000
1932–33	Everton (*Stein, Dean, Dunn*)	Manchester City	3–0	93,000
1933–34	Manchester C. (*Tilson 2*)	Portsmouth (*Rutherford*)	2–1	93,500
1934–35	Sheffield Wed. (*Rimmer 2, Palethorpe, Hooper*)	W.B.A. (*Boyes, Sandford*)	4–2	93,000
1935–36	Arsenal (*Drake*)	Sheffield Utd.	1–0	93,500
1936–37	Sunderland (*Gurney, Carter, Burbanks*)	Preston N.E. (*F. O'Donnell*)	3–1	93,500
1937–38	Preston N.E. (*Mutch—pen.*)	Huddersfield T.	†1–0	93,500
1938–39	Portsmouth (*Parker 2, Barlow, Anderson*)	Wolves (*Dorsett*)	4–1	99,000
1939–45	No competition—Second World War			
1945–46	Derby County (*H. Turner own goal, Doherty, Stamps 2*)	Charlton A. (*H. Turner*)	†4–1	98,000
1946–47	Charlton A. (*Duffy*)	Burnley	†1–0	98,000
1947–48	Manchester U. (*Rowley 2, Pearson, Anderson*)	Blackpool (*Shimwell—pen., Mortensen*)	4–2	99,000
1948–49	Wolves (*Pye 2, Smyth*)	Leicester City (*Griffiths*)	3–1	100,000

180

Season	Winners	Runners-up	Result	Attendance
1949–50	Arsenal (*Lewis 2*)	Liverpool	2–0	100,000
1950–51	Newcastle U. (*Milburn 2*)	Blackpool	2–0	100,000
1951–52	Newcastle U. (*G. Robledo*)	Arsenal	1–0	100,000
1952–53	Blackpool (*Mortensen 3, Perry*)	Bolton W. (*Lofthouse, Moir, Bell*)	4–3	100,000
1953–54	W.B.A. (*Allen 2—1 pen., Griffin*)	Preston N.E. (*Morrison, Wayman*)	3–2	100,000
1954–55	Newcastle U. (*Milburn, Mitchell, Hannah*)	Manchester C. (*Johnstone*)	3–1	100,000
1955–56	Manchester C. (*Hayes, Dyson, Johnstone*)	Birmingham C. (*Kinsey*)	3–1	100,000
1956–57	Aston Villa (*McParland 2*)	Manchester U. (*Taylor*)	2–1	100,000
1957–58	Bolton W. (*Lofthouse 2*)	Manchester U.	2–0	100,000
1958–59	Nott'm Forest (*Dwight, Wilson*)	Luton Town (*Pacey*)	2–1	100,000
1959–60	Wolves (*McGrath own goal, Deeley 2*)	Blackburn R.	3–0	100,000
1960–61	Tottenham H. (*Smith, Dyson*)	Leicester C.	2–0	100,000
1961–62	Tottenham H. (*Greaves, Smith, Blanchflower—pen.*)	Burnley (*Robson*)	3–1	100,000
1962–63	Manchester U. (*Law, Herd 2*)	Leicester C. (*Keyworth*)	3–1	100,000
1963–64	West Ham U. (*Sissons, Hurst, Boyce*)	Preston N.E. (*Holden, Dawson*)	3–2	100,000
1964–65	Liverpool (*Hunt, St. John*)	Leeds United (*Bremner*)	†2–1	100,000
1965–66	Everton (*Trebilcock 2, Temple*)	Sheffield Wed. (*McCalliog, Ford*)	3–2	100,000

Season	Winners	Runners-up	Result	Attendance
1966–67	Tottenham H. (*Robertson, Saul*)	Chelsea (*Tambling*)	2–1	100,000
1967–68	W.B.A. (*Astle*)	Everton	†1–0	100,000
1968–69	Manchester C. (*Young*)	Leicester City	1–0	100,000
1969–70	Chelsea	Leeds United	*†2–1	62,000

(*Replay at Old Trafford, Manchester—after †2–2 draw at Wembley—att: 100,000*)

Scorers at Wembley Chelsea : *Houseman, Hutchinson.*
Leeds : *Charlton, Jones.*

Scorers in replay Chelsea : *Osgood, Webb.* Leeds : *Jones.*

Season	Winners	Runners-up	Result	Attendance
1970–71	Arsenal (*Kelly, George*)	Liverpool (*Heighway*)	†2–1	100,000
1971–72	Leeds Utd. (*Clarke*)	Arsenal	1–0	100,000
1972–73	Sunderland (*Porterfield*)	Leeds United	1–0	100,000
1973–74	Liverpool (*Keegan 2, Heighway*)	Newcastle U.	3–0	100,000
1974–75	West Ham U. (*A. Taylor 2*)	Fulham	2–0	100,000
1975–76	Southampton (*Stokes*)	Manchester U.	1–0	100,000
1976–77	Manchester U. (*Pearson, Greenhoff, J.*)	Liverpool (*Case*)	2–1	100,000
1977–78	Ipswich Town (*Osborne*)	Arsenal	1–0	100,000

Summary of F.A. Cup Winners

Aston Villa	7	Bury	2	Charlton	1
Blackburn	6	Liverpool	2	Chelsea	1
Newcastle	6	Nottingham F.	2	Clapham Rovers	1
Tottenham	5	Old Etonians	2	Derby	1
Wanderers	5	Preston	2	Huddersfield	1
West Bromwich	5	Sunderland	2	Ipswich Town	1
Arsenal	4	West Ham Utd.	2	Leeds Utd.	1
Bolton	4	Barnsley	1	Notts Co.	1
Manchester City	4	Blackburn Olym.	1	Old Carthusians	1
Sheffield Utd.	4	Blackpool	1	Oxford	1
Wolves	4	Bradford C.	1	Portsmouth	1
Manchester U.	4	Burnley	1	Royal Engineers	1
Everton	3	Cardiff	1	Southampton	1
Sheffield Wed.	3				

FOOTBALL LEAGUE CUP WINNERS

For the first 6 seasons, before the fixture was taken to Wembley, the Football League Cup Final was played on a home-and-away basis.

Season	Winners	Runners-up	Aggregate	Home	Away
1960–61	Aston Villa	Rotherham U.	3–2	3–0	0–2
1961–62	Norwich City	Rochdale	4–0	1–0	3–0
1962–63	Birmingham	Aston Villa	3–1	3–1	0–0
1963–64	Leicester	Stoke City	4–3	3–2	1–1
1964–65	Chelsea	Leicester	3–2	3–2	0–0
1965–66	West Brom.	West Ham	5–3	4–1	1–2

Results, with scorers, of League Cup Finals at Wembley:

			Result	Attendance
1966–67	Q.P.R. (*R. Morgan, Marsh, Lazarus*)	W.B.A. (*Clark 2*)	3–2	97,952
1967–68	Leeds United (*Cooper*)	Arsenal	1–0	100,000
1968–69	Swindon (*Rogers 2, Smart*)	Arsenal (*Gould*)	†3–1	100,000
1969–70	Man. City (*Doyle, Pardoe*)	W.B.A. (*Astle*)	†2–1	100,000
1970–71	Tottenham (*Chivers 2*)	Aston Villa	2–0	100,000
1971–72	Stoke City (*Conroy, Eastham*)	Chelsea (*Osgood*)	2–1	100,000
1972–73	Tottenham (*Coates*)	Norwich City	1–0	100,000
1973–74	Wolves (*Hibbitt, Richards*)	Man. City (*Bell*)	2–1	100,000
1974–75	Aston Villa (*Graydon*)	Norwich City	1–0	100,000
1975–76	Man. City (*Barnes, Tueart*)	Newcastle (*Gowling*)	2–1	100,000
1976–77	Aston Villa (*Little 2, Nicholl*)	Everton (*Latchford, Lyons*)	*†3–2	54,749 (at Man. Utd.)

* After Aston Villa 0, Everton 0: Wembley, 100,000—and Aston Villa 1 (Kenyon, o.g.), Everton 1 (Latchford) : Sheffield Wed., 55,000.

(† = After extra time)

SCOTTISH LEAGUE CHAMPIONS

Season		Points	Season		Points
1890–91	Rangers } Dumbarton	29	1930–31	Rangers	60
			1931–32	Motherwell	66
1891–92	Dumbarton	37	1932–33	Rangers	62
1892–93	Celtic	29	1933–34	Rangers	66
1893–94	Celtic	29	1934–35	Rangers	55
1894–95	Hearts	31	1935–36	Celtic	66
1895–96	Celtic	30	1936–37	Rangers	61
1896–97	Hearts	28	1937–38	Celtic	61
1897–98	Celtic	33	1938–39	Rangers	59
1898–99	Rangers	36	1939–46	*No competition*	
1899– 1900	Rangers	32	1946–47	Rangers	46
1900–01	Rangers	35	1947–48	Hibernian	48
1901–02	Rangers	28	1948–49	Rangers	46
1902–03	Hibernian	37	1949–50	Rangers	50
1903–04	Third Lanark	43	1950–51	Hibernian	48
1904–05	Celtic	41	1951–52	Hibernian	45
1905–06	Celtic	49	1952–53	Rangers	43
1906–07	Celtic	55	1953–54	Celtic	43
1907–08	Celtic	55	1954–55	Aberdeen	49
1908–09	Celtic	51	1955–56	Rangers	52
1909–10	Celtic	54	1956–57	Rangers	55
1910–11	Rangers	52	1957–58	Hearts	62
1911–12	Rangers	51	1958–59	Rangers	50
1912–13	Rangers	53	1959–60	Hearts	54
1913–14	Celtic	65	1960–61	Rangers	51
1914–15	Celtic	65	1961–62	Dundee	54
1915–16	Celtic	67	1962–63	Rangers	57
1916–17	Celtic	64	1963–64	Rangers	55
1917–18	Rangers	56	1964–65	Kilmarnock	50
1918–19	Celtic	58	1965–66	Celtic	57
1919–20	Rangers	71	1966–67	Celtic	58
1920–21	Rangers	76	1967–68	Celtic	63
1921–22	Celtic	67	1968–69	Celtic	54
1922–23	Rangers	55	1969–70	Celtic	57
1923–24	Rangers	59	1970–71	Celtic	56
1924–25	Rangers	60	1971–72	Celtic	60
1925–26	Celtic	58	1972–73	Celtic	57
1926–27	Rangers	56	1973–74	Celtic	53
1927–28	Rangers	60	1974–75	Rangers	56
1928–29	Rangers	67	1975–76	Rangers	54
1929–30	Rangers	60	1976–77	Celtic	54
			1977–78	Rangers	55

Summary of Scottish League Champions

Rangers	*37	Hibernian	4	Kilmarnock	1
Celtic	30	Dumbarton	*2	Motherwell	1
Hearts	4	Aberdeen	1	Third Lanark	1
		Dundee	1		

184

(* Includes one shared title)

SCOTTISH F.A. CUP WINNERS

(* = Replay)

Season	Winners	Runners-up	Result
1873–74	Queen's Park	Clydesdale	2–0
1874–75	Queen's Park	Renton	3–0
1875–76	Queen's Park	Third Lanark	*2–0
			(after 1–1 draw)
1876–77	Vale of Leven	Rangers	*3–2
			(after 0–0, 1–1 draws)
1877–78	Vale of Leven	Third Lanark	1–0
1878–79	Vale of Leven	(Rangers did not appear for replay after 1–1 draw)	
1879–80	Queen's Park	Thornlibank	3–0
1880–81	Queen's Park	Dumbarton	3–1
1881–82	Queen's Park	Dumbarton	*4–1
			(after 2–2 draw)
1882–83	Dumbarton	Vale of Leven	*2–1
			(after 2–2 draw)
1883–84	Queen's Park	(Vale of Leven did not appear for Final)	
1884–85	Renton	Vale of Leven	*3–1
			(after 0–0 draw)
1885–86	Queen's Park	Renton	3–1
1886–87	Hibernian	Dumbarton	2–1
1887–88	Renton	Cambuslang	6–1
1888–89	Third Lanark	Celtic	2–1
1889–90	Queen's Park	Vale of Leven	*2–1
			(after 1–1 draw)
1890–91	Hearts	Dumbarton	1–0
1891–92	Celtic	Queen's Park	5–1
1892–93	Queen's Park	Celtic	2–1
1893–94	Rangers	Celtic	3–1
1894–95	St Bernard's	Renton	2–1
1895–96	Hearts	Hibernian	3–1
1896–97	Rangers	Dumbarton	5–1
1897–98	Rangers	Kilmarnock	2–0
1898–99	Celtic	Rangers	2–0
1899–1900	Celtic	Queen's Park	4–3
1900–01	Hearts	Celtic	4–3
1901–02	Hibernian	Celtic	1–0
1902–03	Rangers	Hearts	*2–0
			(after 1–1, 0–0 draws)
1903–04	Celtic	Rangers	3–2
1904–05	Third Lanark	Rangers	*3–1
			(after 0–0 draw)

Season	Winners	Runners-up	Result
1905–06	Hearts	Third Lanark	1–0
1906–07	Celtic	Hearts	3–0
1907–08	Celtic	St Mirren	5–1
1908–09	*Cup withheld because of riot following two drawn games (2–2, 1–1) between Celtic and Rangers.*		
1909–10	Dundee	Clyde	*2–1
			(after 2–2, 0–0 draws)
1910–11	Celtic	Hamilton	*2–0
			(after 0–0 draw)
1911–12	Celtic	Clyde	2–0
1912–13	Falkirk	Raith Rovers	2–0
1913–14	Celtic	Hibernian	*4–1
			(after 0–0 draw)
1914–19	*No competition*		
1919–20	Kilmarnock	Albion Rovers	3–2
1920–21	Partick Thistle	Rangers	1–0
1921–22	Morton	Rangers	1–0
1922–23	Celtic	Hibernian	1–0
1923–24	Airdrieonians	Hibernian	2–0
1924–25	Celtic	Dundee	2–1
1925–26	St Mirren	Celtic	2–0
1926–27	Celtic	East Fife	3–1
1927–28	Rangers	Celtic	4–0
1928–29	Kilmarnock	Rangers	2–0
1929–30	Rangers	Partick Thistle	*2–1
			(after 0–0 draw)
1930–31	Celtic	Motherwell	*4–2
			(after 2–2 draw)
1931–32	Rangers	Kilmarnock	*3–0
			(after 1–1 draw)
1932–33	Celtic	Motherwell	1–0
1933–34	Rangers	St Mirren	5–0
1934–35	Rangers	Hamilton	2–1
1935–36	Rangers	Third Lanark	1–0
1936–37	Celtic	Aberdeen	2–1
1937–38	East Fife	Kilmarnock	*4–2
			(after 1–1 draw)
1938–39	Clyde	Motherwell	4–0
1939–46	*No competition*		
1946–47	Aberdeen	Hibernian	2–1
1947–48	Rangers	Morton	*1–0
			(after 1–1 draw)
1948–49	Rangers	Clyde	4–1
1949–50	Rangers	East Fife	3–0
1950–51	Celtic	Motherwell	1–0
1951–52	Motherwell	Dundee	4–0

186

Season	Winners	Runners-up	Result
1952–53	Rangers	Aberdeen	*1–0
			(after 1–1 draw)
1953–54	Celtic	Aberdeen	2–1
1954–55	Clyde	Celtic	*1–0
			(after 1–1 draw)
1955–56	Hearts	Celtic	3–1
1956–57	Falkirk	Kilmarnock	*2–1
			(after 1–1 draw)
1957–58	Clyde	Hibernian	1–0
1958–59	St Mirren	Aberdeen	3–1
1959–60	Rangers	Kilmarnock	2–0
1960–61	Dunfermline	Celtic	*2–0
			(after 0–0 draw)
1961–62	Rangers	St Mirren	2–0
1962–63	Rangers	Celtic	*3–0
			(after 1–1 draw)
1963–64	Rangers	Dundee	3–1
1964–65	Celtic	Dunfermline	3–2
1965–66	Rangers	Celtic	*1–0
			(after 0–0 draw)
1966–67	Celtic	Aberdeen	2–0
1967–68	Dunfermline	Hearts	3–1
1968–69	Celtic	Rangers	4–0
1969–70	Aberdeen	Celtic	3–1
1970–71	Celtic	Rangers	*2–1
			(after 1–1 draw)
1971–72	Celtic	Hibernian	6–1
1972–73	Rangers	Celtic	3–2
1973–74	Celtic	Dundee United	3–0
1974–75	Celtic	Airdrieonians	3–1
1975–76	Rangers	Hearts	3–1
1976–77	Celtic	Rangers	1–0
1977–78	Rangers	Aberdeen	2–1

Summary of Scottish F.A. Cup Winners

Celtic	25	Falkirk	2	Dumbarton	1
Rangers	22	Hibernian	2	Dundee	1
Queen's Park	10	Kilmarnock	2	East Fife	1
Hearts	5	Renton	2	Morton	1
Clyde	3	Third Lanark	2	Motherwell	1
Vale of Leven	3	St Mirren	2	Partick	1
Aberdeen	2	Airdrieonians	1	St Bernard's	1
Dunfermline	2				

SCOTTISH LEAGUE CUP WINNERS

(* = Replay)

Season	Winners	Runners-up	Result
1945–46	Aberdeen	Rangers	3–2
1946–47	Rangers	Aberdeen	4–0
1947–48	East Fife	Falkirk	*4–1
			(after 1–1 *draw*)
1948–49	Rangers	Raith Rovers	2–0
1949–50	East Fife	Dunfermline	3–0
1950–51	Motherwell	Hibernian	3–0
1951–52	Dundee	Rangers	3–2
1952–53	Dundee	Kilmarnock	2–0
1953–54	East Fife	Partick Thistle	3–2
1954–55	Hearts	Motherwell	4–2
1955–56	Aberdeen	St Mirren	2–1
1956–57	Celtic	Partick Thistle	*3–0
			(after 0–0 *draw*)
1957–58	Celtic	Rangers	7–1
1958–59	Hearts	Partick Thistle	5–1
1959–60	Hearts	Third Lanark	2–1
1960–61	Rangers	Kilmarnock	2–0
1961–62	Rangers	Hearts	*3–1
			(after 1–1 *draw*)
1962–63	Hearts	Kilmarnock	1–0
1963–64	Rangers	Morton	5–0
1964–65	Rangers	Celtic	2–1
1965–66	Celtic	Rangers	2–1
1966–67	Celtic	Rangers	1–0
1967–68	Celtic	Dundee	5–3
1968–69	Celtic	Hibernian	6–2
1969–70	Celtic	St Johnstone	1–0
1970–71	Rangers	Celtic	1–0
1971–72	Partick Thistle	Celtic	4–1
1972–73	Hibernian	Celtic	2–1
1973–74	Dundee	Celtic	1–0
1974–75	Celtic	Hibernian	6–3
1975–76	Rangers	Celtic	1–0
1976–77	Aberdeen	Celtic	2–1

Summary of Scottish League Cup Winners

Celtic	8	Dundee	3	Hibernian	1
Rangers	8	East Fife	3	Motherwell	1
Hearts	4	Aberdeen	3	Partick Thistle	1

ALL-TIME RECORDS
Record Scores

British record for first-class match: Arbroath 36, Bon Accord 0 (Scottish Cup—1st Round, 1885).

Football League: Stockport County 13, Halifax Town 0 (Div. 3 North, 1934); Newcastle United 13, Newport County 0 (Div. 2, 1946).

Highest Football League aggregate: 17 goals Tranmere Rovers 13, Oldham Athletic 4 (Div. 3 North, 1935).

Scottish League Championship: Celtic 11, Dundee 0 (1895).

F.A. Cup: Preston North End 26, Hyde United 0 (1st Round, 1887).

Football League Cup: Leyton Orient 9, Chester 2 (3rd Round, 1962–63); Workington 9, Barrow 1 (1st Round, 1964–65).

England: 13–0 v. Ireland (1882). **Scotland:** 11–0 v. Ireland (1901).

Ireland: 7–0 v. Wales (1930). **Wales:** 11–0 v. Ireland (1888).

Individual Match Scoring

13 by John Petrie in Arbroath 36, Bon Accord 0 (Scottish Cup—1st Round, 1885); 10 by Joe Payne in Luton Town 12, Bristol Rovers 0 (Div. 3 South, 1936); 9 by Ted MacDougall in Bournemouth 11, Margate 0 (F.A. Cup—1st Round, 1971); 9 by 'Bunny' Bell in Tranmere Rovers 13, Oldham Athletic 4 (Div. 3 North, 1935).

First Division: 7 by James Ross in Preston North End 7, Stoke City 1 (1888); 7 by Ted Drake in Aston Villa 1, Arsenal 7 (1935).

Second Division: 7 by Tommy Briggs in Blackburn Rovers 8, Bristol Rovers 3 (1955); 7 by Tim Coleman in Stoke City 8, Lincoln City 0 (1957)—all-time record for a winger.

Third Division: 5 by Barrie Thomas in Scunthorpe United 8, Luton Town 1 (1965); 5 by Keith East in Swindon Town 6, Mansfield Town 2 (1965); 5 by Steve Earle in Halifax Town 7, Fulham 8 (1969); 5 by Alf Wood in Shrewsbury Town 7, Blackburn Rovers 1 (1971).

Fourth Division: 6 by Bert Lister in Oldham 11, Southport 0 (1962).

Football League Cup: 5 by Derek Reeves in Southampton 5, Leeds United 4 (4th Round, 1960–61); 5 by Alan Wilks in Queen's Park Rangers 5, Oxford United 1 (3rd Round, 1967–68).

Scottish League: 8 by Jimmy McGrory in Celtic 9, Dunfermline Athletic 0 (1928).

England: 5 by Steve Bloomer v. Wales (9–1, 1896); 5 by G. O. Smith v. Ireland (13–2, 1899); 5 by Willie Hall v. Ireland (7–0, 1938); 5 by Malcolm Macdonald v. Cyprus (5–0, 1975).

Ireland: 6 by Joe Bambrick v. Wales (7–0, 1930).

Scotland: 5 by Charles Heggie v. Ireland (7–2, 1886).

Wales: 4 by Jimmy Price v. Ireland (7–1, 1882); 4 by John Doughty v. Ireland (11–0, 1888); 4 by Mel Charles v. Ireland (4–0, 1962).

Most Goals (by clubs) in League Season

Football League—Div. 1: 128 by Aston Villa (1930–31);
Div. 2: 122 by Middlesbrough (1926–27); **Div. 3:** 111 by
Queen's Park Rangers (1961–62); **Div. 4:** 134 by Peterborough
United (1960–61); **Div. 3 South:** 127 by Millwall (1927–28);
Div. 3 North: 128 by Bradford City (1928–29).
Scottish League Championship—Div. 1: 132 by Heart of
Midlothian (1957–58); **Div. 2:** 142 by Raith Rovers (1937–38).

Most Individual League Goals in Season

Football League—Div. 1: 60 by W. R. ('Dixie') Dean (Everton,
1927–28); **Div. 2:** 59 by George Camsell (Middlesbrough,
1926–27); **Div. 3:** 39 by Derek Reeves (Southampton, 1959–60);
Div. 4: 52 by Terry Bly (Peterborough United, 1960–61);
Div. 3 South: 55 by Joe Payne (Luton Town, 1936–37);
Div. 3 North: 55 by Ted Harston (Mansfield Town, 1936–37).
Scottish League Championship—Div. 1: 52 by Willie McFadyen
(Motherwell, 1931–32); **Div. 2:** 66 by Jim Smith (Ayr United,
1927–28).

Most League Goals in Career

Football League: 434 by Arthur Rowley, 1946–65 (4 for West
Bromwich Albion, 27 for Fulham, 251 for Leicester City, 152 for
Shrewsbury Town).
Scottish League: 410 by Jimmy McGrory, 1922–38 (397 for
Celtic, 13 for Clydebank).

Most League Appearances in Career

Football League: When Terry Paine, 36-year-old former England
winger, played for Hereford United at home to Peterborough on
25 October 1975, he took his total of Football League appearances
to 765, beating the record of 764 by Jimmy Dickinson for Portsmouth
from 1946–64. Dickinson's total remains a record number of
appearances for a single club. Paine played 713 League matches
for Southampton, with whom he began his career in 1957, and by
the time he retired in May 1977 had played 824 League games. The
record number of *consecutive* League appearances: 401 by
Tranmere centre-half Harold Bell (Div. 3 North) from 1946–55.
Scottish League: 626 appearances by Bob Ferrier for Motherwell
(1918–37).

International Appearances and Goals

Appearances
England: 108 by Bobby Moore
Ireland: 68 by Pat Jennings
Scotland: 55 by Denis Law
Wales: 68 by Ivor Allchurch

Goals
England: 49 by Bobby Charlton
Ireland: 13 by Billy Gillespie
Scotland: 30 by Denis Law
Wales: 23 by Trevor Ford

Most Points in Season

Football League—Div. 1 67 by Leeds United, 1968–69; **Div. 2**
70 by Tottenham Hotspur, 1919–20; **Div. 3** 70 by Aston Villa,

1971–72; **Div. 4** 74 by Lincoln City, 1975–76; **Div. 3 South** 70 by Nottingham Forest, 1950–51; **Div. 3 North** 72 by Doncaster Rovers, 1946–47.
Scottish League Championship 76 by Rangers, 1920–21; **Div. 2** 69 by Morton, 1966–67.

Record Crowds

World: 200,000 Brazil v. Uruguay (World Cup Final, Rio de Janeiro, 1950).
Britain: 149,547 Scotland v. England (Hampden Park, Glasgow, 1937).
England: 126,047 Bolton Wanderers v. West Ham United (F.A. Cup Final, Wembley, 1923).
European Cup: 135,826 Celtic v. Leeds United (semi-final, Hampden Park, Glasgow, 1970).
Biggest Football League crowd: 82,950 Manchester United v. Arsenal (Maine Road, Manchester, 1948).
Record attendance for English club ground: 84,569 Manchester City v. Stoke City (F.A. Cup—6th Round, 1934).
Football League record season's aggregate: 41,271,424 in season 1948–49.
Football League highest single-day aggregate: 1,269,934 on 27 December 1949.
Smallest League match attendance: 13 for Stockport County v. Leicester City (Div. 2) played at Old Trafford, Manchester on 7 May 1921.
Smallest League attendance since the 2nd World War: 450 for Rochdale v. Cambridge United (Div. 3) on 5 February 1974.

Transfer Records

Britain
First £1,000 transfer: Alf Common, Sunderland to Middlesbrough, 1905.
First £10,000 transfer: David Jack (£10,890), Bolton to Arsenal, 1928.
First £50,000 transfer: Denis Law (£55,000), Huddersfield to Man. City, 1960.
First £100,000 transfer: Denis Law (£100,000), Man. City to Torino, Italy, 1961.
First £200,000 transfer: Martin Peters (part-exchange), West Ham to Tottenham, 1970.
First £300,000 transfer: Bob Latchford (£350,000 in part-exchange), Birmingham to Everton, 1974.
British record cash deal: £500,000—Gordon McQueen, Leeds to Manchester United, February 1978.
World record: Giuseppe Savoldi (Italy) valued at £1,400,000 in part-exchange deal when he joined Napoli from Bologna, 1975.

The Field of Play

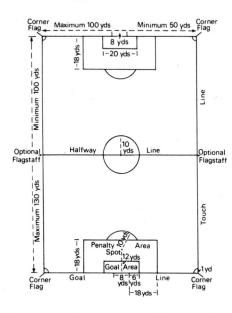

The International Board has approved this table of measurements:

	metres			metres
130 yards	120	10 yards		9·15
120 yards	110	8 yards		7·32
110 yards	100	6 yards		5·50
100 yards	90	1 yard		1
80 yards	75	8 feet		2·44
70 yards	64	5 feet		1·50
50 yards	45	28 inches		0·71
18 yards	16·50	27 inches		0·68
12 yards	11	5 inches		0·12